Production and Utilization of Legumes - Progress and Prospects

Edited by Mirza Hasanuzzaman

Published in London, United Kingdom

Production and Utilization of Legumes - Progress and Prospects
http://dx.doi.org/10.5772/intechopen.104283
Edited by Mirza Hasanuzzaman

Contributors
John R. Caradus, Marissa Roldan, Christine Voisey, Derek R. Woodfield, Manuel Marín-Bravo, Enoc Jara Peña, Doreen R. Masvodza, Moosa M. Sedibe, Alina M. Mofokeng, Rajan Sagar Chaudhary, Suman Dhakal, Briggx Xavier, Klaudija Carović-Stanko, Monika Vidak, Boris Lazarević, Jerko Gunjača, Marisa Jacqueline Joseau, Sandra Rodriguez Reartes, Javier Eduardo Frassoni, Stephanie A. Misquitta, Deepika N. Kshirsagar, Pooja R. Dange, Vikram G. Choudhari, Mukund M. Kabra, Marko Flajšman, Darja Kocjan Ačko

First published in London, United Kingdom, 2023 by IntechOpen
IntechOpen is the global imprint of INTECHOPEN LIMITED, registered in England and Wales, registration number: 11086078, 5 Princes Gate Court, London, SW7 2QJ, United Kingdom

British Library Cataloguing-in-Publication Data
A catalogue record for this book is available from the British Library

Additional hard and PDF copies can be obtained from orders@intechopen.com

Production and Utilization of Legumes - Progress and Prospects
Edited by Mirza Hasanuzzaman
p. cm.
Print ISBN 978-1-83768-646-9
Online ISBN 978-1-83768-647-6
eBook (PDF) ISBN 978-1-83768-648-3

Meet the editor

Dr. Mirza Hasanuzzaman is a professor of agronomy at Sher-e-Bangla Agricultural University, Dhaka, Bangladesh. He received his Ph.D. from Ehime University, Japan, and completed his postdoctoral research at the University of the Ryukyus, Japan. He also received an Australian Government Endeavour Research Fellowship for postdoctoral research as an adjunct senior researcher at the University of Tasmania. Dr. Hasanuzzaman has published over 250 articles in peer-reviewed journals, edited ten books, and written over 40 book chapters on important aspects of plant physiology, plant stress tolerance, and crop production. According to Scopus®, Dr. Hasanuzzaman's publications have received over 16,000 citations with an h-index of 66, and he has been named a Highly Cited Researcher by Clarivate. He is an editor and reviewer for more than 50 peer-reviewed international journals and was a recipient of the Publons Peer Review Award in 2017, 2018, and 2019. He received the World Academy of Science (TWAS) Young Scientist Award 2014, the University Grants Commission (UGC) Gold Medal 2018, the Global Network of Bangladeshi Biotechnologists (GNOBB) Award 2021, and Society for Plant Research Young Scientist Award (Agriculture) 2023. He is a fellow of the Bangladesh Academy of Sciences (BAS), the Royal Society of Biology, and the International Society of Environmental Botanists.

Contents

Preface

Legumes, or members of the Fabaceae family, mainly comprise herbaceous plants, including some shrubs and a few trees. Legumes rank second after cereals globally in both production and nutritional terms. They contain significant amounts of many other mineral components, making them an economically more feasible source of protein than animal sources, particularly in developing countries. Legumes are not only beneficial as human food, but they are also known to have promising positive effects on soil properties: in agronomic studies, they are classed as restorative crops, green manuring crops, or cover crops. Legumes have also been shown to have moderate tolerance properties under different abiotic stress conditions.

The nine chapters in this book deal with the biology and physiology of legume crops as well as their production technologies and responses to various environmental conditions. The book provides the reader with a comprehensive overview of various aspects of legume production technology, agronomic management, and the role of legumes in future food security. We believe the book will be useful for undergraduate and graduate students, teachers, and researchers, particularly in the fields of agronomy and crop science.

We would like to thank all the authors for their outstanding and timely contributions. We are very grateful to Marijana Josipovic, Commissioning Editor, and to Blanka Gugic and Mirna Papuga, Author Service Managers, at IntechOpen for their prompt responses during the production of this book. We also thank Ayesha Siddika for her reviews and formatting.

Mirza Hasanuzzaman
Department of Agronomy,
Sher-e-Bangla Agricultural University,
Dhaka, Bangladesh

Chapter 1

New Age of Common Bean

Monika Vidak, Boris Lazarević, Jerko Gunjača and Klaudija Carović-Stanko

Abstract

Common bean (*Phaseolus vulgaris* L.) is a plant with high nutritional value that occupies an important place in human nutrition worldwide. Its yields vary widely and are often below the genetic potential of the species, given the diversity of cropping systems and climatic changes. Common bean landraces are a source of great genetic variability and provide excellent material for the selection and improvement of numerous agronomic traits and the creation of modern cultivars. It is also important to use high quality seed of high-yielding cultivars in production, because in common bean, in addition to yield and resistance to abiotic and biotic stress factors, traits such as nutritional value and digestibility are also the focus of interest. The success of common bean production depends to a large extent on the quality of the seed, the production approach and new breeding programs.

Keywords: breeding, common bean production, climate changes, genetic variability, landraces

1. Introduction

Grain legumes production have been neglected regardless of their potential to provide nutrition and food security [1]. They are at the crossroads of many societal challenges affecting agriculture, such as climate change, sustainability and food security [2]. Due to their high content of proteins, fibers, carbohydrates, vitamins and minerals, they play a crucial role in the development of a plant-based diet and are important nutritional components to eliminate hunger and malnutrition [1, 2]. In addition, they improve soil fertility, for example by fixing nitrogen through symbiosis with rhizobia, and at the same time keep crop yields high [3]. Nowadays, however, the trend is changing and many consumers are demanding local food for economic reasons (increasing farmers' income, adding more value to local stakeholders, etc.), social reasons (i.e. maintaining the population in the area), environmental reasons (reducing traffic and gas emissions, landscape conservation and biodiversity, etc.) and because local products are perceived to be fresher or of better quality [4]. The COVID-19 pandemic and the Russian-Ukrainian war have led to drastic fluctuations in energy prices and disruptions in energy and food supply chains, access to fertilizers is limited, and future harvests are uncertain [5–8]. As a result, the availability and supply of an extensive range of food commodities and end products are under threat, with notable implications for sourcing, production, processing and logistics, and world markets have recently experienced

IntechOpen

an increase in food prices [6]. Both crises initially seemed to be an opportunity for a low-carbon energy transition: the pandemic because it accelerated the transition from carbon-intensive energy to modern renewables (such as solar and wind) and illustrated the scale of changes in lifestyle and behavior in a short period of time, and the war because it highlighted the need for greater diversification of energy supply and reliance on local, renewable energy sources [6, 7]. However, early indications suggest that policymakers around the world are focusing on short-term, seemingly quicker solutions, such as supporting the established energy industry in the post-pandemic period to save the economy and finding new fossil fuel supply routes to increase energy security after the war [7]. Accordingly, interest in the use of grain legumes and their components in food is growing in many developed countries. Factors contributing to this trend include the fact that legumes are grown in almost all climatic conditions, as well as their nutritional and health benefits [9].

The aim of this chapter is therefore to highlight the importance of common bean as one of the most important legumes in the world and to point out the possibility of creating new cultivars with desirable traits using new technologies (GWAS and high-throughput phenotyping).

2. Common bean importance

Although its Latin and English names (*Phaseolus vulgaris* L.; common bean) suggest that it is an ordinary plant species, considering the nutritional properties and genetic structure of the common bean, it can be concluded that, on the contrary, it is an exceptional species that represents a potential crop for future food and nutrient security [10, 11]. It originated in Mexico and, through later diversification and spread throughout the Americas and the world, has become the most ecologically adapted species of the genus Phaseolus, quickly becoming popular for its nutritional qualities [12]. The common bean is the most widely cultivated legume in the world for direct human consumption and a staple food that does not require industrial processing [2, 13]. It is mainly grown as a grain (i.e. dried beans) and as a fresh vegetable (i.e. snap beans, green beans) [2]. In 2021, global production of dry common bean is estimated at more than 27 million tons on more than 34 million ha [14], feeding more than 300 million people linked to the global agricultural economy [15]. An outstanding feature of the germplasm of common bean is its particularly high diversity [16]. It is grown all over the world in different local environments and climates, with extremely diverse cultivation methods, uses and range of environments to which it is adapted, which has contributed to the great diversity of common bean in terms of growth type, seed characteristics and maturity period [16, 17], but unfavorable environmental conditions, especially drought and salinity in soils, affect its overall performance and reduce productivity and harvest but also consequently the nutritional value [10, 18]. As a food source, it can help reduce global food shortages in the coming years [11]. Common bean is a food with high nutritional value, but also with medicinal properties, which is why it plays an important role in human nutrition and is valued as a functional food [19, 20]. It contains all amino acids but is low in sulfur-containing amino acids such as methionine, cysteine and tryptophan, and is an excellent substitute for meat when combined with cereals, which contain plenty of them [21]. Although the nutrient composition of common bean seeds depends on factors such as origin, genotype and environmental conditions [22], it has the highest content of minerals in its seeds of all legumes [23]. In fact, the common bean is among the most nutrient-dense foods available and is often referred to as the "poor man's meat", "the near-perfect food" and "the grain of hope" for poor communities [11, 24–26]. It is considered a potential food to address malnutrition [27]. In addition, the common bean properties are also recognized in other areas. For example, the use of common bean protein as a fish meal substitute and the production of functional fermented beverages from germinated bean seeds have recently been demonstrated [23, 28]. In addition, the N2-fixing capacity of this crop is well known to minimize the need for synthetic N fertilizer to increase yield and quality [29].

3. Common bean breeding

It is of great importance to make synergistic efforts to advance the efficiency and accuracy of common bean breeding and to develop genetic gain opportunities by integrating common bean genetic and genomic resources and improved phenotyping methods into breeding activities [11, 30].

Breeding of common beans is often done locally and focuses on improving response to biotic and abiotic stresses, which are particularly challenging in certain locations [30]. Among abiotic stressors, drought is the number one environmental stress because of temperature dynamics, lighting intensity and lack of rain, affecting 60% of total crop production worldwide [31, 32]. Farmers' preferences in seed selection and seed lot management had a significant role in the evolutionary development of domesticated beans, their genetic diversity, population structure and chemical composition, which change over time and also depend on agroecological growing conditions [9]. In this context, various researchers around the world use local populations or samples of common bean landraces as reference sets to study their genetic diversity and population structure [9]. Although conventional plant breeding and a collection of global germplasm were the primary sources of improvements in common bean to produce cultivars with greater yield potential [30, 33], in the cases where the study samples come from gene banks, this diversity has remained static over the years [9]. Conventional plant breeding is also designed to address limited requirements and the specific needs of farmers and certain growing environments [30].

In common beans, in addition to yield and resistance to abiotic and biotic stress factors, traits such as nutritional value and digestibility are also the focus of interest [13, 30, 34]. For years, a variety of breeding activities have been carried out to improve several key traits [11] but researchers recognize that current breeding projects would not be sufficient to meet expected future food needs under current climatic conditions [35]. However, to improve the efficiency and accuracy of bean breeding and increase genetic gain, there are tremendous opportunities such as the use of genomic tools and improved phenotyping methods [30]. Thus, common bean variability and a large number of local populations can be used for breeding purposes to create new cultivars with desirable traits (high yielding, adapted to abiotic stresses and with increased nutritional value), and new technologies such as genome-wide association studies (GWAS) and high-throughput phenotyping (HTP) can help to quickly select for these desirable traits.

4. GWAS for biofortification

Hidden hunger is generally a nutritional deficiency that occurs when the quality of food is inadequate for normal growth and development, i.e. as a result of an energy-rich but nutrient-poor diet [36]. It is estimated that more than two billion people worldwide are affected, with young children and women of reproductive age living in low-income countries most at risk [36, 37].

Biofortification is a multidisciplinary strategy to improve staple foods in terms of mineral or vitamin content as a means to combat malnutrition in developing countries [24]. It can be achieved through a variety of approaches such as fertilizer application to the soil or foliage, conventional plant breeding or genetic engineering with genetic modification and transgenesis, using expertise from different fields [34]. Biofortification of common bean is an important strategy to reduce mineral deficiencies, especially in regions of the world where this crop plays a key role in nutrition [38]. Since iron, phosphorus and zinc deficiencies are among the most important nutrient deficiencies in the human diet, research on the genetic control of seed composition focuses mainly on the study of these minerals [10, 39–42]. Iron is essential for the prevention of anemia and for the proper functioning of many metabolic processes, while zinc is essential for proper growth and resistance to gastrointestinal and respiratory infections, especially in children [24]. In recent years, many efforts have been made to achieve Fe biofortification of common beans with two main objectives: to increase the Fe concentration in common bean seeds and to reduce the content of phytic acid (PA), which is known to reduce the absorption of dietary iron [24, 38, 43]. Finally, research on Fe nutrition has shown that biofortified Fe in common beans can improve the nutritional status of the target population [44].

Recent advances in molecular markers, sequencing technologies and the finishing of the common bean genome sequence have opened up numerous opportunities for fine mapping and characterization of genes [9, 45–47]. The application of marker-assisted selection (MAS) for more complex traits, such as yield, has recently shifted to genomic selection approaches that are based on genome-wide association studies (GWAS) [33]. Genome-wide association studies (GWAS) have become a widely accepted strategy for studying traits of importance to agriculture, thanks to the introduction of NGS-based SNP markers to decipher genotype–phenotype associations in many species [48]. Recently, a number of GWAS studies on diseases [49–52], abiotic stress [53, 54], agronomic traits [55–57], cooking time and culinary quality traits [58] and root traits [59, 60] have been conducted on common beans. In addition, the GWAS results can serve as a basis for understanding the genetic architecture of the nutritional properties of bean seeds, with the aim of increasing the macro- and micronutrient content in the bean breeding program [61].

4.1 Case study: Croatian common bean landraces

Although the common bean is an important food crop in Croatia, production is almost exclusively based on landraces, as there are no current breeding programs that would create new varieties [62]. On the other hand, in the course of the long tradition of bean cultivation in Croatia, many landraces with great genetic and morphological diversity have developed (**Figure 1**), known by their vernacular names, which are mainly based on the morphological characteristics of the seeds, i.e. the color and mosaic of the seed coat [62–64]. Landraces are an important source of genes for adaptation to local growing conditions and disease resistance [60, 65]. Furthermore, compared to modern cultivars, landraces are essential sources of key nutritional components for food security and a healthy food supply [66]. However, due to complex socio-economic changes in rural communities in recent decades, such as the low profitability of smaller farms and the aging of farmers who grow modern common bean cultivars and/or other

Figure 1.
Diversity of Croatian common bean landraces.

more profitable crops instead of landraces, there is a risk of genetic erosion of landraces [67]. In addition, current abiotic and biotic stress factors are also affecting Croatia, with a focus on drought, reducing agricultural production [68].

Accordingly, the aim of our studies was first to collect landraces of common bean throughout Croatia, in such a way as to include the most cultivated landraces that could be clearly distinguished based on seed morphological characteristics and accordingly divided into 10 morphotypes [62]. Subsequently, by combining phaseolin genotyping, analysis of SSR and SNP markers and morphological traits, 174 accessions of Croatian common bean landraces were evaluated for their origin, genetic diversity, population structure and morphological diversity, and a set of true-type morphogenetic groups was created. The 122 accessions were classified into 14 morphogenetic groups: (1) Mesoamerican (H1A) ('Biser', 'Kukuruzar', 'Tetovac', 'Trešnjevac'), (2) Andean indeterminate type (H2B1) ('Dan noć', 'Sivi', 'Puter', 'Sivi prošarani', 'Trešnjevac') and (3) Andean determinate type (H3B2) ('Bijeli', 'Dan noć', 'Puter', 'Trešnjevac', 'Zelenčec'). Fifty-two accessions are putative hybrids between morphogenetic groups [69]. As published in Carović-Stanko et al. [62], the STRUCTURE analysis based on 26 SSRs identified $K = 2$ as the most likely number of clusters ($\Delta K = 20{,}533, 24$) and assigned the accessions of Mesoamerican origin (phaseolin type 'S') to cluster A, while the accessions of Andean origin (phaseolin type 'H'/'C' or 'T') formed cluster B, which split into two clusters (B1 and B2) at $K = 3$ ($\Delta K = 1935.93$) and separated the vast majority of phaseolin type 'H'/'C' accessions from those with phaseolin type 'T'. Thus, at $K = 3$, 48 (27.59%) accessions were assigned to cluster A, 29 (16.67%) to cluster B1 and 80 (45.96%) to cluster B2. For 17 accessions (9.77%), the membership probabilities $Q < 75\%$ for any of the clusters and they were therefore considered as "mixed origin". The Q values of each accession obtained at $K = 3$ were used to control for genetic background in the GWAS.

The created panel of accessions was then used for GWAS based on DArTseq-derived SNP markers with the aim of identifying quantitative trait nucleotides (QTNs) associated with variation in seed nutrient content (N, P, K, Ca, Mg, Fe, Zn and Mn) for which phenotypic data on nutrient content were collected from a broader panel of 226 accessions in the research of Palčić et al. [70].

DArTseq analysis was carried out by Diversity Arrays Technology Pty Ltd., Bruce, Australia (https://www.diversityarrays.com/). The quality of the SNP markers derived from DarTseq was determined using the parameters 'reproducibility' (percentage of technical replicate pairs that score identically for a given marker), 'call-rate' (percentage of samples for which a given marker was scored) and 'MAF' (minor- allele frequency) [71]. The marker sequences were aligned against the reference genome of *P. vulgaris* [46] using BLASTN [72]. By excluding all SNPs with MAF < 0.05 and all SNPs with >0.05 heterozygotes, a final quality control of the SNP data was performed, resulting in the final set of 6311 high-quality DArTseq-derived SNPs. The missing SNP data were imputed using the Beagle 5.1 genotype imputation method [73]. The imputed dataset was then used to construct a kinship matrix using four methods implemented in the software TASSEL 5 [74]: (1) centered IBS [75], (2) normalized IBS [76], (3) dominance-centered IBS [77] and (4) dominance-normalized IBS [78]. In addition, as suggested by Diniz et al. [79], we have used the corrected kinship matrix.

Linkage disequilibrium, the random association between alleles at different loci was measured by the squared value of the coefficient of determination (r^2). Bias caused by relatedness and/or population structure was removed by correcting r^2: (a) for relatedness using different relatedness matrices (r_V^2), (b) for population structure using Q values obtained with STRUCTURE (r_S^2), or (c) for both (r_{VS}^2) [80]. The Hill and Weir model [81] was used to represent the decline of LD as a function of distance between loci. According to the uncorrected r^2 estimate, the strength of LD did not decrease at all even at a distance of 10 Mbp, and the value of r^2 remained above 0.3, even for pairs of loci at opposite ends of the chromosome. The bias caused by consanguinity is stronger than the bias caused by population structure. There was almost no difference between the correction for consanguinity alone and for consanguinity and population structure, in both cases the r^2 value fell below 0.1 at about 1 Mbp. Although the differences between the curves for the different kinship matrices were not so pronounced, the centralized IBS matrix was used for GWAS as it gave a slightly better result.

Before performing GWAS, missing phenotypic data were imputed with the method PHENIX which was implemented in the R package of the same name [82]. Before imputation, outliers with the option "trim" in "phenix" were removed (trim. sds = 1.96). GWAS was performed using single-locus models fitted in TASSEL 5 [83] and multi-locus models used in the R package MLMM [84]. In both cases, mixed linear models were fitted with corrections for population structure and genetic relatedness (Q and K matrices). TASSEL "raw" p-values were subjected to adjustment for multiple testing using the "qvalue" package for R [85], with a q-value of 0.2 chosen as the significance threshold. The distribution of TASSEL "raw" p-values was visualized using Manhattan plots created with the "CMplot" package for R [86]. In creating the Manhattan plots, an approximate threshold was calculated for each trait as the p-value of a hypothetical SNP that would have a q-value of 0.2. A similar approximate significance threshold was calculated for MLMM, by using zero-step p-values to estimate the p-value of a hypothetical SNP that would have a q-value of approximately 0.2. Violin plots were created to visualize the distribution of alleles across subpopulations for each QTN.

DOI: http://dx.doi.org/10.5772/intechopen.110437

On chromosomes Pv01, Pv02, Pv03, Pv05, Pv07, Pv08 and Pv10 were detected 22 QTNs which were associated with nitrogen content of the seeds (**Figure 2**). A total of five QTNs were associated with seed phosphorus content, four on chromosome Pv07 and one on Pv08. On chromosome Pv09, one QTN was found for seed calcium content and on chromosome Pv08 one for seed magnesium content. On chromosome Pv06, two QTNs were found for the zinc content of the seeds.

As expected, fitting the multilocus model to the MLMM resulted in significantly fewer discoveries of marker-trait associations. Of the 22 QTNs found by TASSEL for N, the MLMM confirmed only two: one of four on chromosome Pv01 and the first of two QTNs on Pv10. Similarly, only one of the four QTNs found by TASSEL for P was on chromosome Pv07. An additional discovery was a QTN found by MLMM for N on chromosome Pv05.

Regarding the relationship between the sizes of the different variance component estimates by MLMM, the comparison of the residual sum of squares (RSS) plots for N and P can be summarized in two key points: (1) population structure explained 40% of the total variability for N and 0% of the total variability for P; (2) the error variability was similar to the genetic variability for N and twice as large for

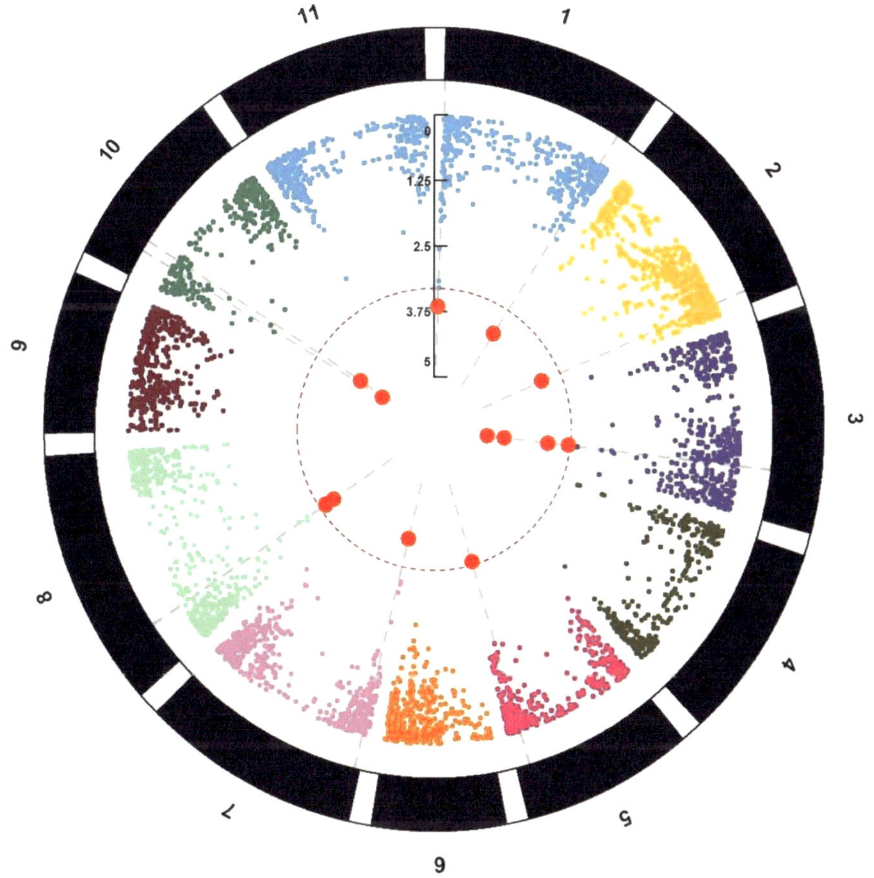

Figure 2.
Circular Manhattan plot for significant markers detected by TASSEL for N.

P. Consequently, MLMM discovered three QTNs with p-values below the threshold for N and only one for P despite the similar relative size of genetic variability for N and P.

The largest proportion of total phenotypic variability is explained by QTN Mg_8, which explains 13% of the total phenotypic variability for Mg. Associated markers were distributed throughout the genome, except on chromosomes Pv04 and Pv11, where none were found. N is the trait associated with the greatest number of markers, but individual marker effects were smaller than for other traits. Most markers were located closer to the ends of the chromosomes and only a few were closer to the centromeric region.

The strong effect of population structure on N may be related to the effect of allelic substitution at the QTN loci. In all subpopulations, the reference allele was always present for all QTNs, and the mean N content of individuals carrying the reference allele in subpopulation A (Mesoamerican origin) always lies somewhere between the mean values of subpopulations B1 and B2 (Andean origin). There are three possible scenarios for the distribution of the SNP alleles. They could be present only in the subpopulations of Andean origin, but their positive effect, which is visible in B1 and B2, has almost disappeared at the level of the total population hidden by the effect of population structure. In the second scenario, the SNP allele is only present in subpopulation A (Mesoamerican origin) and has an obvious negative effect that is attenuated by the effect of population structure. Finally, if an SNP allele is present in all subpopulations, its effect varies from one subpopulation to another and becomes almost invisible at the population level. The same scenarios occur with other elements, e.g., with P (**Figure 3**).

This result will serve as a basis for breeding and improving common beans for nutrient content.

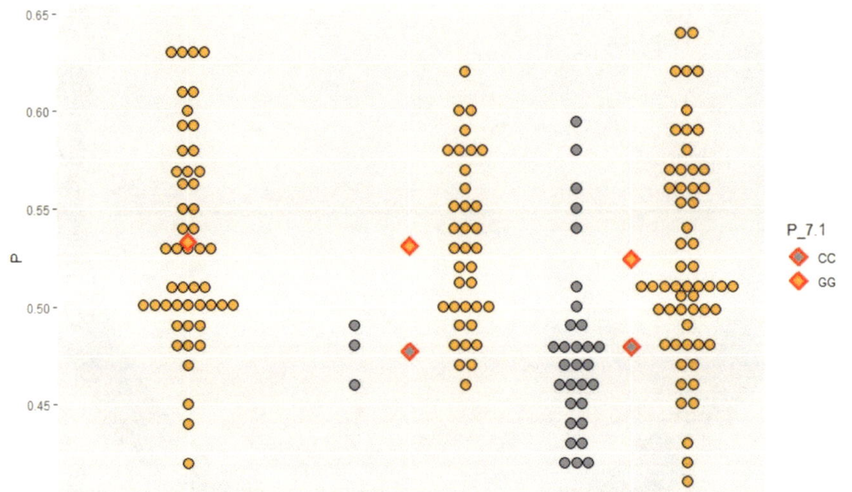

Figure 3.
P seed content distribution for different allele classes within subpopulations (A Mesoamerican; B1 Andean; B2 Andean). Diamonds designate subpopulation means for reference allele homozygotes (gray) and SNP homozygotes (yellow).

5. Phenotyping

Climate change and growing populations have led to the need to develop integrated biotechnological approaches to increase agricultural production while coping with environmental threats. This has led to the concept of developing "climate-proof crop varieties" [31]. In plant breeding and quantitative genetics, a large number of measurements are usually made to select superior individuals or identify regions in the genome that control a trait, which requires high-throughput phenotyping [87]. The tools and applied methods of phenotyping differ in the various -omics disciplines, but basically, they are all used to assess and measure complex traits related to growth, yield, quality and adaptation to various biotic and abiotic stress factors [88]. Therefore, it is necessary to monitor the plant during its growth and development for the early detection of plant responses to stress in each growing season (because each season is different) [89]. This can be done by using new non-destructive automated phenotyping techniques with integrative and simultaneous quantification of multiple morphological and physiological traits, allowing early detection and quantification of different stress factors on a whole-plant basis, i.e. timely identification of how certain stress factors such as drought or e.g. nutrient deficiencies affect the plant [90]. That is, high-throughput phenotyping (HTP) technology plays a crucial role in developing new or better crops through traditional or molecular breeding using marker-assisted selection or genetic selection [35]. The most widely used methods for the non-destructive investigation of phenotypic traits of plants under stress conditions, combining different techniques for measuring gas exchange and techniques for imaging and analyzing the images obtained, are multispectral imaging and multispectral 3D scanning, and chlorophyll fluorescence imaging [90]. These methods provide precise insight into the physiological state of plants under specific environmental conditions, excellently detect morphological and biochemical changes such as light utilization by the photosystem II (PSII) and the underlying biochemical processes, leaf pigment content, chemical composition of leaves, morphological and architectural features of leaves and shoots, etc., and enable rapid data collection and processing [90, 91]. HTP enables objective, fast and precise quantification of morphological, anatomical, physiological and biochemical properties of plants and modeling of ideotypes of agricultural crops adapted to growing in specific agroecological conditions [92]. By growing plants in controlled conditions of growth chambers that enable the management and control of environmental factors such as temperature, duration, spectral composition and intensity of light, availability of nutrients and water, in combination with the latest available methods of spectral analysis (VIS, NIR, IR), chlorophyll fluorescence and measurements of gas exchange, the phenotypic properties of plants, i.e. the complex interaction of genotypes with their environment, are analyzed in an innovative way [88].

In recent years, HTP technology has revolutionized phenotyping and accelerated plant breeding in screening large numbers of plants at different phenological stages [35]. To increase the accuracy and efficiency of plant trait evaluation non-destructive and high-throughput methods have been developed [93]. By using advanced sensors and data acquisition systems, HTP platforms can take full advantage of monitoring, quantifying and evaluating specific phenotypes for large-scale agricultural experiments [94]. Platforms can be used in the laboratory and in the field under controlled and natural conditions and are not necessary to wait for the plants to mature in the field, as the desired traits can be studied quickly in the early stages [35]. This is a crucial step in breeding to select better performing cultivars in terms of yield, abiotic and biotic stress tolerance to accelerate crop improvement programs [35].

To improve the production and quality of common beans, it is necessary to possess in-depth knowledge of its genetic diversity, the genome and the functions of the genes, but also to be familiar with the new phenotyping techniques [35, 95].

As drought is one of the significant environmental stressors due to its significant detrimental effects, there is an increasing need to create tolerant genotypes of agricultural crops [32]. The analysis of gas exchange is based on the fact that drought stress causes rapid closure of stomata [96]. By closing the leaves, the plant saves water, but also reduces the diffusion of CO_2 needed for photosynthesis from the atmosphere into the leaf. By measuring stomatal conductance (gas exchange) it is possible to quantify drought stress and select tolerant genotypes [97]. The analysis of chlorophyll fluorescence is based on the fact that the light energy absorbed by the chlorophyll molecules in the photosystems can undergo one of three processes: It can be used to initiate photosynthesis (photochemical reactions), it can be released as heat or it can be re-emitted as long-wave light radiation, i.e., fluorescence. These three processes are interdependent, i.e., any increase in one process leads to a decrease in the value of the other two. Photosystem two (PSII), located in the thylakoid membranes of chloroplasts, is responsible for the uptake of light energy and the initiation of photosynthesis, and at the same time is very sensitive to abiotic stress. Therefore, the measurement of chlorophyll fluorescence, which provides information on changes in the efficiency of photosynthesis, is one of the most commonly used methods for stress assessment in plants [98]. Multispectral analyses are based on the reflection of light of different wavelengths. Many physiological and chemical properties of plants affect the way their tissues absorb and reflect light. When a plant is exposed to stress, these properties can change and thus the intensity of the light reflected by the leaves also changes [99]. The spectral reflectance data of the leaves are used to calculate vegetation indices. Some of the commonly used vegetation indices to assess abiotic stress are the normalized differential vegetation index (NDVI), anthocyanin index (ARI) and chlorophyll index (CHI) [100, 101]. Since drought stress leads to physical and biochemical changes (reduction of leaf area, wilting of the plant, closure of stomata, closure of PSII, disruption of gas exchange, decrease in the intensity of photosynthesis, changes in the composition of pigments, etc.), these parameters can be used to assess the tolerance of genotypes to drought.

Also, for the successful production of beans and obtaining a high yield, a good supply of nutrients to the plant is necessary [102]. Their level can be determined by analyzing the soil, but the nutritional status of beans can be determined by analyzing plant material (leaves). Nutrient deficiency in plants leads to specific symptoms that can be easily detected, for example, by 3D scans with PlantEye F500 multispectral 3D scanner (**Figure 4**) and chlorophyll fluorescence measurements with CropReporter™ (PhenoVation B.V.,Wageningen, The Netherlands) (**Figure 5**) [103].

Current ground-based phenotyping platforms are likely to be replaced by new and specialized UAVs (drones) and will facilitate next-generation breeding programs to develop improved varieties [35].

The combination of HTP methods with advanced high-throughput genotyping techniques in genome-wide association studies (GWAS) will allow the identification of gene regions and genes associated with specific phenotypic traits (such as drought resistance, increased efficiency of nutrient utilization or disease resistance). The implementation of the results of this research into breeding programs through

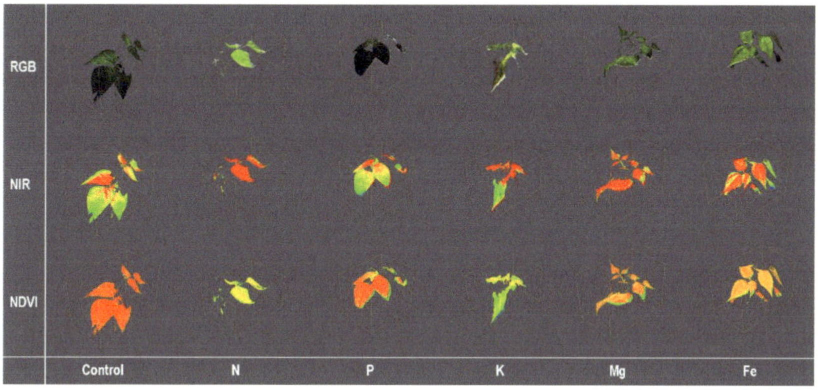

Figure 4.
Color [red, green, and blue (RGB)] and pseudo-color [near infra-red (NIR) and normalized differential vegetation index (NDVI)] images of 3D common bean plants grown for 9 days (MT3) in treatment solutions [12 modified Hoagland's solution (control), and solutions without nitrogen (N), phosphorus (P), potassium (K), magnesium (Mg), and iron (Fe)] [103].

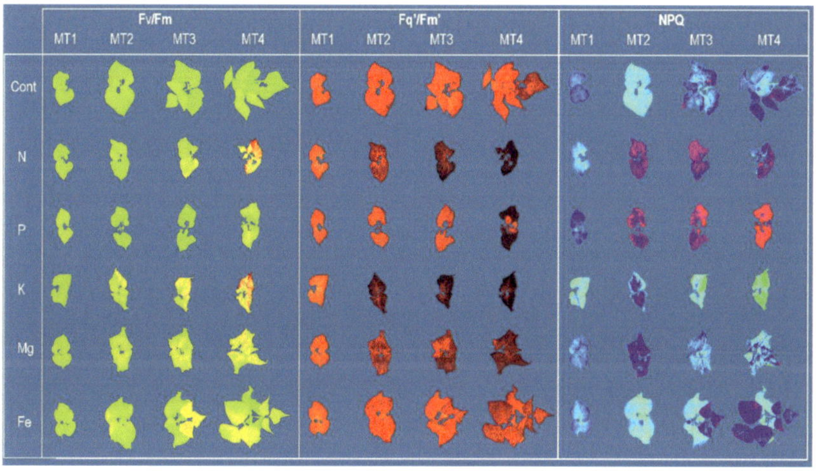

Figure 5.
Color and pseudo-color images of common bean plants with maximum quantum yield of PSII (Fv/Fm), effective quantum yield of PSII (Fq'/Fm') and non-photochemical quenching (NPQ) taken during four measurements (MT1-MT4), for 12 days every 3 days of growth in the control [12 modified Hoagland solution (Cont)] and solutions without nitrogen (N), phosphorus (P), potassium (K), magnesium (Mg) and iron (Fe) [103].

marker-assisted breeding will enable a faster and more efficient breeding process that will produce new, more efficient and more productive crop genotypes.

6. Conclusion and future perspectives

In these challenging times (climate change, sustainability and food security), the success of common bean production depends not only on seed quality and production approach, but also to a large extent on breeding programs. The implementation of the results of GWAS and phenotyping research into breeding programs through marker-assisted breeding will enable a faster and more efficient breeding process that will produce new, more efficient and more productive common bean genotypes. The combination of advanced high-throughput genotyping techniques in genome-wide association studies (GWAS) will enable the identification of gene regions and genes associated with specific phenotypic traits (e.g. mineral content, drought resistance, increased nutrient utilization or disease resistance).

Acknowledgements

This paper was supported by the project KK.01.1.1.01.0005 Biodiversity and Molecular Plant Breeding, Centre of Excellence for Biodiversity and Molecular Plant Breeding (CoE CroPBioDiv), Zagreb, Croatia and by Croatian Science Foundation under the project UIP-11-2013-3290.

Conflict of interest

The authors declare no conflict of interest.

Author details

Monika Vidak, Boris Lazarević, Jerko Gunjača and Klaudija Carović-Stanko*
Centre of Excellence for Biodiversity and Molecular Plant Breeding
(CoE CroP-BioDiv), University of Zagreb Faculty of Agriculture, Zagreb, Croatia

*Address all correspondence to: kcarovic@agr.hr

References

[1] Mecha E, Figueira ME, Vaz Patto MC, do Rosário Bronze M. Two sides of the same coin: The impact of grain legumes on human health: Common bean (*Phaseolus vulgaris* L.) as a case study. In: Jimenez-Lopez JC, Clemente A, editors. Legume Seed Nutraceutical Research [Internet]. London, UK: IntechOpen; 2018. p. 18. Available from: https://www.intechopen.com/chapters/62359. DOI: 10.5772/intechopen.78737

[2] Murube E, Beleggia R, Pacetti D, Nartea A, Frascarelli G, Lanzavecchia G, et al. Characterization of nutritional quality traits of a common bean germplasm collection. Foods. 2021;**10**(7):1-26

[3] Allito BB, Ewusi-Mensah N, Logah V. Legume-rhizobium strain specificity enhances nutrition and nitrogen fixation in faba bean (Vicia faba L.). Agronomy. 2020;**10**(6):1-21

[4] Mallor C, Barberán M, Aibar J. Recovery of a common bean landrace (*Phaseolus vulgaris* L.) for commercial purposes. Frontiers in Plant Science. 2018;**871**(1440):1-7

[5] Ben Hassen T, El Bilali H. Impacts of the Russia-Ukraine war on global food security: Towards more sustainable and resilient food systems? Food. 2022;**11**(15):1-17

[6] Jagtap S, Trollman H, Trollman F, Garcia-Garcia G, Parra-López C, Duong L, et al. The Russia-Ukraine conflict: Its implications for the global food supply chains. Food. 2022;**11**(14):1-23

[7] Zakeri B, Paulavets K, Barreto-Gomez L, Echeverri LG, Pachauri S, Boza-Kiss B, et al. Pandemic, war, and global energy transitions. Energies. 2022;**15**(17):1-23

[8] Li K, Qi S, Shi X. The COVID-19 pandemic and energy transitions: Evidence from low-carbon power generation in China. Journal of Cleaner Production. 2022;**368**(132994):1-9

[9] Chávez-Servia JL, Heredia-García E, Mayek-Pérez N, Aquino-Bolaños EN, Hernández-Delgado S, Carrillo-Rodríguez JC, et al. Diversity of common bean (*Phaseolus vulgaris* L.) landraces and the nutritional value of their grains. In: Goyal AK, editor. Grain Legumes. London, UK: IntechOpen; 2016. pp. 1-33

[10] Losa A, Vorster J, Cominelli E, Sparvoli F, Paolo D, Sala T, et al. Drought and heat affect common bean minerals and human diet—What we know and where to go. Food and Energy Security. 2022;**11**(1):1-28

[11] Nadeem MA, Yeken MZ, Shahid MQ, Habyarimana E, Yılmaz H, Alsaleh A, et al. Common bean as a potential crop for future food security: An overview of past, current and future contributions in genomics, transcriptomics, transgenics and proteomics. Biotechnology & Biotechnological Equipment [Internet]. 2021;**35**(1):758-786. DOI: 10.1080/13102818.2021.1920462

[12] Bitocchi E, Rau D, Bellucci E, Rodriguez M, Murgia ML, Gioia T, et al. Beans (*Phaseolus* ssp.) as a model for understanding crop evolution. Frontiers in Plant Science. 2017;**8**(722):1-21

[13] Castro-Guerrero NA, Isidra-Arellano MC, Mendoza-Cozatl DG, Valdes-Lopez O. Common bean: A legume model on the rise for unraveling responses and adaptations to iron, zinc, and phosphate deficiencies. Frontiers in Plant Science. 2016;**7**(600):1-7

[14] Food and Agricultural Organization of the United Nations. Crops and livestock products [Internet]. 2023. Available from: https://www.fao.org/faostat/en/#data

[15] Nasar S, Shaheen H, Murtaza G, Tinghong T, Arfan M, Idrees M. Socioeconomic evaluation of common bean (*Phaseolus vulgaris* L.) cultivation in providing sustainable livelihood to the mountain populations of Kashmir Himalayas. Plants. 2023;**12**(1):1-12

[16] Sedlar A, Marjetka K, Šuštar-Vozlič J, Pipan B, Zadražnik T, Meglič V. Drought stress response in agricultural plants: A case study of common bean (*Phaseolus vulgaris* L.). In: Ondrasek G, editor. Drought- Detection and Solutions [Internet]. London, UK: IntechOpen; 2019. Available from: https://www.intechopen.com/books/advanced-biometric-technologies/liveness-detection-in-biometrics

[17] Caldas DGG, Konzen ER, Recchia GH, Pereira ACVZ, Tsai SM, Caldas DGG, et al. Functional genomics of biotic and abiotic stresses in *Phaseolus vulgaris*. In: Abiotic and Biotic Stress in Plants - Recent Advances and Future Perspectives. London, UK: IntechOpen; 2016. pp. 121-151. Available from: https://www.intechopen.com/chapters/49750

[18] Mazón-Suástegui MJ, Ojeda-Silvera CM, García-Bernal M, Avilés-Quevedo AM, Abasolo-Pacheco F, Batista-Sánchez D, et al. Agricultural homoeopathy: A new insight into organics. In: Multifunctionality and Impacts of Organic and Conventional Agriculture. London, UK: IntechOpen; 2016. pp. 1-18. DOI: 10.5772/intechopen.84482

[19] Câmara C, Urrea C, Schlegel V. Pinto beans (*Phaseolus vulgaris* L.) as a functional food: Implications on human health. Agriculture. 2013;**3**(1):90-111

[20] Angeles JGC, Villanueva JC, Uy LYC, Mercado SMQ, Tsuchiya MCL, Lado JP, et al. Legumes as functional food for cardiovascular disease. Applied Sciences. 2021;**11**(12):1-39

[21] Bennetau-Pelissero C. Plant proteins from legumes. In: Reference Series in Phytochemistry [Internet]. Cham: Springer; 2019 [cited 2022 Dec 8]. pp. 223-265. DOI: 10.1007/978-3-319-78030-6_3

[22] Gouveia CSS, Freitas G, de Brito JH, Slaski JJ, de Carvalho MAÂP. Nutritional and mineral variability in 52 accessions of common bean varieties (*Phaseolus vulgaris* L.) from Madeira Island. Agricultural Sciences. 2014;**5**(4):317-329

[23] Veber A, Zaręba D, Ziarno M. Functional fermented beverage prepared from germinated white kidney beans (*Phaseolus vulgaris* L.). In: Ziarno M, editor. Milk Substitutes - Selected Aspects [Internet]. London, UK: IntechOpen; 2021. Available from: https://www.intechopen.com/books/advanced-biometric-technologies/liveness-detection-in-biometrics

[24] Blair MW. Mineral biofortification strategies for food staples: The example of common bean. Journal of Agricultural and Food Chemistry. 2013;**61**(35):8287-8294

[25] Kotue T, Marlyne J, Wirba L, Amalene S, Nkenmeni D, Kwuimgoin I, et al. Nutritional properties and nutrients chemical analysis of common beans seed. MedCrave Online Journal of Biology and Medicine. 2018;**3**(2):41-47

[26] CIAT. Common bean: The nearly perfect food. The importance of common bean. CIAT in Focus Crop Commitment. 2019

[27] Jannat S, Shah AH, Sabir SM. Nutraceutical characterisation of

common bean (*Phaseolus vulgaris* L.) germplasm from Pakistan. International Food Research Journal. 2019;**26**(2):1835-1843

[28] Delgado E, Reyes-Jaquez D. Extruded aquaculture feed: A review. In: Qamar SZ, editor. Extrusion of Metals, Polymers, and Food Products. [Internet]. London, UK: IntechOpen; 2018. p. 21. Available from: https://www.intechopen.com/books/advanced-biometric-technologies/liveness-detection-in-biometrics

[29] Karavidas I, Ntatsi G, Vougeleka V, Karkanis A, Ntanasi T, Saitanis C, et al. Agronomic practices to increase the yield and quality of common bean (*Phaseolus vulgaris* L.): A systematic review. Agronomy [Internet]. 2022;**12**(2):271. Available from: https://www.mdpi.com/2073-4395/12/2/271/htm

[30] Assefa T, Assibi Mahama A, Brown AV, Cannon EKS, Rubyogo JC, Rao IM, et al. A review of breeding objectives, genomic resources, and marker-assisted methods in common bean (*Phaseolus vulgaris* L.). Molecular Breeding. 2019;**39**(2):1-23

[31] Zargar SM, Mahajan R, Nazir M, Nagar P, Kim ST, Rai V, et al. Common bean proteomics: Present status and future strategies. Journal of Proteomics. [Internet]. 2017;**169**:239-248. DOI: 10.1016/j.jprot.2017.03.019

[32] Seleiman MF, Al-Suhaibani N, Ali N, Akmal M, Alotaibi M, Refay Y, et al. Drought stress impacts on plants and different approaches to alleviate its adverse effects. Plants. 2021;**10**(2):1-25

[33] Reinprecht Y, Qi Y, Shahmir F, Smith TH, Pauls KP. Yield and antiyield genes in common bean (*Phaseolus vulgaris* L.). Legume Science. 2021;**3**(3):1-17

[34] Cominelli E, Rodiño AP, De Ron AM, Sparvoli F. Genetic approaches to improve common bean nutritional quality: Current knowledge and future perspectives. In: Quality Breeding in Field Crops. Cham: Springer; 2019. pp. 109-138. DOI: 10.1007/978-3-030-04609-5_5

[35] Jangra S, Chaudhary V, Yadav RC, Yadav NR. High-throughput phenotyping: A platform to accelerate crop improvement. Phenomics [Internet]. 2021;**1**(2):31-53. DOI: 10.1007/s43657-020-00007-6

[36] Lowe NM. The global challenge of hidden hunger: Perspectives from the field. The Proceedings of the Nutrition Society. 2021;**80**(3):283-289

[37] Muthayya S, Rah JH, Sugimoto JD, Roos FF, Kraemer K, Black RE. The global hidden hunger indices and maps: An advocacy tool for action. PLoS One. 2013;**8**(6):1-12

[38] Caproni L, Raggi L, Talsma EF, Wenzl P, Negri V. European landrace diversity for common bean biofortification: A genome-wide association study. Scientific Reports [Internet]. 2020;**10**(1):1-13. DOI: 10.1038/s41598-020-76417-3

[39] Blair MW, Astudillo C, Grusak MA, Graham R, Beebe SE. Inheritance of seed iron and zinc concentrations in common bean (*Phaseolus vulgaris* L.). Molecular Breeding. 2009 Feb;**23**(2):197-207

[40] Cichy KA, Caldas GV, Snapp SS, Blair MW. QTL analysis of seed iron, zinc, and phosphorus levels in an Andean Bean population. Crop Science. 2009;**49**(5):1742-1750

[41] Gregory PJ, Wahbi A, Adu-Gyamfi J, Heiling M, Gruber R, Joy EJM, et al.

Approaches to reduce zinc and iron deficits in food systems. Global Food Security. Dec 2017;**1**(15):1-10

[42] Bindraban PS, Dimkpa CO, Pandey R. Exploring phosphorus fertilizers and fertilization strategies for improved human and environmental health. [cited 2022 Dec 12]; DOI: 10.1007/s00374-019-01430-2

[43] Blair MW, Hurtado N, Sharma P. New gene-derived simple sequence repeat markers for common bean (*Phaseolus vulgaris* L.). Molecular Ecology Resources. 2012;**12**(4):661-668

[44] Bouis HE, Saltzman A. Improving nutrition through biofortification: A review of evidence from HarvestPlus, 2003 through 2016. Global Food Security. [Internet]. 2017;**12**:49-58. DOI: 10.1016/j.gfs.2017.01.009

[45] Gioia T, Logozzo G, Attene G, Bellucci E, Benedettelli S, Negri V, et al. Evidence for introduction bottleneck and extensive inter-gene pool (Mesoamerica x Andes) hybridization in the European common bean (*Phaseolus vulgaris* L.) germplasm. PLoS One. 2013;**8**(10):1-14

[46] Schmutz J, McClean PE, Mamidi S, Wu GA, Cannon SB, Grimwood J, et al. A reference genome for common bean and genome-wide analysis of dual domestications. Nature Genetics [Internet]. 2014;**46**(7):707-713. DOI: 10.1038/ng.3008

[47] Valdisser PAMR, Pereira WJ, Almeida Filho JE, Müller BSF, Coelho GRC, de Menezes IPP, et al. In-depth genome characterization of a Brazilian common bean core collection using DArTseq high-density SNP genotyping. BMC Genomics. 2017;**18**(1):1-19

[48] Xiao Y, Liu H, Wu L, Warburton M, Yan J. Genome-wide association studies in maize: Praise and stargaze. Molecular Plant [Internet]. 2017;**10**(3):359-374. DOI: 10.1016/j.molp.2016.12.008

[49] Perseguini J, Oblessuc PR, Rosa J, Gomes KA, Chiorato AF, Carbonell S. Genome-wide association studies of anthracnose and angular leaf spot resistance in common bean (*Phaseolus vulgaris* L.). PLoS One. 2016;**11**(3):150506

[50] Wu J, Zhu J, Wang L, Wang S. Genome-wide association study identifies NBS-LRR-encoding genes related with anthracnose and common bacterial blight in the common bean. Frontiers in Plant Science. 2017;**8**(August):1-15

[51] Campa A, García-Fernández C, Ferreira JJ. Genome-wide association study (GWAS) for resistance to sclerotinia sclerotiorum in common bean. Genes (Basel). 2020;**11**(12):1-16

[52] Dramadri IO, Amongi W, Kelly JD, Mugisha MC. Genome-wide association analysis of resistance to Pythium ultimum in common bean (*Phaseolus vulgaris*). Plant Breeding. 2020;**139**(6):1168-1180

[53] Oladzad A, Porch T, Rosas JC, Moghaddam SM, Beaver J, Beebe SE, et al. Single and multi-trait GWAS identify genetic factors associated with production traits in common bean under abiotic stress environments. G3 Genes, Genomes, Genetics. 2019;**9**(6):1881-1892

[54] Valdisser PAMR, Müller BSF, de Almeida Filho JE, Morais Júnior OP, Guimarães CM, Borba TCO, et al. Genome-wide association studies detect multiple QTLs for productivity in Mesoamerican diversity panel of common bean under drought stress. Frontiers in Plant Science. 2020;**11**:1-22

[55] Kamfwa K, Cichy KA, Kelly JD. Genome-wide association study of agronomic traits in common bean. Plant Genome [Internet]. 2015;**8**(2):1-12. Available from: https://onlinelibrary.wiley.com/doi/full/10.3835/plantgenome2014.09.0059

[56] Moghaddam SM, Mamidi S, Osorno JM, Lee R, Brick M, Kelly J, et al. Genome-wide association study identifies candidate loci underlying agronomic traits in a Middle American diversity panel of common bean. Plant Genome [Internet]. 2016;**9**(3):1-21. Available from: https://onlinelibrary.wiley.com/doi/full/10.3835/plantgenome2016.02.0012

[57] Nkhata W, Shimelis H, Melis R, Chirwa R, Mzengeza T, Mathew I, et al. Genome-wide association analysis of bean fly resistance and agro-morphological traits in common bean. PLoS One [Internet]. 2021;**16**(4):e0250729. Available from: https://journals.plos.org/plosone/article?id=10.1371/journal.pone.0250729

[58] Cichy KA, Wiesinger JA, Mendoza FA. Genetic diversity and genome-wide association analysis of cooking time in dry bean (*Phaseolus vulgaris* L.). Theoretical and Applied Genetics. 2015;**128**(8):1555-1567

[59] Ambachew D, Blair MW. Genome wide association mapping of root traits in the Andean genepool of common bean (*Phaseolus vulgaris* L.) grown with and without Aluminum toxicity. Front. Plant Science. 2021;**12**:1-14

[60] Wu L, Chang Y, Wang L, Wu J, Wang S. Genetic dissection of drought resistance based on root traits at the bud stage in common bean. Theoretical and Applied Genetics [Internet]. 2021;**134**(4):1047-1061. Available from: https://link.springer.com/article/10.1007/s00122-020-03750-6

[61] Gunjača J, Carović-Stanko K, Lazarević B, Vidak M, Petek M, Liber Z, et al. Genome-wide association studies of mineral content in common bean. Frontiers in Plant Science [Internet]. 2021;**12**. Available from: https://www.frontiersin.org/articles/10.3389/fpls.2021.636484/full

[62] Carović-Stanko K, Liber Z, Vidak M, Barešić A, Grdiša M, Lazarević B, et al. Genetic diversity of Croatian common bean landraces. Frontiers in Plant Science. 2017;**8**:1-8

[63] Čupić T, Gantner R, Popović S, Tucak M, Sudar R, Stjepanović M. Widespread annual legumes in Croatia. In: Stipešević B, Sorić R, editors. Proceedings & Abstracts 5th International Scientific/Professional Conference. Osijek, Croatia: Glas Slavonije d.d; 2012. pp. 220-225

[64] Vidak M, Malešević S, Grdiša M, Šatović Z, Lazarević B, Carović-Stanko K. Phenotypic diversity among Croatian common bean (*Phaseolus vulgaris* L.) landraces. Agriculturae Conspectus Scientificus. 2015;**80**(3):133-137

[65] Azeez MA, Adubi AO, Durodola FA. Landraces and crop genetic improvement. In: Grillo O, editor. Rediscovery of Landraces as a Resource for the Future [Internet]. London: IntechOpen; 2018. p. 1-19. Available from: http://www.intechopen.com/books/trends-in-telecommunications-technologies/gps-total-electron-content-tec-prediction-at-ionosphere-layer-over-the-equatorial-region%0AInTec

[66] Celmeli T, Sari H, Canci H, Sari D, Adak A, Eker T, et al. The nutritional content of common bean (*Phaseolus vulgaris* L.) landraces in comparison to modern varieties. Agronomy. 2018;**8**(9):1-9

[67] Yin L, Zhang H, Tang Z, Xu J, Yin D, Yuan X, et al. rMVP: A memory-efficient, visualization-enhanced, and parallel-1 accelerated tool for genome-wide association study. Genomics Proteomics Bioinforma. 2021;**19**(4):619-628

[68] Pandžić K, Likso T, Curić O, Mesić M, Pejić I, Pasarić Z. Drought indices for the Zagreb-Grič observatory with an overview of drought damage in agriculture in Croatia. Theoretical and Applied Climatology. 2020;**142**(1-2):555-567

[69] Vidak M, Šatović Z, Liber Z, Grdiša M, Gunjača J, Kilian A, et al. Assessment of the origin and diversity of Croatian common bean germplasm using Phaseolin type, SSR and SNP markers and morphological traits. Plants. 2021;**10**(4):665, 1-23. DOI: 10.3390/plants10040665

[70] Palčić I, Karažija T, Petek M, Lazarević B, Herak Ćustić M, Gunjača J, et al. Relationship between origin and nutrient content of Croatian common bean landraces. Journal of Central European Agriculture. 2018;**19**(3):490-502

[71] Wenzl P, Carling J, Kudrna D, Jaccoud D, Huttner E, Kleinhofs A, et al. Diversity arrays technology (DArT) for whole-genome profiling of barley. Proceedings of the National Academy of Sciences of the United States of America. 2004;**101**(26):9915-9920

[72] Zhang Z, Schwartz S, Wagner L, Miller W. A greedy algorithm for aligning DNA sequences. Journal of Computational Biology. 2000;**7**(1-2):203-214

[73] Browning BL, Zhou Y, Browning SR. A one-penny imputed genome from next-generation reference panels. American Journal of Human Genetics. 2018;**103**(3):338-348

[74] Bradbury PJ, Zhang Z, Kroon DE, Casstevens TM, Ramdoss Y, Buckler ES. TASSEL: Software for association mapping of complex traits in diverse samples. Bioinformatics. 2007;**23**(19):2633-2635

[75] Endelman JB, Jannink JL. Shrinkage estimation of the realized relationship matrix. G3-Genes Genomes Genetics. 2012;**2**(11):1405-1413

[76] Yang J, Lee SH, Goddard ME, Visscher PM. GCTA: A tool for genome-wide complex trait analysis. American Journal of Human Genetics. 2011;**88**(1):76-82

[77] Muñoz PR, Resende MFR, Gezan SA, Resende MDV, de los Campos G, Kirst M, et al. Unraveling additive from nonadditive effects using genomic relationship matrices. Genetics. 2014;**198**(4):1759-1768

[78] Zhu Z, Bakshi A, Vinkhuyzen AAE, Hemani G, Lee SH, Nolte IM, et al. Dominance genetic variation contributes little to the missing heritability for human complex traits. American Journal of Human Genetics. 2015;**96**(3):377-385

[79] Diniz WJS, Mazzoni G, Coutinho LL, Banerjee P, Geistlinger L, Cesar ASM, et al. Detection of co-expressed pathway modules associated with mineral concentration and meat quality in nelore cattle. Frontiers in Genetics. 2019;**10**:1-12

[80] Mangin B, Siberchicot A, Nicolas S, Doligez A, This P, Cierco-Ayrolles C. Novel measures of linkage disequilibrium that correct the bias due to population structure and relatedness. Heredity (Edinb). 2012;**108**(3):285-291

[81] Hill WG, Weir BS. Variances and covariances of squared linkage disequilibria in finite populations. Theoretical Population Biology. 1988;**33**(1):54-78

[82] Dahl A, Iotchkova V, Baud A, Johansson S, Gyllensten U, Soranzo N, et al. A multiple-phenotype imputation method for genetic studies. Nature Genetics. 2016;**48**(4):466-472

[83] Yu J, Pressoir G, Briggs WH, Bi IV, Yamasaki M, Doebley JF, et al. A unified mixed-model method for association mapping that accounts for multiple levels of relatedness. Nature Genetics. 2006;**38**(2):203-208

[84] Segura V, Vilhjálmsson BJ, Platt A, Korte A, Seren Ü, Long Q, et al. An efficient multi-locus mixed-model approach for genome-wide association studies in structured populations. Nature Genetics. 2012;**44**(7):825-830

[85] Storey JD, Bass AJ, Dabney A, Robinson D. qvalue: Q-value estimation for false discovery rate control version 2.22.0 from bioconductor [Internet]. 2020. Available from: https://rdrr.io/bioc/qvalue/

[86] Yin L, Zhang H, Tang Z, Xu J, Yin D. rMVP: A memory-efficient, visualization-enhanced, and parallel-accelerated tool for genome-wide association study. Genomics Proteomics Bioinforma. 2020;**19**(4):619-628

[87] Walter A, Liebisch F, Hund A. Plant phenotyping: From bean weighing to image analysis. Plant Methods. 2015;**11**(1):1-11

[88] Kondić-Špika A, Mikić S, Mirosavljević M, Trkulja D, Marjanović Jeromela A, Rajković D, et al. Crop breeding for a changing climate in the Pannonian region: Towards integration of modern phenotyping tools. Journal of Experimental Botany. 2022;**73**(15):5089-5110. Available from: https://academic.oup.com/jxb/article/73/15/5089/6583379

[89] Yao Y, Yang Y, Li C, Huang D, Zhang J, Wang C, et al. Plants research progress on the functions of gasotransmitters in plant responses to abiotic stresses. 2019 [cited 2022 Dec 12]; Available from: www.mdpi.com/journal/plants

[90] Lazarević B, Šatović Z, Nimac A, Vidak M, Gunjača J, Politeo O, et al. Application of phenotyping methods in detection of drought and salinity stress in basil (*Ocimum basilicum* L.). Frontiers in Plant Science. 2021;**12**:1-13

[91] Brestic M, Zivcak M. PSII fluorescence techniques for measurement of drought and high temperature stress signal in crop plants: Protocols and applications. In: Molecular Stress Physiology of Plants [Internet]. 2013; [cited 2022 Dec 12]. pp. 87-131. Available from: https://link.springer.com/chapter/10.1007/978-81-322-0807-5_4

[92] Roth L, Barendregt C, Bétrix CA, Hund A, Walter A. High-throughput field phenotyping of soybean: Spotting an ideotype. Remote Sensing of Environment. 2022;**269**:1-13

[93] Sankaran S, Quirós JJ, Miklas PN. Unmanned aerial system and satellite-based high resolution imagery for high-throughput phenotyping in dry bean. Computers and Electronics in Agriculture. [Internet]. 2019;**165**:1-38. DOI: 10.1016/j.compag.2019.104965

[94] Li D, Quan C, Song Z, Li X, Yu G, Li C, et al. High-throughput plant phenotyping platform (HT3P) as a novel tool for estimating agronomic traits from the lab to the field. Frontiers in Bioengineering and Biotechnology. 2021;**8**:1-24

[95] Zargar SM, Nazir M, Rai V, Hajduch M, Agrawal GK, Rakwal R. Towards a common bean proteome atlas: Looking at the current state of research and the need for a comprehensive proteome. Frontiers in Plant Science. 2015;**6**:1-4

[96] Taiz L, Zeiger E. Plant Physiology. 3rd ed. Massachusetts, USA: Sinauer Associates; 2002

[97] Farooq M, Hussain M, Wahid A, Siddique KHM. Drought stress in plants: An overview. In: Plant Responses to Drought Stress: From Morphological to Molecular Features [Internet]. Berlin Heidelberg: Springer-Verlag; 2012. [cited 2022 Dec 12]. pp. 1-33. Available from: https://link.springer.com/chapter/10.1007/978-3-642-32653-0_1

[98] Maxwell K, Johnson GN. Chlorophyll fluorescence—A practical guide. Journal of Experimental Botany [Internet]. 2000;**51**(345):659-668. Available from: https://academic.oup.com/jxb/article/51/345/659/652534

[99] Zubler AV, Yoon JY. Proximal methods for plant stress detection using optical sensors and machine learning. Biosens [Internet]. 2020;**10**(12):193. Available from: https://www.mdpi.com/2079-6374/10/12/193/htm

[100] Gitelson AA, Merzlyak MN, Chivkunova OB. Optical properties and nondestructive estimation of anthocyanin content in plant leaves. Photochemistry and Photobiology. 2001;**74**(1):38

[101] Gitelson AA, Gritz Y, Merzlyak MN. Relationships between leaf chlorophyll content and spectral reflectance and algorithms for non-destructive chlorophyll assessment in higher plant leaves. Journal of Plant Physiology. 2003;**160**(3):271-282

[102] Kandel H, Endres G. Dry Bean Production Guide. North Dakota: NDSU Extension; 2019. pp. 1-128

[103] Lazarević B, Carović-Stanko K, Živčak M, Vodnik D, Javornik T, Safner T. Classification of high-throughput phenotyping data for differentiation among nutrient deficiency in common bean. Frontiers in Plant Science. 2022;**13**(931877):1-17

Chapter 2

The Role of the Internal Structure of Fabaceae Seeds in the Processes of Dormancy and Germination

Enoc Jara-Peña and Manuel Marín-Bravo

Abstract

The germination processes of Fabaceae seeds are well studied based on physiological parameters. However, in many cases, especially in wild seeds, there is a predominance of dormancy processes that must be reversed to finally produce germination, generally applying scarification processes. In the anatomical studies of seeds, a certain conformation of the structure of the cover is appreciated, with a predominance of sclerenchymatic tissues and waxy covers that are the cause of the difficulty of the entry of water to produce the imbibition of the seed. Mechanical or chemical scarifications are usually recommended to produce effective scarification. The characterization of the anatomical details of the seed coat allows us to predict the appropriate scarification technique with which optimal seed germination can be obtained.

Keywords: anatomy, seminal seed coat, mechanical scarification, ecological restoration, Fabaceae seeds

1. Introduction

The seed is the main reproductive organ of the spermatophytes. In nature, the seed is a basic food source for many animals and can be stored alive for long periods, thus ensuring the preservation of valuable plant species and varieties [1]. The seed plays a fundamental role in the dispersal, renewal, persistence of plant populations, forest regeneration, and ecological succession. For this reason, it is considered to be one of the main resources for the agricultural and silvicultural management of plant populations, for reforestation and the conservation of plant germplasm.

Knowledge about the germination of native species is considered the initial step in ecological restoration processes [2]. This knowledge is not only related to germination requirements, but also includes storage techniques to ensure its availability in the medium and long term [3]. Although there are few studies on the propagation of native Andean species [4], the importance of the ecological requirements of seeds in relation to ecological restoration programs is currently recognized [5]. Among the physiological processes that control germination is dormancy, which allows the seeds to remain for long periods of time in the soil until the environmental conditions are favorable for the establishment of seedlings [6]. Several types of dormancy have been described, including physical dormancy, which is determined by the characteristics of the seed (or fruit) cover and prevents the absorption of water by the embryo [7]. This type of dormancy is considered one of the most evolved in angiosperms and one of the families that presents them in a notorious way is the Fabaceae, which has the so-called hard seeds in which the characteristics of the thickening of the seed coat that prevent the adequate hydration of the embryo and therefore the triggering of the germination process; [8, 9]. The identification of the anatomical components of physical dormancy in seeds and the methods for the seed to get out of this state are key to understanding the germination and dispersal process of species that present this type of dormancy [9, 10]. This paper reports the effects of mechanical scarification in the germination of three promising Fabaceae seeds from the Peruvian Andean zone in relation to the structural anatomical characteristics of the seed coat.

2. Taxonomics aspects

The Fabaceae is one of the largest and most important families of angiosperms and is considered monophyletic in both morphological and molecular analyses [11]. Geographically, the Fabaceae are trees, shrubs, and herbs distributed in the South American Neotropics. In Peru around 145 genera and 1000 species have been registered, the endemic species occupy mainly the so-called Mesoandean regions, such as the humid and dry puna and the humid montane forests, between 1100 and 4800 meters of altitude [12]. The genus with the largest number of endemic species is *Lupinus*, in contrast to the genus *Astragalus* with few endemic species. Many of the Fabaceae species are promising phytostabilizing species, and there is a priority need to carry out detailed taxonomic studies and a greater collection of specimens of these genera [12]. *Astragalus garbancillo* Cav. (**Figure 1A**, **D**), It is a species that forms dense shrubby perennial tufts that in very cold places are small-sized plants, frequently glabrous and erect or sometimes decumbent stems. The fruit is an oblong

Figure 1.
Evaluated species and their seeds. A, D Astragalus garbancillo. *B, E* Lupinus ballianus. *C, F* Lupinus condensiflorus.

legume, sometimes compressed and puberulent with 3–4 seeds [13]. *Lupinus ballianus* C.P. Sm. (**Figure 1B** and **E**), is a shrub approximately 1.50 meters tall, with branches and petioles with an attenuated pubescence [13]. *Lupinus condensiflorus* C.P.Sm. (**Figure 1C** and **F**), is a shrubby species 60 to 110 cm long, with sericeous-adpressed stems and branches. Fruits are 2.9 cm x 2.9 cm x 0.8 cm broad, hairy, with 3–5 seeds, and rostrate [14].

3. Methodology

3.1 Method of collecting fruits of species of *Astragalus* and *Lupinus*

The fruits of the seeds of the evaluated species were collected in different localities of the Peruvian high Andean region (**Table 1**). Aspects of the reproductive phenology of the species were previously defined, through a previous visit to the natural populations of these species, taking into account that the beginning of flowering, fruiting, fruit ripening, and seed dispersal; they are different if we compare it with the fruits of non-domesticated plants [15]. The ripe fruits were manually detached from the floral clusters and then stored in Kraft paper bags. Once the collection was finished, the fruits were wrapped with a paper towel to reduce humidity [16]. The criteria established to determine the maturity of the fruits were the change in coloration and the reduction in moisture content. It was observed that in most of the fruits and seeds of the high Andean plant species, maturation ends in the month of July, while the dispersal of the seeds begins in the month of August and ends in the month of October, this physiological process coincides with the dry season that prevails in the Andean region of the country.

3.2 Determination of seed moisture content

Seed moisture was determined based on dry weight (dw) by weighing them in Petri dishes on an analytical balance. For each species, five replicates and 20 seeds per Petri dish were weighed in the case of Lupinus ballianus and L. condensiflorus and 100 seeds in the case of *Astragalus garbancillo*, because the seeds are small in the latter. For the determination of the dry weight, the seeds were dried in an oven at 105°C for 4 hours. Seed moisture content was expressed in terms of the weight of water contained in seed as a percentage of the total weight of the seed before drying, known as wet weight based on fresh weight (fw) [17, 18] and was calculated using the following equation [19]:

$$\text{Moisture Content}(\%\text{dw}) = (\text{fresh weight}) - (\text{dry weight}) / (\text{dry weight})] \times 100 \quad (1)$$

3.3 Seed pre-treatment by mechanical scarification

A part of the evaluated seeds was subjected to a mechanical scarification treatment to ensure their hydration and ensure the appropriate conditions to achieve optimal germination. The outer coverings of the seeds were scraped using fine sandpaper, taking care not to deeply damage the testa. The scarified seeds were disinfected in a 30% sodium hypochlorite solution for 20 minutes, rinsed several times in distilled

Localities	District	Province	Region	Altitude (m)	Coordinates UTM
Santa Rosa	Aquia	Bolognesi	Ancash	3, 798	265,166, 8,894,157
Cerro bendita	Lachaqui	Canta	Lima	3, 780	322,491, 8,722,856
Caruya-Rio blanco	Chicla	Huarochiri	Lima	3, 889	363,325, 8,701,373

Table 1.
Places of origin, altitude and geographic coordinates (UTM) of fruits, and seeds of Andean species of Astragalus *and* Lupinus *evaluated.*

water and then sown in Petri dishes conditioned with filter paper and sterile water, hermetically covered and incubated in a growth chamber at 21°C during the day, 15°C at night, with a photoperiod of 12 hours of light and 12 hours of darkness and with a relative humidity of 80% during the day and 90% at night. A germinated seed was considered when it presented the emergence of a radicle of at least 0.5 mm long. Finally, on the tenth day, the calculation of the accumulated percentage of germinated and non-germinated seeds was made according to the species and treatment evaluated.

3.4 Experimental design and statistical treatment

The experiment was carried out under laboratory conditions using a completely randomized experimental design. They were evaluated under two light conditions (with and without light) and with two scarification treatments (with mechanical scarification, and without scarification). For each species, four treatments were evaluated, with five repetitions for each treatment (Number of Petri dishes). For the germination test, 20 pre-treated seeds of each species were added to each Petri dish. The distribution of the experimental units (Petri dishes with seeds) within the growth chamber was carried out at random. In the statistical analysis, it was carried out according to the experimental design, and the variance analysis (ANOVA) was carried out, and the multiple comparison test of means by Tukey (α = 0.01), using the Infostat program version 2016e.

3.5 Observation of the internal structure of the seed

Representative seeds of the evaluated species were cut transversally by freehand, rinsed in 50% sodium hypochlorite, washed, stained with 1% toluidine blue, and mounted in diluted glycerine for observation at 100 and 400 magnifications in light microscopy [20]. For the observation of the seeds in scanning electron microscopy, the material was treated following the steps of fixation with Carnovsky, post fixation with 1% osmium tetroxide, dehydration with a battery of alcohols, drying of the samples at a critical point with CO_2. Mounting of the samples with double-sided adhesive tape, conductive tape, and gold plating on an ion coating. [21]. Observations were made between 90 and 5000 magnifications in the INSPECT S50 Scanning Electron Microscope (FEI, Hillsboro, Oregon), from the equipment laboratory of the Faculty of Biological Sciences of the National University of San Marcos.

4. Results

4.1 Moisture content of *Astragalus* and *Lupinus* seeds

Significant statistical differences ($p < 0.0093$) were obtained in the moisture content of *Astragalus garbancillo* seeds compared to *Lupinus ballianus* and *L. condensiflorus* seeds. The highest moisture content in the seeds was registered in *Astragalus garbancillo*, while in the *Lupinus* species the moisture content remained at values below 10% (**Table 2**).

4.2 Germination of the seeds of *Astragalus* and *Lupinus* species

In the germination of the seeds of the species, significant statistical differences ($p < 0.001$) were obtained in the analysis of variance (ANOVA) between the evaluated treatments. In the mean separation analysis by Tukey's test of the number of germinated seedlings, differences were obtained, being the highest values obtained in the number of germinated seeds with the treatment with mechanical scarification in the species of *Astragalus garbancillo* and *Lupinus condensiflorus* compared with the lower value obtained by the seeds of *Lupinus ballianus*. Additionally, the seeds of *A. garbancillo* presented the least thickness in the seed coat (**Table 3**).

In the germination of the seeds of the evaluated species, statistically significant differences ($p < 0.001$) were obtained with the scarification and light factors according to the analysis of variance (ANOVA). The seeds with mechanical scarification of the testa and light treatment were the ones that germinated in the highest quantity (except *L. ballianus*) (**Table 4**).

Species	Seed moisture content (%)
Astragalus garbancillo	11.74 [a]
Lupinus condensiflorus	9.12 [b]
Lupinus ballianus	8.95 [b]
Least significant difference	2.15

a, b indicates significant differences between treatments (Tukey, α = 0.0093).

Table 2.
Moisture content of the seeds of the evaluated species.

Scarification factor	Number of germinated seeds		
	A. garbancillo	*L. condensiflorus*	*L. ballianus*
With mechanical scarification	18.33 [a]	18 [a]	13 [a]
Without mechanical scarification	1.6 [b]	3.8 [b]	1.83 [b]
Least significant difference	0.72	2.1	3.51
Seed coat thickness (μm)	7.95	8.30	9.0

a, b indicates significant differences between treatments (Tukey, α = 0.01).

Table 3.
Accumulated number of germinated seeds of the evaluated species in relation to scarification and thickness of the seed coat.

Scarification factor and light	Number of germinated seeds		
	A. garbancillo	*L. condensiflorus*	*L. ballianus*
With mechanical scarification	19.4 [a]	15.9 [a]	15.4 [a]
Without mechanical scarification	7.1 [b]	2.5 [b]	4.1 [b]
With lighting	13.6 [a]	10.2 [a]	7.6 [b]
In darkness	12.9 [a]	8.2 [b]	11.9 [a]
Least significant difference	1.25	2.19	1.91

a, b indicates significant differences between treatments (Tukey, $\alpha = 0.01$).

Table 4.
Number of germinated seeds accumulated in the species according to the scarification factor and light evaluated in laboratory conditions.

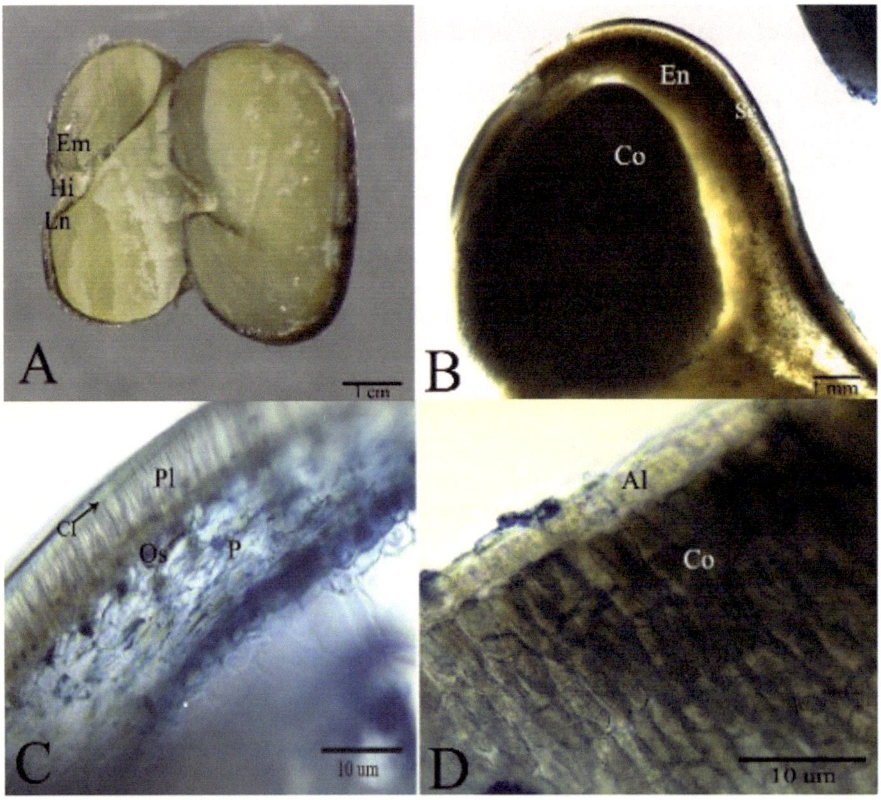

Figure 2.
Anatomical characteristics of the Astragalus garbancillo *seed. A, internal view of the seed. B, sagittal section of the seed. C, detail of the seed coat. D, detail of the aleurone layer and cotyledon. Em, embryo. Hi hilum. Ln, lens. Co, cotyledon. Sc, seed coat. Cl, clear line. Pl, palisade layer. Os, osteosclereids layer. P, parenchyma. Al, aleurone layer.*

4.3 Internal anatomical structure of the seed

In the transverse plane, the internal structure of the seminal layer of the seeds of the evaluated species shows a characteristic color for the species (**Figures 1A–3A**). An epidermal coat composed of a compact uniseriate layer of palisade sclereids (macrosclereid type), with non-uniformly thickened walls, about 10 microns thick, thicker in *Lupinus ballianus* and thinner in *Astragalus garbancillo* (**Figures 2B, C, 3B,** and **4B**). At the level of the hilum region, the palisade layer is thickened. On the outer wall of this palisade layer, there is a refringent linear region in the cell walls, thick in *L. ballianus*, thin in *A. garbancillo*, and intermediate in *L. condensiflorus*. **Table 3** shows the comparative results of the seminal coat thickness for the three species. The cells of the adjacent sub-epidermal layer differentiate into hourglass-shaped cells called osteosclereids (**Figures 2C, 3B,** and **4B**). The tissue underlying this layer is a type of colorless large elongated cell parenchyma with a tangentially collapsed appearance. Next, a single-stratified inner layer of quadrangular cells containing Aleurone granules. The innermost tissue, with a positive reaction to Lugol, corresponds to the cotyledon with starch-reserving parenchyma (**Figures 2D–4D**).

Under the scanning microscopy view, the thin cuticular surface of the testa appears finely rough and uniform in *Astragalus garbancillo* (**Figure 5A**), smooth and uniform in *Lupinus ballianus* (**Figure 6A**). and irregularly alveolate in *L. condensiflorus* (**Figure 7A**). In the region of the hilum, the funicular tissue can be seen, made up of a fine pubescence with a loose appearance, leaving in the central part the fine fissure of the hilar groove, oriented longitudinally in *Lupinus* species (**Figures 6B** and **7B**) and transversally oriented in *A. garbancillo* (**Figure 5C**). thin refringent line of this palisade layer of sclereids can be highlighted on its outer part (**Figures 5D, 6D,** and **7C**). In this hilar region, the palisade cell layer of the seed

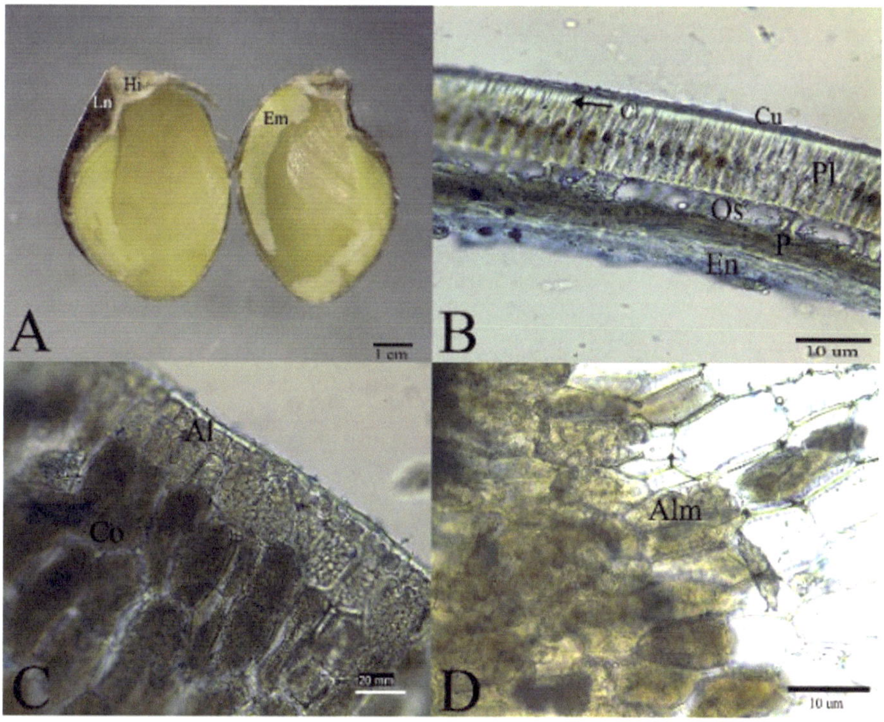

Figure 3.
Anatomical characteristics of the seed of Lupinus ballianus. *A, internal view of the seed. B, detail of the seed coat. C, detail of the aleurone layer and cotyledon D, cotyledon storage parenchyma. Em, embryo. Hi hilum. Ln, lens. Co, cotyledon. Sc, seed coat. Cl, clear line. Pl, palisade layer. Os, osteosclereids layer. P, parenchyma. En, endosperm. Al, aleurone layer.*

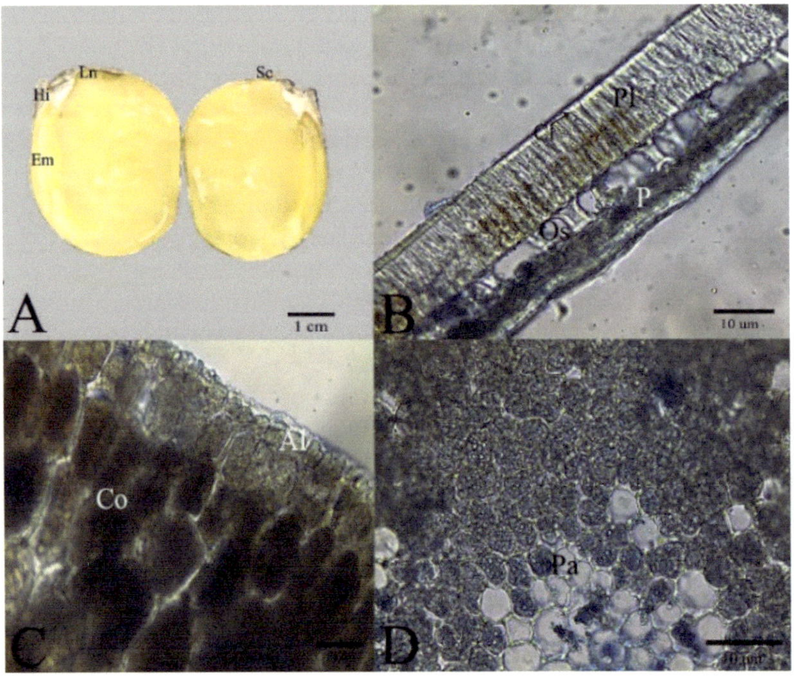

Figure 4.
Anatomical characteristics of the seed of Lupinus condensiflorus. *A, internal view of the seed. B, detail of the seed coat. C, detail of the aleurone layer and cotyledon D, cotyledon storage parenchyma. Hi hilum. Ln, lens. Co, cotyledon. Sc, seed coat. Cl, clear line. Pl, palisade layer. Os, osteosclereids layer. P, parenchyma. En, endosperm. Al, aleurone layer. Pa, storage parenchyma.*

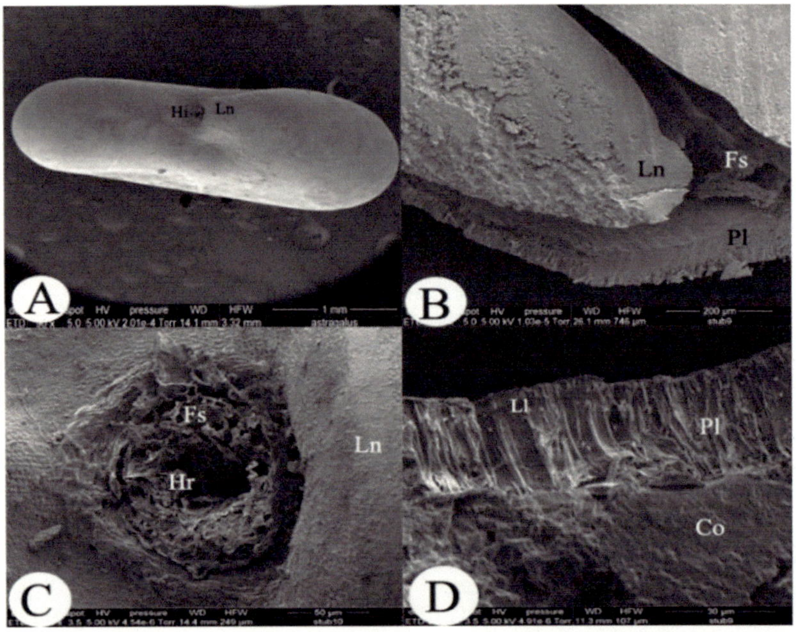

Figure 5.
Scanning microscopy images of Astragalus garbancillo *seeds. A. Detail of the surface of testa. B. Longitudinal section at the level of the hilum. C. Surface view of the hilar region. D. Cross section of the seed coat.*

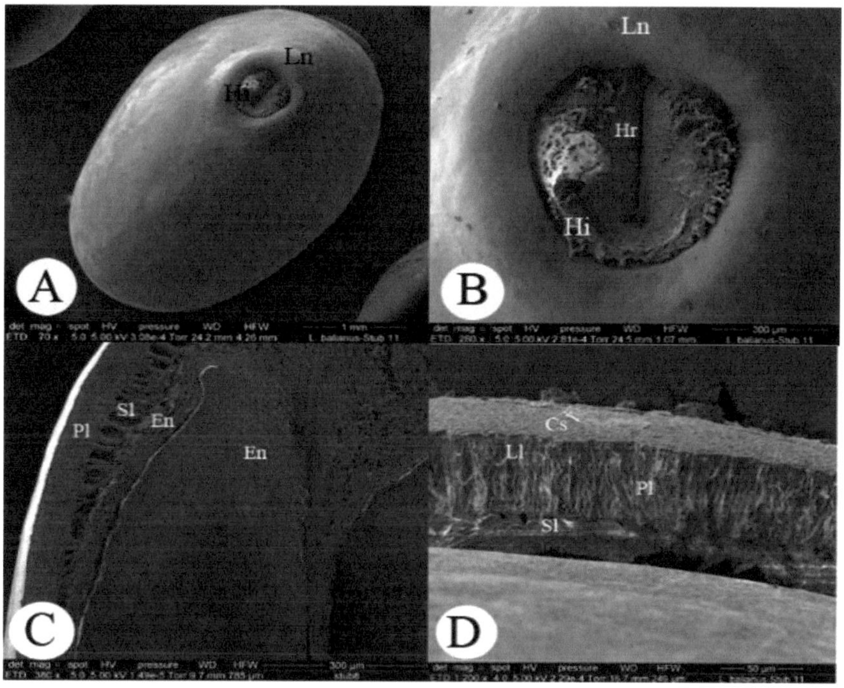

Figure 6.
Scanning microscopy images of Lupinus ballianus *seeds. A. Detail of the surface of testa. B. Detailed view of the hilar region. C. Longitudinal section of the seed. D. Cross section of seed coat.*

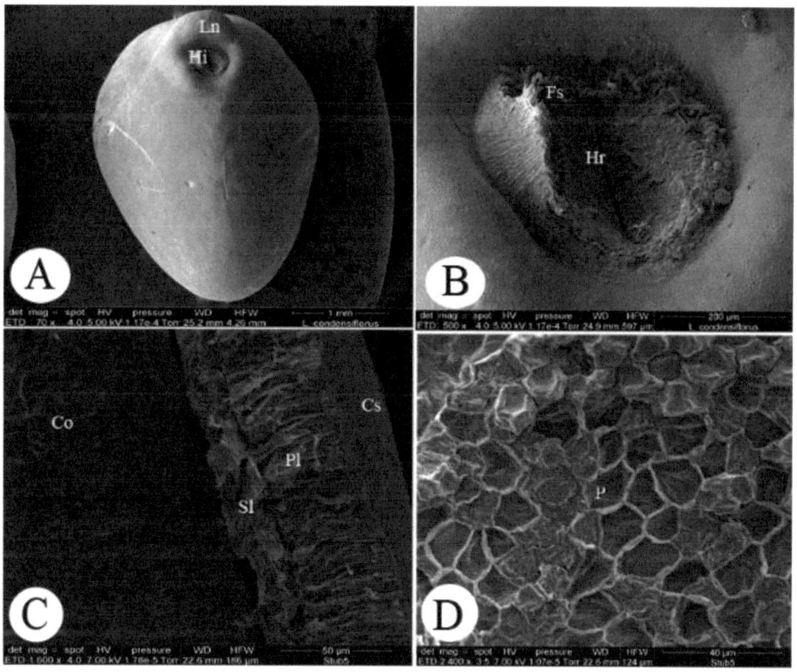

Figure 7.
Scanning microscopy images of Lupinus condensiflorus *seeds. A. Detail of the surface of testa. B. Detailed view of the hilar region. C. Longitudinal section of the seed. D. Detail of the seed storage parenchyma.*

coat is particularly thickened (**Figures 5B, 6C**, and **7C**). In *L. condensiflorus*, the endosperm cells are irregularly polygonal in shape (**Figure 7D**).

5. Discussion

The seeds of *Astragalus garbancillo* had the smallest diameter of the seed coat, associated with the palisade layer of sclereids (**Figure 2C**), which would explain the greater effectiveness of mechanical scarification expressed in the greater number of germinated seeds (**Table 3**). On the contrary, the seeds of *Lupinus ballianus* presented the thickest seed coat associated with the largest diameter of the palisade layer and the lowest germination percentages, which indicates that mechanical scarification was not effective for this species. A separate case represents the seeds of *L. condensiflorus*, which presented a thick seed coat and yet had a high percentage of germination. In the seeds of this species, its seminal coat was characterized by presenting a thin refringent line (**Figure 4B**), if we compare it with the thick refringent line shown by *L. ballianus* (**Figure 3B**), hence we associate this characteristic with effective mechanical scarification and its high percentage of germination. In fact, both species, *A. garbancillo* and *L. condensiflorus*, presented high germination percentages with the light factor associated with its thin refringent line (**Table 4**). Indeed, the presence of the thickened line on the outside of the seed coat and its hydrophobic cuticular layer would be determining a certain degree of impermeability of the seed coat to water and oxygen, which can be broken with a simple mechanical scarifying action. Seed dormancy refers to the state by which viable seed does not germinate when provided with favorable conditions for germination, such as adequate moisture, an appropriate temperature regime, normal atmosphere, and, in some cases, light [22]. This form of dormancy found in the evaluated seeds would correspond to the so-called physical dormancy, where the seminal seed coats (or fruit pericarps) are impermeable to water. This type of impermeability is considered to be one of the most evolved types of dormancy [23]. In this type of dormancy, the impermeability of water in the seed is caused by the presence of palisade cells, which constitutes an impermeable layer to water, so it forms a barrier to its entry [24]. For this reason, the effectiveness of scarification is demonstrated, which is a mechanical or chemical method, by which germination is induced through breakage, abrasion, or softening of the seed coat, making it more permeable to the inhibition of humidity [1].

Dormancy is considered to have evolved as a strategy to avoid germination in conditions where seedling survival is low [15, 19]. Seed dormancy breaking also depends on a balance between growth inhibitors and growth promoters. Among the numerous plant germination inhibitors, some are located in the fruit wall or in the seed coat. The stimulating effect of the elimination of the seed coat and the covers associated with germination determines that this is considered in itself as one of the inhibitory sources of germination. In this sense, in Fabaceae seeds, it is usual to find that the quality of light does not greatly affect the germination process [25]. Germination and seedling establishment are critical stages in the biological cycle of plants [26]. Seedling emergence is the event most important phenological of a crop's establishment. It represents the moment in which a seedling becomes independent of the non-renewable seminal reserves and when photosynthetic autotrophism begins. Emergence time often determines whether a plant competes successfully with its neighbors, whether it is consumed by herbivores, infested by diseases, and whether it flowers, reproduces, and matures at the end of its growth stage [27].

The seed coats of some species have characteristics that help germination and seed emergence. The testa of seeds eaten by animals and by humans can resist digestive processes and allow them to pass through the intestinal tract unharmed and thus facilitate seed dispersal. However, the use of corrosive chemical agents such as sulfuric acid may not always be considered the appropriate simile of this biological process [28]. In studies carried out on the emergence of seedlings in other *Lupinus* species under greenhouse conditions, it is mechanical scarification that determines the highest percentage of seedling emergence obtained with testa scarification, presenting up to 80% efficiency compared to chemical scarification with sulfuric acid [29]. Although the International Rules for Seed Testing (ISTA) recommends using concentrated sulfuric acid, for 2 to 45 minutes depending on the species, to scarify the test, this method is mentioned to be expensive and dangerous and should be followed with caution [19]. Under natural conditions, it has also been suggested that exposure of the seeds to high temperatures will be responsible for the release of dormancy [30].

The humidity factor is one of the conditions for triggering the seed germination processes. It is considered that the thread acts as a hygroscopic valve, by forming a fissure capable of interacting with the moisture content from the outside [7]. It is known that the combination of an impermeable testa with the valvular action of the thread allows reaching a high degree of desiccation in the hard seeds of Fabaceae, thus obtaining a certain percentage of humidity that is not affected by fluctuations in the external humidity content. of the seed [31]. This moisture is kept in equilibrium with the environment outside the seed and is the most important factor in determining the rate at which seeds deteriorate. For this reason, the moisture content within the seed is also an important aspect to consider in the postharvest of the crop. The determination of the moisture content before storing the seeds makes it possible to accurately predict the storage life potential of the accessions [19]. The highest moisture content recorded for *Astragalus garbancillo* (**Table 2**) seeds indicates their greatest potential to preserve their germination power for longer periods of time in relation to the dry season in the Andean region, in fact, we associate this feature with the shorter length of the hilar fissure compared to *Lupinus* species (**Figures 5C, 6B**, and **7B**). Additionally, we know of the influence of factors such as soil depth and its composition on the germination of especially hard cover seeds, such as Fabaceae seeds, and that they can effectively plan the establishment of species in projects of ecological restoration projects [32].

6. Conclusions

It is concluded that seed dormancy of the studied Andean Fabaceae species is related to the structural characteristics of the seed coat, especially the sclereid layer. Under the evaluated conditions, *Astragalus garbancillo* seeds had the thinnest sclereid layer compared to seeds of species of the genus *Lupinus*, with a thicker seed coat. Based on the germination percentages obtained, the mechanical scarification carried out on the seeds of *A. garbancillo* was the most effective method that allows them to come out of dormancy. The seeds of this species with a thin seminal coat also had a higher moisture content, which is why they have a greater potential for conservation in function and are ideal for ecological restoration programs.

Author details

Enoc Jara-Peña[1] and Manuel Marín-Bravo[2]*

1 Faculty of Biological Sciences, Applied Phytology Laboratory, National University of San Marcos, Lima, Perú

2 Faculty of Biological Sciences, Anatomy and Pharmacognosy Laboratory, National University of San Marcos, Lima, Perú

*Address all correspondence to: mmarinb@unmsm.edu.pe

References

[1] Azcón-Bieto J, Talón M. Fundamentos de fisiología Vegetal. 2nd ed. Madrid: McGraw-Hill Interamericana; 2008

[2] Perez-Suarez B. Observaciones sobre la germinación de tres especies delgenero Citharexylum Jacqm empleadas en restauración ecológica. Colombia Forestal. 2011;**14**(2):137-143. https://doi.org/10.14483/udistrital.jour.colomb.for.2011.2.a02

[3] Vargas O, Perez-Martinez LV. Semillas de plantas de paramo: ecología y métodos de germinación aplicados a la restauración ecológica. Bogota, Colombia: Grupo de Restauración Ecológica. Universidad Nacional de Colombia; 2014

[4] Castañeda SL, Garzón AE, Cantillo MA, Torres MP, Silva LJ. Análisis de la respuesta de ocho especies nativas del bosque alto andino ante dos métodos de propagación. Colombia Forestal. 2006;**10**(20):79-90. https://doi.org/10.14483/udistrital.jour.colomb.for.2007.1.a04

[5] Pedrini S, Dixon KW. International principles and standards for native seeds in ecological restoration. Restoration Ecology. 2020;**28**:286-303. DOI: 10.1111/rec.13155

[6] Fenner M, Thompson K. The Ecology of Seeds. Cambridge: Cambridge University Press; 2005

[7] Baskin CC, Baskin JM. Seeds: Ecology, Biogeography and Evolution of Dormancy and Germination. San Diego: Academic Press; 2014

[8] Galíndez G, Malagrina G, Ceccato D, Ledesma L-L, T.L., Ortega Baes P. Dormición física y conservación ex situ de semillas de Amburana cearensis y Myroxylon peruiferum (Fabaceae). Boletín de la Sociedad Argentina de Botánica. 2015;**50**(2):153-161

[9] Galussi AA, Argüello JA, Cerana MM, Maximino M, Moya ME. Características anatómicas y químicas del tegumento seminal de Medicago sativa L. (alfalfa) cv. Baralfa 85 y su asociación con la dormición. Phyton. 2015;**84**:163-117

[10] Mira S, Schnadelbach A, Correa E, Pérez-García F, González-Benito ME. Variability of physical dormancy in relation to seed mechanical properties of three legume species. Seed Science and Technology. 2017;**45**:540-556. DOI: 10.15258/sst.2017.45.3.11

[11] LPWG (Legume Phylogeny Working Group). A new subfamily classification of the Leguminosae based on a taxonomically comprehensive phylogeny. Evolution. 2017;**55**(9):1762-1780. DOI: 10.12705/661.3

[12] Baldeón S, Flores M, Roque J. Fabaceae endémicas del Perú. Revista peruana de biología Special number. 2006;**13**(2):302-337

[13] Carrillo FE. Las Leguminosas del Valle del Rímac, [Thesis]. Lima: National University of San Marcos; 1970

[14] Flores, M. La familia leguminosae en el valle del Chillón-Parte media y alta, [Thesis]. Lima, National University of San Marcos. 1997

[15] Schmidt L. Guide to Handling of Tropical and Subtropical Forest Seed, Humlebaek. Denmark: Danida Forest Seed Centre; 2000

[16] Ailstock MS, Shafer DJ, Magoun AD. Effects of planting depth, sediment grain

size, and nutrients on Ruppia maritima and Potamogeton perfoliatus seedling emergence and growth. Restoration Ecology. 2010;**18**(4):574-583

[17] Pablo-Perez M, Lagunes-Espinoza C, López-Upton J, Ramos-Juarez J, Aranda-Ibanez EM. Morfometría, germinación y composición mineral de semillas de Lupinus silvestre. Bioagro. 2013;**25**(2):101-108

[18] ISTA. International Rules for Seed Testing. 2023 edition. International Seed Testing Association. Bassersdorf, Suiza. 2005. Available from: https://www.seedtest.org/en/publications/international-rules-seed-testing.html. Accessed December 5, 2022.

[19] Rao NK, Hanson J, Dullo ME, Ghosh K, Novell D, Larinde M. Manual para el manejo de semillas en bancos de germoplasma, Manuales para Bancos de Germoplasma No. 8. Roma: Biodiversity International; 2007

[20] D'ambrogio de Argüeso A. Manual de Técnicas en Histología Vegetal. 1ra. ed. Buenos Aires. Editorial Hemisferio sur. 1996 p. 42-48

[21] Nath D, Dasgupta T. Study of some Vigna species following scanning electron microscopy (SEM). International Journal of Scientific and Research Publications. 2015;**5**(1):1-6. http://www.ijsrp.org/research-paper-0915.php?rp=P454575

[22] Baskin JM, Baskin CC. A classification system for seed dormancy. Seed Science Research. 2004;**14**:1-16

[23] Baskin JM, Baskin CC. Some considerations for adoptions of Nikolaeva's system in to seed dormancy classification. Seed Science Research. 2008;**18**:131-137

[24] Baskin CC, Baskin JM. Seeds: Ecology, Biogeography and Evolution of Dormancy and Germination. San Diego: Academic Press; 1998

[25] Corona Mora A, Gómez Romero M, Lindig Cisneros RA. Efecto de la escarificación y la calidad de la luz en la germinación de Lupinus elegans. Biológicas. 2007;**9**(1):47-54

[26] Harper J. Population Biology of Plant. London: Academic Press; 1977

[27] Forcella F, Benech RL, Sanchez R, Ghersab CM. Modeling seedling emergence. Field Crops Research. 2000;**67**(2):123-139. DOI:10.1016/ S0378-4290(00)00088-5

[28] Ortega Baes P, Viana ML, Larenas G, Saravia M. Germinación de semillas de Caesalpinia paraguariensis (Fabaceae): agentes escarificadores y efecto del ganado. Revista de Biología Tropical. 2001;**49**(1):301-304

[29] De La Cruz-Landero N, Hernández VE, Guevara E, López MA, Santos AT, Ojeda-Trejo E, et al. Lupinus versicolor response in soils contaminated with heavy metals from a petroleum extraction field. Journal of Applied Science. 2010;**10**(1):694-669

[30] Mackay WA, Davis TD, Sankhla D, Rimenschneider DE. Factors influencing seed germination of lupines perennis. Journal of Environmental Horticulture. 1996;**14**(4):167-169

[31] Esau K. Anatomy of Seed Plants. 2nd ed. New York: Wiley; 1977

[32] Bushman BS, Johnson DA, Connors KJ, Jones TA. Germination and seedling emergence of three semiarid Western north American legumes. Rangeland Ecology & Management. 2015;**68**:501-506. DOI: 10.1016/j.rama.2015.08.002

Chapter 3

The Legumes of *Neltuma spp.* (ex *Prosopis spp*.) and Their Properties for Human and Animal Food

Marisa Jacqueline Joseau, Sandra Rodriguez Reartes and Javier Eduardo Frassoni

Abstract

The objective of this chapter is to present the advances in the use of *Neltuma* (*ex Prosopis*) pods for human and animal consumption, taking into account their distribution in Argentina. Images of the distribution of principal species used in forest cultivation, types of pods, nutritional tables and possible uses are included. Fruit threshing machine to obtain seeds and flour from the National Germplasm Bank of *Prosopis* of the Faculty of Agricultural Sciences of the National University of Córdoba, and some regional recipes are described.

Keywords: Algarrobo, morphological characteristic, fruit, flour, recipes

1. Introduction

The word "*algarrobo*" refers to several species of the genus *Fabaceae*, a word deriving from the Spanish Arabic dialect ("*al jarruba*") [1] which means "the tree." This was the name given to the specimens of the species *Ceratonia siliqua* L., which were spontaneously distributed along the coasts of the Mediterranean Sea and Middle East [2]. When Spanish people arrived in America, they assigned the name "*algarrobo*" to specimens of *Neltuma* (*ex Prosopis*) and coincidentally the native communities called it "*taku*" which also means "the tree." These species coincide in being legumes with similar aspects in their shape and use, mainly food for animals and humans [3]. All of these species present pods as fruit. An example of the component of the typical pods is shown in **Figure 1**. The vulgar name for these pods is "*algarroba*."

The genus *Neltuma* (*ex Prosopis*) has a wide diffusion in various phytogeographical regions of the country, extending from Prepuna to Patagonia, mainly in the Provinces of Monte, Chaco and Espinal [4, 5]. Hughes *et al.* [6], divide the genus *Prosopis sensu* Burkart [7] into three genera: *Anonychium, Neltuma and Strombocarpa*, two of which are present in Argentina with 39 recognised taxa amongst species, varieties and subspecies (**Table 1**).

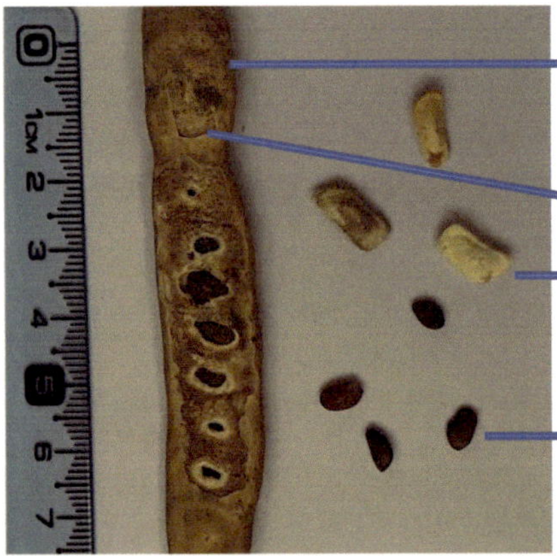

Figure 1.
Components of a typical Neltuma pods (algarroba).

Scientific name		Vulgar name
N. x vinalillo	(Stuck.) C.E. Hughes & G.P. Lewis	
N. affinis	(Spreng.) C.E. Hughes & G.P. Lewis	*ñandubay, espinillo*
N. alba	(Griseb.) C.E. Hughes & G.P. Lewis	*árbol, algarrobo blanco, ibopé-pará*
N. alba var. *panta*	(Spreng.) C.E. Hughes & G.P. Lewis	*algarrobo panta*
N. alpataco	(Phil.) C.E. Hughes & G.P. Lewis	*alpataco*
N. alpataco var. *lamaro*	(Phil.) C.E. Hughes & G.P. Lewis	*alpataco*
N. alpataco f. *rubra*	(Phil.) C.E. Hughes & G.P. Lewis	*alpataco*
N. argentina	(Burkart) C.E. Hughes & G.P. Lewis	*algarrobilla, algarrobo de guanaco*
N. caldenia	(Burkart) C.E. Hughes & G.P. Lewis	*caldén, huichru*
N. calingastana	(Burkart) C.E. Hughes & G.P. Lewis	*cusqui*
N. campestris	(Griseb.) C.E. Hughes & G.P. Lewis	
N. castellanosii	(Burkart) C.E. Hughes & G.P. Lewis	
N. chilensis	(Molina) C.E. Hughes & G.P. Lewis	*algarrobo de chile, algarrobo blanco*
N. chilensis var. *catamarcana*	(Molina) C.E. Hughes & G.P. Lewis	
N. chilensis var. *riojana*	(Molina) C.E. Hughes & G.P. Lewis	
N. denudans	(Benth.) C.E. Hughes & G.P. Lewis	*algarrobo patagónico*
N. denudans var. *patagonica*	(Benth.) C.E. Hughes & G.P. Lewis	
N. denudans var. *stenocarpa*	Benth.) C.E. Hughes & G.P. Lewis	
N. elata	(Burkart) C.E. Hughes & G.P. Lewis	*algarrobillo, huschillo*
N. fiebrigii	(Harms) C.E. Hughes G.P. Lewis	
N. flexuosa	(DC.) C.E. Hughes & G.P. Lewis	
N. flexuosa var. depressa	(DC.) C.E. Hughes & G.P. Lewis	
N. flexuosa var. fruticosa		
N. flexuosa f. subinermis	(Burkart) C.E. Hughes & G.P. Lewis	*algarrobo, algarrobo negro*

Scientific name		Vulgar name
N. hassleri	(Harms) C.E. Hughes G.P. Lewis	*algarrobo paraguayo*
N. hassleri var. *nigroides*	(Harms) C.E. Hughes G.P. Lewis	
N. humilis	(Gillies ex Hook.) C.E. Hughes & G.P. Lewis	*algarrobilla, barba de tigre*
N. kuntzei	(Harms ex Kuntze) C.E. Hughes & G.P. Lewis	*itín, palo mataco*
N. nigra	(Griseb.) C.E. Hughes & G.P. Lewis	*algarrobo negro, ibopé-hú*
N. nigra var. *longispina*	(Griseb.) C.E. Hughes & G.P. Lewis	
N. nigra var. *ragonesei*	(Griseb.) C.E. Hughes & G.P. Lewis	
N. pugionata	(Burkart) C.E. Hughes & G.P. Lewis	*algarrobo de las salinas, algarrobo*
N. ruizlealii	(Burkart) C.E. Hughes & G.P. Lewis	
N. ruscifolia	(Griseb.) C.E. Hughes & G.P. Lewis	*vinal, ibopémorotí*
N. sericantha	(Gillies ex Hook.) C.E. Hughes & G.P. Lewis	
Strombocarpa abbreviata	(Benth.) Hutch.	
S. ferox	(Griseb.) C.E. Hughes & G.P. Lewis	*churqui, churqui jujeño*
S. reptans	(Benth.) A. Grey	*mastuerzo, retortuño*
S. torquata	(Cav. ex Lag.) Hutch.	*tintitaco, tusca*

Table 1.
Taxa present in Argentina of the genus Neltuma *and* Strombocarpa *(ex* Prosopis*).*

Tree and shrub carobs are multiple-use species [8]. The aboriginal populations and the conquerors knew about these attributes [4, 9]. Species in this genus provide not only wood forest products (WFP), but also non-wood forest products (N-WFP). The tree species of this genus offer a wood that is highly appreciated for its hardness, stability and preservation. It is used in carpentry and for furniture. It is also used for poles, rods and in the manufacture of charcoal (calorific value: 4200 kcal/kg) [10].

Amongst the N-WFP of plant origin, the genus *Neltuma* (*ex Prosopis*) provides leaves, fruits and seeds that are an important source of food for animals. The fruits and their derivatives can also be used as human food. The leaves have high protein value. They contain 22% crude protein, 15% digestible protein and 55% dry matter digestibility [10].

There are numerous uses of the N-WFP of vegetable origin offered by the species of the genus *Neltuma*, amongst of them are: resin, gum, bark and fruits. For example, tannin is extracted from the bark, which is used in the tanning of leather and also in dyes [11]. The fruits, seeds, bark and flowers also have a medical use [11]. Ethyl alcohol can be obtained from the fermentation of the fruits [10, 12]. *Neltuma* species can act as biocontrol agents. Proof of this is the stem extracts of *N. chilensis* that are effective in the control of a Homoptera [13].

Other N-WFP that are obtained in *Neltuma* forests are animals and animal products, such as cattle, goats, sheep [14] from which products like meat, leather, milk, cheese and wool are obtained. The species of this genus are good producers of nectar and pollen, so beekeeping becomes important and favoured, generating other resources of animal origin, such as honey, wax, propolis and pollen [10, 15].

Neltuma is also important because it provides services to the forest. It acts as a protective source by providing nitrogen to the soil through the symbiotic association with fixing bacteria and also shade for cattle. Some indirect benefits are: the pasture under its canopies is of better quality, and it supplies abundant organic matter to the soil for present semi-persistent foliage, etc. [10].

In North America, soils under *Neltuma* canopy have more than 1000 kg/ha of nitrogen and more than 8000 kg/ha of carbon than soils outside tree canopies [16]. The contributions of organic matter, nitrogen and phosphorus of *N. flexuosa* forest are significant in the phytogeographical regions of Central Monte of Argentina, constituting true islands of fertility [17]. This species has not only to create edaphic heterogeneity in the region, but also contributed to create climatic heterogeneity, modifying the microclimate, water regime and light conditions under its canopy. This environmental heterogeneity allows a different spatial distribution of species and increases diversity at a regional scale [18]. In India, *Neltuma* has been used to improve high pH (10.4) soils. On the other hand, *Neltuma* species can grow in saline concentrations equal to ocean water [16].

The rural inhabitants of the southern sector of the Calchaquí Valley, province of Catamarca, recognise the use of pods of three species that they call "white," "black" and "*panta,*" identified from the morphology of its fruit and depending on its flavour. As regards the possible production, a total of 9 products obtained from the pod were mentioned (flour, coffee, fodder, liquor, "*añapa,*" "*aloja,*" "*arrope,*" "*aguardiente*" and seedlings), being used by families as a source of fodder, food, drink and medicine [19].

"*Patay*" is defined as a kind of dry bread, floury and sweet paste that is obtained by drying, grinding and sifting the fruits, compressing the flour obtained and then proceeding to cook it. It is marketed locally. The "*chuningo*" is similar to the previous one, but the ground dough is soaked and eaten without baking. The drinks are: the "*aloja,*" a native alcoholic fermented drink obtained by fermenting the pods of "*algarrobo*" which is made by grinding the fruits with water; the "*añapa,*" which is a non-fermented, sweet and refreshing drink, is prepared simply by crushing the fruits in a mortar with water. The sweet product is the "*arrope,*" which is a type of honey obtained by cooking, grinding and sifting. (4). Amongst the flours are: whole fruit flour (FF), mesocarp flour (MF), seedless fruit flour (SFF), seed flour (SF), cotyledon flour (CF) and meso- endocarp residue (R). When the flour is toasted, it can be used to prepare substitutes for chocolate and coffee [20].

2. National Germplasm Bank of *Prosopis* of the Faculty of Agricultural Sciences of the National University of Córdoba (BNGP)

The BNGP's main objective is the conservation and commercialization of seeds of quality and known origin. It currently has 1650 accessions in the Passive Bank corresponding to 1106 trees of 9 *Neltuma* (*ex Prosopis*) tree species from different regions of Argentina [21]. In the last 8 years, it has managed to register 24 Seed-Producing Areas (10 for *N. alba*, 5 for *N. chilensis*, 3 for *N. flexuosa*, 2 for *N. nigra*, 3 of *N. chilensis* x *N. flexuosa*, 1 of *N. alba x N.* sp.), and 2 Seed Stands (*N. alba and N. flexuosa*), from which it obtains seeds to respond to the needs of afforestation and restoration. **Figure 2** shows some of the locations of the species present in the BNGP.

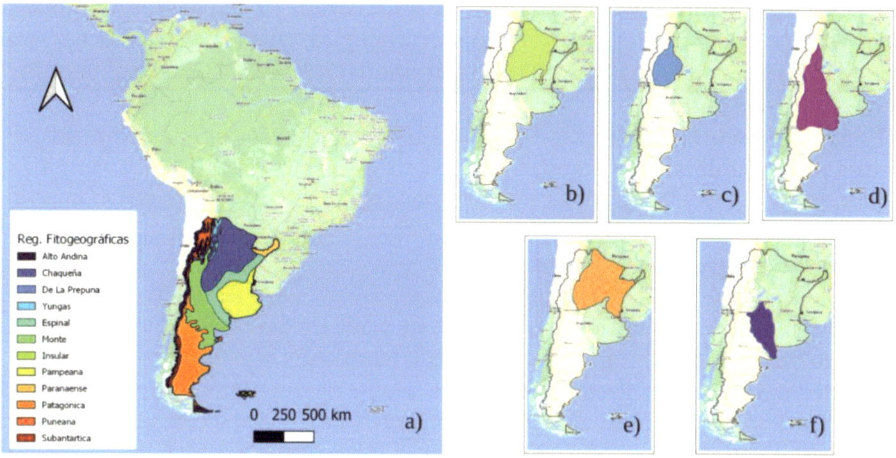

Figure 2.
a) Phytogeographic Regions of Argentina. Distribution of the main Neltuma species in Argentina: b) N. alba, c) N. chilensis, d) N. flexuosa, e) N. nigra and f) N. caldenia.

3. Characterisation of *Neltuma* species

The collected species are morphologically characterised in the laboratory. A measurement of leaf and fruit characters is carried out to confirm the taxon of belonging following the specifications proposed by Verga [22] and Joseau *et al.* [21, 23].

Figure 3.
View of leaves and fruits of a) N. chilensis, b) N. alba, c) N. nigra, d) N. caldenia and e) N. flexuosa.

INASE [24] establishes marketing categories according to the degree of improvement. For a seed-producing area (APS) a morphological characterisation is necessary, whilst for a higher category (seeds from seed stands) a morphological and genetic analysis are required.

Figure 3 presents some examples of leaves and fruits according to taxon, where the existing variability is observed.

4. *Neltuma* ("*algarrobo*") flour

*Algarrob*o flour is a traditional food product made by the communities that inhabit the Chaco Semiarid and Monte ecoregion [25]. However, "*algarrobo*" trees are also distributed in other phytogeographic regions [4, 5].

Articles 680, 681, 681 bis, 681 tris of Chapter IX of the Argentine Food Code provide specifications for the commercialization of flour from the species of the genus *Neltuma* (*ex Prosopis*) and define "*algarrobo*" flour as "the product of the grinding of the clean, healthy and dry seeds" of *N alba* and/or *N. nigra* and/or *N. chilensis* and/or *N. flexuosa* (Art.681) and of *N ruscifolia* (Art. 680). It also defines "*algarrobo*" "fruit flour" (complete pod with its seeds) as "the product of grinding the complete fruits" of *N. alba* and/or *N. nigra* and/or *N. chilensis* and/or *N. flexuosa* (Art. 681 tris). Likewise, the concept of "*Patay*" is incorporated in the same code as "made by kneading '*algarrobo*' flour, in any of its types: seed or fruit, with water; shaping dough into loaves before taking it to the oven to bake it" [26].

In general, the whole fruit is used to obtain flour. The types the flours obtained after drying the pods are used as substitutes for cocoa and coffee because they do not contain stimulating substances such as caffeine and theobromine. In addition, it constitutes a suitable ingredient in the preparation of sweet products such as cakes, muffins and cookies due to its high sugar content and good aroma and flavour [27]. The roasted white "*algarrobo*" seeds can also be used as a coffee substitute [15].

The fruits of the genus *Neltuma* (ex *Prosopis*) are legumes with a high content of proteins, carbohydrates, fibres and minerals. The legumes which vary in size, colour and chemical characteristics depending on the species [3]. Correa *et al.* [28] found differences between clones of *N. alba* in terms of protein and fibre content, on the one hand, and phenolic component content, on the other hand, in the SF of this species. Hence, when producing on a large scale it is necessary to know the genetic materials to be established in implanted forests.

Flour is gaining great importance in the diet for celiacs, as it is free of gliadins and gluteins. It is considered a building food as it contains protein and energy due to its sugars; in addition to providing mineral salts and vitamins [4, 29].

González-Montemayora *et al.* [20] carried out a review to incorporate legumes such as pods of some *Neltuma* species in the food industry. Some of them produce functional bread-making, protein-fortifying wheat flour with these legumes and enhancing the bioactive content of bread. These authors state that one of the main challenges of adding any legume to a bakery product is the rheological changes in the dough and the final product. Pereira de Gusmão *et al.* [30, 31], quoting González-Montemayora *et al.* [20], concluded that the use of flour from *Neltuma* fruits with a size between 500 and 100 μm is suitable for products such as bread, cakes and cookies. The rheology, tenacity and extensibility of the dough decreases as the concentration of "*algarrobo*" flour increases and the more quantity is added, the weaker the remaining dough. Escobar *et al.* [32] produce CF from *N. chilensis* added a percentage

Variables	MF %	SF %	R %	FF %	FF %	FF %	FF %	FF %	FF %
	N. ruscifolia	*N. ruscifolia*	*N. ruscifolia*	*N. ruscifolia*	*N. alba*	*N. nigra*	*N. alpataco*	*N. chilensis*	*N. flexuosa*
Ashes	6.07	3.40	4.40	4.45	3.2	3.2	3.33	3.4	3.9
Protein	10,5	33.81	8.34	12.70	7.8	7.8	10.2 (protein) 2.6 (mucilage)	11.48–13.2	13.1
Fats	5.59	5.94	3.73	4.32	0.68	6.59	3.23	2.4–3.02	1.7
Carbohydrates	77.84	56.80	83.58	78.52	53.0 saccharose 2.5 fructose	53.0 saccharose 2.e fructose	62.0	39	46
Crude fibre	6.50	5.80	22.56	17.82	20.0	23.0	25.5	27.20–35.3	29.9
Calcium	0.153	0,078			0.1860	0.1610			
Phosphorus	0.472	0.187							
Potassium	0.589	0.905			0.9030	1.0600			
Magnesium	0.044	0.040			0.0560	0.0690			
Iron	4.570	25.420			0.0049	0.0026			
Zinc	3.890	1.480							
Manganese	15.30	0.840			0.0047	0.0077			
Copper	21.70	1.620							
Polyphenols					0.6210	1.0810		0.29–0.31	0.35–0.37
Antioxidant capacity					0.5450	0.9350			
References:	[33]				[34]		[35]	[36, 37]	

MF: Mesocarp flour, SF: Seed flour, R: Meso-endocarp residue, FF: Fruits flour

Table 2.
Composition of grinding fractions of ***N. ruscifolia*** *fruit and whole fruit (dry basis) of* ***N. ruscifolia, N. alba, N. nigra, N. alpataco, N. chilensis*** *and* ***N. flexuosa.***

of 10% to wheat flour to make cookies and fried flakes, increasing the contribution of available lysine, its protein and dietary fibre content, improving the soluble/insoluble fibre ratio, without affecting its physical characteristics or sensory acceptability. "*Algarrobo*" flour does not have the binding characteristic of wheat flour. It has sweetening properties, natural flavouring and mineral and protein content, making it interesting for the food industry [20].

There are many other *Neltuma* which beans are used for flour. They have some differential characteristics: for example, *N. chilensis* flour contains fewer carbohydrates than *N. alba* flour, and together with *N. flexuosa* they have higher amounts of fibre and protein than *N. alba* flour (**Table 2**). **Table 2** also shows that the flours of *N. ruscifolia* and *N. alpataco* stand out for the high amount of carbohydrates, whilst that of *N. nigra* stands out in the amount of fats.

5. Methods of elaboration of *Neltuma* flours

These vary from precarious systems with some degree of technology to industrial-scale projects.

The traditional production process involves the collection of the pods, drying by direct exposure to solar radiation (**Figure 4a**) and finally their manual grinding in mortar [25].

5.1 Fruit collection

When the fruits are ripe, they are collected by placing them in plastic burlap bags that allow aeration. Collection seasons are generally: December–January for *N. flexuosa* and *N. chilensis*; December to February for *N. alba*, late January to February for *N. nigra* and May–April for *N. caldenia*. If the collection is possible, it is done from the tree manually or by placing a mesh to catch the fruits at the time of shaking for phytosanitary reasons.

The collected bags should be stored in a dry environment with air circulation to avoid deterioration and proliferation of insects. The collected fruits are selected, separating the healthy fruits from others in poor condition, foreign matter and insects.

The fruits are generally attacked by insects belonging to the *Bruchidae* family [38]. One method to eliminate bruchids is to place the bags kept in dried conditions in the freezer at a temperature of −18°C for 10 days (**Figure 4b**) [21].

Silva *et al.* [39] conclude that the chemical and physical quality of fruits stored for animal feed is maintained with the use of closed bins with a capacity of 40 kg with the addition of dry insect repellent plants (*Capparis atamisquea* Kuntze and *Ocimum basilicum* L.) placed at the base, in the middle and at the top.

5.2 Fruit washing

The fruits are washed with 5% sodium hypochlorite to eliminate adhering substances and microorganisms with subsequent rinsing, draining and air-drying on meshes placed for this purpose.

5.3 The grinding of fruits

This varies according to the region. The Institute of Popular Culture [40] processes dry and healthy fruits with a 3000 rpm hammer mill with a 6 HP TEKNE 400 brand

Figure 4.
Components of the "algarrobo" threshing machine (Cosiansi, 1991): a) pods hopper, b) shredder, c) threshing cylinder I, d) sieves, e) flour tray, f) knuckles tray, g) seed tray, h) hopper for knuckles, i) threshing cylinder II.

gasoline engine [41], which processes 40 to 50 kg of fruits per hour. The granulometry of the grinding obtained goes through a 12 mm diameter sieve. If it absorbs moisture, it is necessary to dry it in a solar dryer. INCUPO [40] performs a second grinding by varying the sieve with a 2 mm diameter mesh. It is necessary to dry it again in the solar dryer, to then mechanically sieve with a 1 mm metal mesh. The product obtained is stored in plastic drums with hermetic closure of 220 litres (80 kg). In these drums the product lasts 1 year if it is kept hermetically closed with low moisture content in storage. The TEKNE 400 hammer mill is also proposed by Cornejo Becker *et al.* [42] who made a proposal to bring flour production to an industrial level, using rotary washers, vibrating sieve, tray dryer, conveyor belt and ground product packaging.

In the Monte region, the company "*El Resurgir del Algarrobal* S.A." collect *N. flexuosa* directly from trees devoid of shrubs and grasses below. When collecting impurities are also collected. Inclined planes and fans are used to clean light remains of fruits. To separate heavy remains they perform immersion in water, so the pods come out clean. The pods are sun-dried and hand-selected. To obtain "*algarrobo*" flour, they use a hammer mill with interchangeable sieves and obtain the desired granulometry by reducing the step. The flour is collected in hermetic jars after sifting and packaging. The destination is human consumption [43].

The community of *Santa María de Catamarca* presented the use of an individual solar dryer and a medium-scale solar dryer as an improvement in the traditional process of drying *Neltuma* fruits to obtain flour [25].

Mom *et al.* [44], studying two species of *Neltuma*, argue that the milling process to obtain flour by dry milling demands the use of previously dried fruits. One of the critical factors is the high sugar content (40%), which requires drying to very low moisture (<6%) to avoid stickiness. In *N. alba* a reduction of 80% was observed in the drying time at 60 and 70°C. A grinding more homogeneous and with very fine granulometry of all the components (soluble in water and insoluble in ethanol) is observed in *N. alba*, whilst that the highest granulometry of *N. flexuosa* is found in the flour and not in the water-insoluble fraction.

Freyre *et al.* [33] for the separation of different fractions of the (N. ruscifolia) used a concentric disc mill that retains the endocarp, and allows the exo-mesocarp mixture to pass through. The endocarps enter in a disc mill with radial grooves that open the endocarp and release the seeds. The separation will be implemented using a pneumatic separator, sieves and manually. In this process three different products were obtained: fraction H or pulp meal (MF), fraction S of pure seeds (SF) and the residual fraction (R), made of the residues obtained in each step. The particle size of each of these fractions was reduced and homogenised using a Cyclotec mill. The proximal composition of these fractions is observed in **Table 2**.

Escobar *et al.* [32] obtained cotyledon meal from pods of *N. chilensis* harvested in April in Chile. To obtain them, the pods were dried in a tunnel with forced air at 60°C until a residual humidity of 8–10%. They extracted the cotyledons from the pods manually and peeled them with a 0.75% w/v solution of sodium hydroxide according to the method of Escobar *et al.* [45]. The cotyledons obtained are thermally treated with moist heat (cotyledon: water ratio of 1:3) at overpressure (1.57 atm) for 9 minutes for the inactivation of heat-sensitive antinutritional compounds. The cotyledons were dried at 35°C until a residual humidity of 8% and they were ground in two stages, a pre-milling until a granulometry of 250 μm (Mill Arthur H. Thomas. C.O.) and a milling.

Peru has established technical standards for the production of products originating from the pods of the "*algarrobos*" and guidelines for the implementation of standards to establish quality and aptitude requirements for the product, process and service, contemplating various aspects of production in a manner to provide sustainable economic development [46].

The BNGP in the threshing process uses the machine designed by Ing. Agr. (M Sc.) Jorge Cosiansi [47], which allows to obtain flour as well as seeds. The machine has a power of 6 HP, a weight of 380 kg, a hopper capacity of 40 kg of pods and a threshing capacity of 20 min for that amount of fruit (**Figure 4**).

5.4 Threshing process

The pods collected in plastic burlap bags by the BNGP go through a cleaning and drying process before the threshing (**Figure 4c**). Cleaning is done by emptying the bag on a table, where with the help of a fan the pods are separated from other elements (grass, branches and insects and other materials). Once clean, the pods are placed in ovens for 48 hours at a temperature of 40°C with forced air circulation for drying until the moisture content drops to approximately 9%. Before being threshed, the fruits are broken into pieces of about 2–3 cm manually using a bucket and a stick as a pylon.

The dried and split pods are incorporated into the pod hopper of the thresher for indehiscent fruits (**Figure 4a**). In the lower part of the hopper there is a shredder (**Figure 4b**), which continues the process of breaking the material and allows the passage of the crushed pods to the threshing cylinder I (**Figure 4c**). The threshing cylinder I is in charge of opening the material and releasing the seeds. All the material falls to a set of sieves (**Figure 4d**), which classifies and transports to three output compartments: one for "*algarrobo*" flour (**Figure 4e**), another for the knuckles

(**Figure 4f**) and a third compartment for the seeds with other impurities (flour and grains, **Figure 4g**). In the case of materials that have smaller knuckles and seeds, the hopper for knuckles (**Figure 4h**) and the threshing cylinder II (**Figure 4i**) can be used, which has the opening elements (tines) closer together.

To obtain a purity of seed of 80% (according to INASE Res. 374/14 standard), the seed obtained must go through a final cleaning process that is carried out with a fan and an inclined plane, where impurities are blown away and escape through the upper part of the inclined plane and the clean seeds are collected at the base of it (**Figure 4c**).

5.5 Performance

An adult of *N. chilensis* tree can produce up to 100 kg of pods. However, pod production does not occur uniformly every year, due to different factors, therefore it can be said that the average is 20 to 60 kg of pods per tree, whilst *N. nigra* varies from 20 to 50 kg per tree [48]. The production of *N. alba* begins around 5 years of the tree's life, and produces 5 to 40 kilogrammes of pods per tree each year [49] (**Figure 5**).

3040 kg of pods yields 1400 kilogrammes of flour and the rest is made up of bran, which is the residue used to make balanced feed for animals (poultry, pigs and cattle) [40]. Cornejo Becker *et al.* [42] diagrammed a "*algarrobo*" flour plant and mention a yield of 42% in Salta.

One hundred kilos of ripe and dry "*algarroba*" (fruit) contain 30 kg of sugar, 20 kg of starch, 8 kg of protein and 2 kg of lipids, nutritive substances and more than 60 kg of cellulose [11].

In summary, it is concluded that the fibre content of "*algarrobo*" flour is higher than that of whole wheat flour, it has less fat with a very good composition of essential fatty acids (linoleic and oleic) and a notable amount of mineral salts (amongst others) Ca; Fe and P. The iron in the white "*algarrobo*" tree reaches values established for the

Figure 5.
a) Previous drying in full sun of the plastic bags with pods b) Cold treatment to eliminate bruchids (−18°C) to bagged and dried fruits, c) P. flexuosa pods prepared for threshing d) seeds of P. alba from Campo Duran Seed.

liver of cattle. The nutritional characteristics and the behaviour of the product define it as a quality flour that can be used in bakery products [50].

6. Animal feeding

"*Algarrobas*" are collected to feed livestock, whole or processed, alone or as part of a ration, fresh or after storage. Researchers have conducted studies on ground carob in cattle feed rations, especially in Brazil and India. "*Algarrobas*" are ground to ensure maximum nutritional value, since most of the seeds are made up of proteins which are not indigestible when passing through the digestive tract of cattle [13].

In the Argentine Chaco Region, "*algarroba*" flour production is in summer, coinciding with the season of greatest pasture production in the area. Its use can be deferred for times of forage scarcity (late autumn and winter). The high energy values of "*algarroba*" flour can significantly improve daily weight gains in cattle [3].

Prokopiuk *et al.* [51] say that pods of *N. alba* have nutritional values (95.3% dry matter, 6.8% crude protein, 35.7% neutral detergent fibre, 33.1% acid detergent fibre, *in vitro* digestibility of dry matter 66.6%, non-structural carbonates 52.3%, ethereal extract 2.2%) indicating that they are located within the main group of feed for ruminants, that of bulky ones, those that have a low weight: volume, with fibre content greater than 18%. Comparatively within this group, they could replace conserved maize and grain sorghum forages.

Prokopiuk *et al.* [3] used coarse fractions of ground "*algarroba*" from *N. alba* as a winter supplement (1 kg/animal/day, 0.5% live weight) for 4 months for 200 kg live weight steers of the Braford breed in the province of Chaco, Argentina, in front of a witness without supplement. All remained on implanted pasture, with an average stocking rate of 0.5 animal/ha, in a continuous grazing system where the predominant species was Gatton panic (*Panicum maximum*). The ground "*algarroba*" supplied a concentration of metabolizable energy of approximately 2.4 Mcal/kg DM. The supplemented steers had significant increases in haematocrit, erythrocytes, haemoglobin and iron and there were no adverse clinical side effects, improving the blood levels of some nutritional indicators, and slightly increasing the weight of the growing animals. No animal registered signs of disease.

Gonzalez- Montemayora *et al.* [20] studied the whole meal of dried pods of *N. alba*, *N. chilensis* and *N. nigra* from Bolivia obtained with a knife mill, and found that *N. nigra* and *N. alba* stood out for their protein, fibre and protein content. Low levels of antinutrients (saponins, lectins, trypsin, polyphenols, nitrates, phytate) and that the antinutritional substances studied do not represent a risk for the population. They also highlighted that the contribution of dietary fibre was higher 45.93% (*N. nigra*), 46.28% (*N. chilensis*) and 48.15% (*N. alba*).

Gonzalez- Montemayora *et al.* [20] found a high protein digestibility *in vitro* for the whole meal of pods of *N. nigra* (60.97%) and *N. alba* (55.37%), the same as Galera [52], although for *N. chilensis* it had the lowest protein digestibility. (45.57%). In this species Silva *et al.* [39] recorded 71.18% and state that it decreases with unprotected storage time, reaching a digestibility of 30%.

Chagra Dib *et al.* [53] cite that milk production at the beginning of lactation increased when Creole goats that were on natural pasture are supplemented in winter with alfalfa hay, commercial balanced and "*algarrobo*" pods. It also improved butterfat and crude milk protein. Weight loss was lower when they received alfalfa hay plus "*algarrobo*" pods.

7. Conclusions

Numerous publications support the need to improve technological production processes to obtain quality "*algarrobo*" flour in order to have a food product of good nutritional quality, high added value, of natural origin both for local residents and those who want to engage in industrial activity. It is recommended to use proven genetic material when forest plantations of the *Neltuma* genus are carried out for industrial purposes. *Algarrobo* flour is a quality food with building properties because it contains proteins and energy due to its sugars, as well as salts, minerals and vitamins that serve as an excellent food for both human and animal consumption. There is a wide variability depending on the taxon and origin of the fruits. Hence, the need to increase research that characterises the physical, chemical and nutritional properties in order to provide consumers with "*algarrobo*" flour. The establishment of technical standards and guides for their implementation similar to those of Peru would be a very useful tool for "*algarrobo*" flour producers since it will allow to homogenise the production and quality of the product obtained to improve competitiveness and commercialization in the national and international market.

8. Supplementary material: "*Algarrobo*" flour recipes

8.1 Benefits and recipes

"*Algarrobo*" flour is obtained by grinding the pods and seeds. It helps regulate digestive and intestinal processes, due to its pectic acid and fibre content. It has low fat content. It has vitamins A, B, D, as well as a significant amount of minerals (magnesium, calcium, potassium, iron and phosphorus). Also, it is suitable for celiacs. Its versatility as a food is a real stimulus to create desserts and infusions. The recipes shown below are an example of this:

8.2 Own recipes

"*Algarrobo*" Cake

Ingredients: 1 cup of sugar, 1 cup of "*algarrobo*" flour, 3 large eggs, 1 teaspoon of vanilla essence, 2 cups of self-rising flour.

Preparation: Beat the eggs, add the sugar and "*algarrobo*" flour. Continue beating until obtaining a cream. Add vanilla essence, add the 2 cups of self-rising flour. Mix well. Finally add 1 cup of liquid yogurt of the flavour you prefer, mix well. Leave 10 minutes for the yogurt bacteria to act.

If it lacks liquid, add a little more yogurt, or lemon juice, or a few drops of cognac, or port. The sugar can be replaced by honey, but the "*algarrobo*" flour tastes like mount honey. Flour a cake pan and place the preparation. Place it in the oven. Cooking can take between 1/2 hour or an hour depending on the depth of the source to be used (**Figure 6a**).

"*Algarrobo*" Bonbons

Ingredients: 50 g of "*algarrobo*" flour, 50 g of rolled oats, 50 g of grated coconut, ½ cup of pastry dulce de leche, liquid yogurt if it is necessary.

Preparation: Mix the "*algarrobo*" flour with the rolled oats, the pastry dulce de leche to form a paste. Add grated coconut and liquid yogurt if it is necessary. Make balls and pass them through grated coconut to cover them (**Figure 6c**).

a)

b

c)

Figure 6.
"Algarrobo" flour recipes: a) Fruit pudding, b) "algarrobo" bonbons and c) "algarrobo" cake.

8.3 "*Paciencia del Monte*" recipes

Moulded Sweet Potato

Ingredients: 1 kg of sweet potato; 250 g pumpkin squash (*), 500 cc of water, 1 tablespoon of natural vanilla, agar-agar, 1 or 2 tablespoons of "*algarrobo*" flour, 3 or 4 tablespoons of honey [54].

Preparation: Peel the sweet potatoes and cut them into cubes under running water so that they do not turn black. Also, peel and cut pumpkin squash into cubes. Place the sweet potatoes together with the pumpkin squash in a container with water. Cook over moderate heat until everything is tender. Remove the preparation and let it warm slightly. Blend until it forms a cream and pour into a saucepan, perfume with vanilla. Bring it back to a low heat, over a diffuser, so that it heats up slowly and does not stick. Add agar-agar, dissolved in a little cold water and continue cooking, stirring with a wooden spoon for 5 more minutes. Remove from heat and add honey and mix. Pour into a mould, moistened with water or brushed with oil. When it begins to take consistency, dissolve the "*algarrobo*" flour with water to form a cream. Pour over the moulding. Mix with a spoon to give a marbled effect. Let it cool and cut it into portions.

(*) It is used to give better colour. If omitted, reduce a little amount of water.

Charlotte

Ingredients: 1/2 cup of "*algarrobo*" flour, 1/2 cup of water, 3 tablespoons of honey, natural vanilla, to taste.

Preparation: Mix the flour with the water trying not to form lumps. Bring the mixture to a low heat, cooking for 3 or 4 minutes, whilst stirring with a wooden spoon. Remove the preparation, sweeten it with honey and perfume it with vanilla. Use hot.

Creams

Ingredients: 1/2 kg pumpkins, ½ litre of water, 3 tablespoons of "*algarrobo*" flour, 1 tablespoon of corn starch, half walnuts to decorate.

Preparation: Peel the pumpkin and cut into cubes and cook them with water. Remove from the heat and blend the preparation. Bring back to the fire, over the diffuser. Separately, mix the "*algarrobo*" flour with the corn starch and dissolve everything with 3 tablespoons of cold water. Add to the previous preparation, stirring with a wooden spoon, until thick. Remove it, flavour it with vanilla, and sweeten it with honey. Pour it into little bowls, when it solidifies decorate each portion with a nuts and take it to the fridge until serving.

Fancy Cookies

Ingredients: 4 cups fine wholemeal flour, 1 cup "*algarrobo*" flour, 1 teaspoon baking soda, 1 tablespoon lemon zest; 3 tablespoons of honey, 1 egg, 3 tablespoons of oil, milk or water, the necessary amount.

Preparation: Arrange in a bowl the flours, the baking soda and the lemon zest. Separately, beat the honey with the egg, oil and vanilla. Mix both preparations as the milk or water is incorporated in sufficient quantity to form a consistent dough. Let it rest for 30 minutes. Stretch it with the help of a rolling pin until it is 1 cm thick. Cut squares 5 cm on each side or other shapes to taste, place the dough on oiled and floured plates. Bake them at a moderate temperature for 10 to 15 minutes. Remove them and let cool on a wire rack. Decorate them with natural jams.

Algarrobo Cream

Ingredients: ½ cup of "*algarrobo*" flour, 1 egg, 3 table spoons of honey, 3 tablespoons of ricotta, 1 teaspoon of natural vanilla.

Preparation: Place the "*algarrobo*" flour, egg, honey, ricotta and vanilla in the blender glass. Blend everything, adding a minimum of liquid (water or cooking liquid from some fruit) used to dip cakes or for decorations.

Lemon Pie

Ingredients: "*Algarrobo*" base for cakes: 1 tablespoon of fresh brewer's yeast, required amount of warm water and 2 tablespoons of oil, 2 tablespoons of honey, 1 teaspoon of natural vanilla, 2 cups superfine wholemeal flour, 3 tablespoons of "*algarrobo*" flour.

Filling: Lemon yolk cream; 2 tablespoons of oil, 2 tablespoons of honey, lemon zest and juice, 2 egg yolks, 2 tablespoons of corn starch, 1 cup of water.

Meringue, according to the recipe.

Preparation: Dissolve the yeast in ½ cup of warm water. Add the oil, honey and vanilla. Separately, combine the flours and arrange them in the shape of a crown. Pour the previous preparation in the centre. Take the dough as water is incorporated: a medium consistency should be obtained. Place the bun in a warm place and let it rest for 30 minutes. Stretch it out.

Filling: Place in the blender glass: the oil, the honey, the zest with the lemon juice, the yolk and the starch. Blend as the water is incorporated. Pour the preparation into a container and take it to a water bath for 30 minutes, stirring with a wooden spoon. Remove the cream and pour it over the cake.

Arrange the meringue on top forming peaks. Gratinate at maximum temperature. Remove, cool and serve.

Fruit Pudding (Figure 6a).

Ingredients: 2 green apples, ½ cup of seedless raisins, 2 tablespoons of honey, 1 teaspoon of natural vanilla, a small bowl of oil, 2 tablespoons of fresh brewer's yeast, required amount of warm water, 4 cups of fine wholemeal flour, 1 cup of "*algarrobo*" flour, 100 g of dried fruit (chopped walnuts and almonds, plums and figs in pieces, etc.).

Preparation: Arrange in the blender glass: cubed apples, raisins, honey, vanilla, oil and yeast, dissolved in 1/2 litre of water. Blend perfectly. Pour the smoothie over the previously mixed flours and combine the ingredients, adding more water, if necessary. It should be a more consistent paste than the sponge cake. Add the dried fruit, and let it rest for 30 minutes in a warm place. Pour into oiled and floured moulds. Let rise for 30 minutes in a preheated and turned off oven. Bake at a moderate temperature for 45 to 60 minutes (depending on the depth and diameter of the moulds used). Remove them, let them warm and unmould on a wire rack.

Cocadas

Ingredients: 3 cups of wholemeal flour, half a cup of "*algarrobo*" flour, 1 cup of grated coconut, ½ teaspoon of baking soda, 3 apples, 3 tablespoons of honey, 1 teaspoon of natural vanilla, the necessary amount of milk.

Preparation: Combine the flours with the coconut and the baking soda. Arrange them in the shape of a crown, placing the grated apples, honey and vanilla in the centre. Take the dough, incorporating the necessary milk to obtain a consistent paste. Let it rest for 30 minutes, place it in a sleeve with a wide curly nozzle. Make crests on oiled and floured plates. Cook the cocadas in the oven at maximum temperature for approximately 10 minutes. Remove them, let them warm and detach them with a spatula. Let them cool on a rack.

Brown Cake

Ingredients: 1 tablespoon of fresh brewer's yeast, 1/2 cup of warm milk, 100 g of defatted ricotta, 2 tablespoons of oil, 4 tablespoons of honey, 1 teaspoon of natural vanilla, 3 cups of superfine wholemeal flour, ½ cup of "*algarrobo*" flour, 1 cup of corn starch, 1 apple, 50 g of seedless raisins. To decorate: 400 g Chantilly, ricotta (or natural jams).

Preparation: Dissolve yeast in warm milk. Beat it and let it rest. Place in the blender glass: the ricotta, the oil, the honey and the vanilla. Blend and reserve. Mix the flours and starch in a large bowl. Make a hole in the centre and pour the yeast and the liquid inside. Work the dough, incorporating the flours on the sides until you achieve a consistency similar to that of a sponge cake. If it is necessary add more warm milk. Add the diced apple, raisins and walnuts, mixing to distribute well. Let the mixture rest in a warm place for 30 minutes, pour it into a 30 cm diameter and 12 cm high pan (or 2 smaller moulds) oiled and floured. Bake at moderate temperature for approximately 40 minutes. The cake is ready when the surface is consistent and detaches from both sides of the mould. Remove it, let it warm and unmould it on a wire rack.

"*Algarrobo*" Jelly

Ingredients: ½ litre of water, 1 tablespoon of agar-agar, 2 tablespoons of "*algarrobo*" flour, 1 tablespoon of lemon zest, 3 or 4 tablespoons of honey.

Preparation: Place the water over low heat. Separately, mix the agar-agar with the carob and add 5 tablespoons of cold water. Add the boiling water, stirring continuously with a wooden spoon. Continue cooking for approximately 10 minutes without stopping stirring, and add the zest. Remove the preparation and add the honey. Mix very well and pour into individual moulds. When the preparation is warm, take them to the fridge and reserve them until dessert time, unmould and decorate with fresh fruit.

***Añapa* (Refreshing Drink)**

Preparation: Mix "*algarrobo*" flour with very cool water, let stand for about an hour and then strain. This drink is more nutritious and natural than all commercial sodas made with industrial flavourings and colourings.

Acknowlegement

The authors of this chapter are grateful for the contributions to writing in English made by by Analia Piacenza, Victoria Ubino and Susi Garcia.

Author details

Marisa Jacqueline Joseau*, Sandra Rodriguez Reartes and Javier Eduardo Frassoni
Faculty of Agricultural Sciences, National University of Córdoba, Cordoba, Argentina

*Address all correspondence to: jajoseau@agro.unc.edu.ar

References

[1] Corominas J. Breve diccionario etimológico de la lengua castellana. Madrid, Spain: Tercera; 1973

[2] Guillén A, Ferrer-Gallego PP, Serena V, Peris JB. El algarrobo (*Ceratonia siliqua* L.), importancia paisajística, económica y perspectivas de futuro. Chron naturae. 2018;7:45-54

[3] Prokopiuk D, Crudeli G, Konrad J. In: Verzino GE, editor. Algarroba (*Prosopis alba* Griseb) como suplemento invernal de novillos. Córdoba, Argentina: Grupo Encuentro; 2013, 1934

[4] Resico C. Estado actual de la información sobre productos Forestales no madereros. Roma: FAO; 2001

[5] Verzino GE, Joseau MJ. In: Verzino GE, editor. Conservación de recursos forestales nativos en Argentina. El Banco Nacional de Germoplasma de *Prosopis*. Córdoba, Argentina; 2005. p. 172

[6] Hughes CE, Ringelberg JJ, Lewis GP, CSA. Disintegration of the genus *Prosopis* L. (*Leguminosae, Caesalpinioideae*, mimosoid clade). PhytoKeys. 2022;**205**:147-189

[7] Burkart A. A monograph of the genus *Prosopis* (*Leguminosae* subfam. *Mimosoideae*). Journal of Arnold Arbor. 1976;**57**(219-49):450-525

[8] de Melo Araujo S. Especies arbóreas y arbustivas para las zonas áridas y semiáridas de América Latina. In: Serie Zonas Áridas y Semiáridas N°12. Santiago, Chile: OEA; 1977. p. 347. Programa conjunto FAO-PNUMA de Control de la Desertificación en América Latina y el Caribe

[9] Roig F. Aportes a la etnobotánica del género *Prosopis*. In: Contribuciones mendocinas a la quinta reunión regional para América Latina y el Caribe de la red de Forestación del CIID Conservación y mejoramiento de especies del género *Prosopis*. Mendoza, Argentina: IADIZA-CRICYT- CIID; 1993. pp. 99-119

[10] Karlin UO, Coirini R, CL y ZR. Especies arbóreas y arbustivas para zonas áridas y semiáridas de América Latina. In: Serie Zonas Áridas y Semiáridas N°12 OEA Programa conjunto FAO-PNUMA de Control de la Desertificación en América Latina y el Caribe. Santiago, Chile; 1997. pp. 41-51

[11] Demaio P, Karlin U, Medina M. Árboles nativos del centro de Argentina. Buenos Aires, Argentina: L.O.L.A. (Literature of Latin America); 2002. p. 210

[12] Serra M. *Prosopis tamarugo*. In: Especies Arboreas y arbustivas para las zonas áridas y semi áridas de América Latina Serie Zonas Áridas y semi áridas N°12. Santiago, Chile: FAO/PNUMA; 1997. pp. 1-9

[13] Pasiecznik N, Felker P, Harris P, Harsh L, Cruz G, Tewari J, et al. The *Prosopis juliflora-Prosopis pallida* Complex: A Monograph. Coventry, UK; 2001

[14] Ragonese AE. Vegetación y ganadería en la República Argentina. Buenos Aires, Argentina: Colección Científica del INTA; 1967. p. 20

[15] Instituto de Cultura Popular (INCUPO). El algarrobo. El monte nos da comida. Reconquista, Argentina; 1991

[16] Felker P, Moss J. *Prosopis*: SemiaridFuelwood and Forage Tree Building Consensus for the Disenfranchised. Washington, D.C; 1996

[17] Alvarez JA, Sauna V, Villagra PE, Rossi BE. Aportes de la materia orgánica por *Prosopis flexuosa* en el Monte Central. In: Actas de la Reunión Nacional del Algarrobo III Reunión Nacional de la Asociación Argentina de *Prosopis*. Mendoza, Argentina; 2000. p. 56

[18] Villagra PE, Rossi BE, Alvarez JA. Efecto de *Prosopis flexuosa* sobre las condiciones microambientales en el Monte central (Reserva de Biósfera de Ñacuñan, Mendoza, Argentina). In: Actas de la Reunión Nacional del Algarrobo III Reunión Nac de la Asoc Arg de *Prosopis*. Mendoza, Argentina; 2000. p. 57

[19] Mallo MF. La algarroba (*Prosopis* sp.) como recurso en las estrategias campesinas al sur del Valle Calchaquí. In: Verzino GEJMJ, editor. Reunión Nacional del Algarrobo Actas. Córdoba. Argentina: Grupo Encuentro; 2013. p. 193

[20] González-Montemayora AM, Flores-Gallegosa AC, Contreras-Esquivela JC, Solanilla-Duqueb JF, Rodríguez-Herrera R. Functional activities and its applications in bakery products. Trends in Food Science and Technology. 2019;**94**:12-19

[21] Joseau MJ, Frassoni JE, Verzino GE, Rodriguez Reartes, S. L. Verga AR, López Lauenstein S. Avances en la conservación y obtención de material selecto del Banco Nacional de Germoplasma de *Prosopis*, Córdoba, Argentina. FAVE Sección Ciencias Agrar. 2021;**20**(1):265-285.

[22] Verga AR. Genetische Untersuchungen an *Prosopis chilensis* und *P. flexuosa* (*Mimosaceae*) im trockenen Chaco Argentiniens. Göttingen Res Notes for Genetics. 1995;**19**(1):96

[23] Joseau MJ, Castro Schule FF. Caracterización del género *Prosopis*. In: Verzino GE, editor. Conservación de recursos forestales nativos en Argentina El Banco Nacional de Germoplasma de *Prosopis*. Córdoba, Argentina; 2005. pp. 81-88

[24] Intituto Nacional de Semillas. INASE Res. 374/14. Argentina; 2014 p. 8

[25] Cruz I, Sauad J, Condorí M. Mejora del proceso tradicional de secado de frutos de algarroba, para la obtención de harina. Aplicación de herramientas de análisis multicriterio para la selección de alternativas tecnológicas. In: Verzino GEJMJ, editor. Reunión Nacional del Algarrobo Actas. Córdoba, Argentina: Grupo Encuentro; 2013. p. 193

[26] Código Alimentario Argentino. Capitulo IX. Buenos Aires, Argentina; 2017

[27] Sciammaro L, Ferrero C, Puppo C. Agregado de valor al fruto de Prosopis alba. Estudio de la composición química y nutricional para su aplicación en bocaditos dulces saludables. Revista de la Facultad de Agronomía. 2015;**14**(1):115-123

[28] Correa Uriburu FM, Cattaneo F, Maldonado LM, Zampini IC, Alberto MR, Isla MI. *Prosopis alba* seed as a functional food waste for food formulation enrichment. Food. 2022;**11**:2857

[29] Draghi C. Las semillas del futuro. La ciencia redescubre cultivos olvidados. La Nación. 2003;**2003**:20

[30] Pereira de Gusmão R, Cavalcanti-Mata ME, Martins-Duarte ME, Souza Gusmão TA. Particle size, morphological, rheological, physicochemical characterization and designation of minerals in mesquite flour (*Prosopis juliflora*). Journal of Cereal Science. 2016;**69**:119-124

[31] Pereira de Gusmão R, Souza-Gusmão TA, Calvancanti-Mata ME,

Martins Duarte ME. Mathematical modeling and determination of effective diffusivity of mesquite during convective drying. American Journal of Plant Sciences. 2016;7(6):814-823

[32] Escobar BA, Estévez MA, Fuentes CG, Venegas DF. Uso de harina de cotiledón de algarrobo (*Prosopis chilensis* (Mol) Stuntz) como fuente de proteína y fibra dietética en la elaboración de galletas y hojuelas fritas. Arch Latinoam Nutr Órgano Of la Soc Latinoam Nutr. 2009;**59**(2):191-198

[33] Freyre M, Astrada E, Blasco C, Baigorria C, Rozycki V, Bernardi C. Valores nutricionales de frutos de vinal (*Prosopis ruscifolia*): consumo humano y animal nutritional. The Journal of Food. 2003;**4**(1):41-46

[34] Sciammaro L, Ferrero C, Puppo C. Comparación entre harinas de dos especies de algarrobo (*Prosopis* sp.) del norte argentino. [Internet]. p. 93. Available from: http://sedici.unlp.edu.ar/bitstream/handle/10915/136450/Resumen.pdf?sequence=1

[35] Boeri P, Piñuel L, Sharry S, Barrio D. Caracterización nutricional de la harina integral de algarroba (*Prosopis alpataco*) de la norpatagonia Argentina. Rev la Fac Agron La Plata. 2017;**116**(1):129-140

[36] Mom MV. Caracterización estructural y propiedades funcionales de las harinas de los frutos de *Prosopis alba* Griseb., *P. chilensis* (Molina) Stuntz emend. Burkart y *P. flexuosa* DC. Desarrollo de un proceso de secado, molienda y mezcla para optimizar la calidad del . Universidad de Buenos Aires; 2012

[37] Labuckas D, Arzac M, Ledesma M, Domina A, Carranza C, Rovetto L, Aguilar R, Silva MP Martinez MJ. Harinas de algarrobas del Noroeste Cordobés: Propiedades Químicas y Funcionales. Artículo de Divulgación [Internet]. 2018; Available from: https://inta.gob.ar/documentos/harinas-de-algarrobas-del-noroeste-cordobes-propiedades-quimicas-y-funcionales-0

[38] Mazzuferi V, Ingaramo P, Joseau MJ. Tratamiento de Calor para el Secado de Frutos y el Control de Insectos en *Prosopis chilensis*. Ağrı. 1994;**XI**:49-53

[39] Silva MP, Martinez MJ, Brunetti MA, Balzarini M, Karlin U. Valoración nutritiva del fruto del algarrobo blanco (*Prosopis chilensis*) bajo distintos tipos de almacenamiento. Multequina. 2000;**9**:65-74

[40] INCUPO/SAGPYA. Instituto de Cultura Popular. Catálogo de tecnologías para pequeños productores agropecuarios. La elaboración de harina de algarrobo. 2003

[41] TEKNYCAMPO. Molinos multiuso Tekne-400. [Internet]. 2022. Available from:.https://teknycampo.com.ar/productos-de-teknycampo/molinos-multiuso-tekne-400/

[42] Cornejo Becker C, Gerbán CA. Proyecto de inversión de una planta de harina de algarrobo. Estudio Técnico. Universidad Católica de Salta; 2017. Available from: http://bibliotecas.ucasal.edu.ar /opac_css/doc_ num.php?explnum_id=1259

[43] Martin L. Comunicación personal. 2022

[44] Mom MP, Tolaba MP, Castro MA. Molienda de frutos de Prosopis alba Griseb. y Prosopis flexuosa DC. Estudio anatómico estructural y propiedades funcionales. In: Verzino GEJMJ, editor. Reunión Nacional del Algarrobo Actas. Córdoba. Argentina: Grupo Encuentro; 2013. p. 193

[45] Escobar B, Romeo M, Baeza G, Soto X, Vásquez M. Caracterización y composición química del fruto de algarrobo (*Prosopis chilensis* Mol Stuntz). Revista Chilena de Nutricion. 1987;**15**(2):113

[46] Instituto Nacional de Defensa de la Competencia y de la Protección de la Propiedad Intelectual (INDECOPI). Algarroba Compendio de Normas Técnicas peruana y Guías para su implementación. 2009. 49

[47] Cosiansi JF. Desarrollo de un mecanismo de trilla para vainas de *Prosopis*. La Plata: U.N; 1991

[48] FAO. El género *Prosopis* "algarrobos" en América Latina y el Caribe. Distribución, bioecología, usos y manejo. The Interne 2000. Available from: https://www.fao.org/3/ad314s/AD314S03.htm

[49] Gómez MI. Propiedades de la harina de algarrobo (*Prosopis alba* Griseb) con vistas a procesos de panificación. In: Verzino GEJMJ, editor. Reunión Nacional del Algarrobo Actas. Córdoba. Argentina: Grupo Encuentro; 2013. p. 193

[50] Secretaria de Agroindustria. Ministerio de Producción y Trabajo. Presidencia de la Nación. Harina de Algarroba: La competencia del chocolate. Ficha 40 [Internet]. 2015. Available from: https://alimentosargentinos.magyp.gob.ar/HomeAlimentos/Nutricion/fichaspdf/Ficha_40_HarinaAlgarroba.pdf

[51] Prokopiuk D, Crudeli G. Caracterización de harinas de algarroba (*Prosopis alba* Griseb) para alimentación de rumiantes. Comunicaciones Científicas y Tecnológicas. 2008:V–042

[52] Galera FM, Los algarrobos. Primera. Córdoba, Argentina: Graziani Gráfica; 2000. p. 269

[53] Chagra Dib EP, Valdivia CL, Vera AT, Leguiza HD. Efecto de la suplementación invernal con fruto de algarrobo y heno de alfalfa sobre la producción de leche de cabras criollas y el crecimiento de los cabritos lechales. Sitio Argentino Prod Anim Estación Agropecu Junín Cent Reg Cuyo. 2002;**1**(12):1-12

[54] Paciencia del Monte. Tuclame. Córdoba. Recetas. [Internet]. Available from: pacienciadelmonte@yahoo.com.ar.

Chapter 4

Soybean Production, Constraints, and Future Prospects in Poorer Countries: A Review

Moosa M. Sedibe, Alina M. Mofokeng and Doreen R. Masvodza

Abstract

This study was carried out to examine patterns of soybean production, constraints, and possible solutions in poorer countries such as Southern African countries. It was observed that the success of soybean in top-producing countries was characterized by large acreage of land, with a good supply of inputs coupled with intensive management and access to competitive markets. Africa is a minor player in the soybean industry as it supplies less than 1% of the world's soybeans. Because the crop is not for direct household consumption, it is produced on a small-scale and treated as a zero inputs crop. This has resulted in a persistent yield gap, with levels reaching only a third of those obtained in developed countries. There is under-usage of inputs such as irrigation, fertilizers, and improved seed. There is need for a definite shift from small to large-scale production. Limited access to inputs, poor adoption of technologies and restricted markets usually also compromise production. The global demand for soybean due to a growing feed industry, biodiesel, industrial demand, and bias for plant-based protein, is going upwards. New soybean frontiers will likely be present in future, and countries whose production levels lag could take advantage of this situation.

Keywords: production patterns, yield gap, biotic factors, technology adoption, soybean production

1. Introduction

Soybean (*Glycine max*) is an economically important oilseed crop with a high protein (40%), high oil content (20%), and of good nutritional quality [1]. It is a non-native and non-staple crop in Sub-Saharan Africa with potential to become a commercial crop owing to its wide range of uses such as food, feed, and as an industrial raw material [2, 3]. After palm oil, soybean oil is the most consumed cooking oil in the world, being also a major export good. The overall sector can have a total retail market value of around USD 146.23 billion [2].

This study will examine production patterns of soybean in poorer countries in contrast to top-producing countries and will discuss the constraints and limitations to soybean production in poorer countries such as those in Southern Africa and suggest their possible solutions. Some of the uses of the crop will also be elaborated.

2. Global production and consumption

Top production of soybean is mainly reported in the United States, Brazil, and Argentina, with India ranking fourth so far [4]. The best three countries together account for 80% of total production and they dominate world exports [5]. United States of America, Brazil, Argentina, China, India, Paraguay, Canada, Ukraine, Russia, and Bolivia are among the top 10 soybean producers globally [6].

Brazil emerges as one of the leading countries in soybean production because it has a significant amount of usable and relatively inexpensive land coupled with yield growth while production in the USA is driven predominantly by yield growth since the 80's, **Table 1** [4]. Soybeans in the USA is also known for its good quality regarding protein content as compared other countries hence its usual good price [9]. China imports the largest quantities of soybean (USD 38.1 billion) followed by the Europe Union which imports mainly soymeal and cake for feed for livestock and soybean oil to produce biodiesel [5].

The introduction of herbicide-resistant, genetically modified (GM) soybeans has also allowed for increased productivity levels and a smaller workforce, enabling the crop's rapid expansion. More than 80% of soybean varieties are genetically modified and given this inherent resistance, they survive better under chemical control of weeds, especially on large scales, and this contributes to better crop yields [5]. According to reports by Debnath and Babu [2], the adoption of genetically modified technology increases yields by an average of 22% relative to traditional varieties.

3. Production in Africa and Sub-Saharan Africa

In Africa and Sub-Saharan Africa, however, there is very little or no significant growth of production of the soybean crop despite its value and important uses and benefits [10]. Southern Africa is one of the regions where the human population

Area	Country	Area harvested 2019 (million ha)	Yield 2019 (t/ha)	2018 Production million tons	2019 Production million tons	2020 Production million tons
International	USA	35.45	3.40	120.51	96.67	112.55
	Brazil	35.90	3.36	117.91	114.32	121.80
	Argentina	16.60	3.33	37.79	55.26	48.80
	Canada	2.54	2.86	7.42	6.15	6.36
	India	11.33	0.96	10.93	13.26	11.023
Africa	South Africa	0.73	1.60	1.54	1.17	1.25
	Zambia	0.19	1.58	0.30	0.28	0.30
	Nigeria	1.00	1.05	0.66	0.70	0.60
	Malawi	0.06	0.4	0.18	0.17	0.18
	Ghana	0.05	0.60	0.18	0.18	0.18

Table 1.
World production, yield, and acreage for the African producers from 2018 to 2019 against top international producers [7, 8].

increases faster than food production and food insecurity is also a major concern. African producers supply less than 1% of the world's soybeans (**Table 1**) [7, 8].

African production levels are rising 48% fast, at a rate of 6.84% per year, although this mostly results from an increase in area under the crop and not from yield [7, 8]. Major production is concentrated in South Africa, which is the leading producer in Africa, contributing about 35% of the total production, followed by Nigeria (27%), Zambia and Uganda (85%) [8]. Other Sub-Saharan African (SSA) countries, including Zimbabwe, Malawi, Ghana, Sudan, and Ethiopia, have also experienced sizeable commercial soybean expansion [10]. Outside of these countries, there is very little soybean production in the rest of SSA [11]. Cereals, such as maize (*Zea mays*), millet (*Panicum* spp.), rice (*Oryza sativa*), sorghum (*Sorghum bicolor*), and wheat (*Triticum aestivum*) are also important crops with regard to calorie intake in Southern Africa [10].

Because soybean is usually not for direct household consumption, it is grown as a secondary crop and this makes it not thrive under subsistence settings [12]. The African continent still has to significantly increase the area under soybean crop and make use of underutilized land to its benefit [10]. The major factors that are expected to drive soybean production include land availability, the investment by private equities, international developmental organizations and banks in corporate farms, growth of the poultry market, growing bias towards plant based protein, and increasing household consumption [13].

Protein deficiency exacts a greater toll from infants, children, and pregnant and lactating women in the Southern African region, than anywhere else in the world, partially because starchy foods are widely consumed and animal protein often is too expensive and out of reach for low-income families. The region accounts for 38 and 27% of global child stunting and wasting, respectively [14]. Soybean has a potential to economically and nutritionally transform African economies and some of the countries actually share similar agro-climatic conditions with countries like Argentina and Brazil [15].

4. Uses of soybean

As the list of its uses continues to expand, soybean may potentially play a role in food globalization among crops like maize, wheat, rice, and potato. Besides its role in the food industry, it is important in the feeds, biodiesel, and other industrial uses as well as improvement of soil nutrients and structure. Its many uses contribute to its widespread production [16]. This section will describe some of the important uses of soybean.

4.1 Soybean-derived foodstuffs

Soybean can be processed into soy milk, a valuable protein supplement in infant feeds and the milk can be processed into curds and cheese [17]. Soybean seed yields edible, semi-drying oil, used as salad oil and also for manufacturing margarine and shortening [13]. Soy foods such as miso, tempeh, and soy sauce are derived either directly from the whole fresh bean or after processing of the bean into soymilk and are consumed either in fermented or non-fermented form. In the recent past, the range of soy foods has expanded to include fresh beans and sprouts, and grain products such as pasta and flour, meat substitutes, and soy spreads and pastes, baked goods, snack bars, noodles, and infant formula [11, 16]. Soybean can be used blended with maize and wheat flour as a source of protein with about 20% oil. Mechanically pressed meal provides low-fat flour with 5–6% oil, and solvent-extracted meal gives defatted flour with about 1% oil [16].

Soybean is used in dietetic foods and in novel products, such as tofu-based ice cream and soybean yogurt. Studies associate the soybean consumption of phytoestrogen-rich diets typical of soybean with a lower risk of lifestyle diseases such as coronary heart diseases, osteoporosis, hormone-dependent forms of cancer, and menopausal symptoms. Soy protein is a primary component in meat analogues consumed by people who prefer foods that are animal-free or lower in saturated fat [16, 17].

4.2 Feeds

The major processed soybean product globally is soybean meal [18]. In Africa, the demand for soybean has increased, driven by the growing feed industry for poultry and aquaculture. The vegetative portions of plants are used for silage, hay, pasture or as fodder [13, 16]. Soy products, like soy cake and full fat soy is increasingly used as substitutes for fishmeal in feed rations because it is cheaper. Soy oilcake is mainly imported from Argentina and then mixed with soy-oil and nutrients to compose a balanced feed ration. These feed rations are cheaper than a ration consisting of full fat soybeans but, however do not give the same performance of production [9]. Soy meal is a very rich protein feed for livestock and it has an increasing demand [17].

4.3 Biodiesel and other and industrial uses

A small but growing proportion of soybean oil is used as a feedstock for biofuel production, but soybean is rarely cultivated with this as the core objective [18]. Industrially, the oil is important in the production of paints and candle wax. It is also used is in the manufacturing of paints, linoleum, oilcloth, printing inks, soap, insecticides, and disinfectants [17]. The straw is used to make paper stiffer than that made from wheat straw.

4.4 Improvement of soil nutrients and structure

Soybean straw may be plowed back into the soil as a green manure [17]. In low-input inter-cropping systems, the crop is known to improve soil properties, through nitrogen fixation and enhanced moisture retention. The combination of improved soil properties and the ability to break lifecycles of pests and diseases makes soybean an ideal crop in cereal rotation programs [1]. This advantage is especially important for crop production in Africa due to the economic limitations in the use of fertilizers. Besides socioeconomic benefits, soybean and associated Rhizobium and Bradyrhizobium microbes contribute to nitrogen fixation in soils. Nitrogen fertilization is tremendously expensive and pauses ecological risks, such as water eutrophication and the emission of greenhouse gases, that contribute to global warming [11].

5. Production constraints and solutions

5.1 Yield gap

Among the constraints faced in the production of soybean, there is a substantial yield gap between the developed and developing countries and it is persistent among Sub-Saharan African farmers [2]. The average soybean yield has stagnated at 1.1 t ha^{-1} in SSA in contrast to the world average of 2.4 t ha^{-1}. This yield gap is primarily due to the under-usage of modern inputs in developing countries. Sub-Saharan Africa imports substantial volumes of processed soybean in the form of oil and cake for animal feed to fill the gaps. As a net importer, Africa is exposed to rising global prices for soybean, oil, and cake.

Yield gaps are not unique for only soybean as they also exist for staple cereal crops like maize and a number of other crops grown under smallholder and subsistence setups [11]. There are a number of constraints that account for yield gaps, such as resource availability, economic issues such as inflation, gender disparities, accessible markets, etc. These may have resulted in limiting farmers in this region from becoming major players in producing soybean [10, 19]. Solving technical issues and taking measures to close the yield gap may go a long way to improve production levels [20].

5.2 Fertilizer usage

One way to close the yield gap is making sure farmers access fertilizer and other inputs. Technical issues such as access to fertilizers, herbicides, and pesticides, seem to linger for all for farmers from small to large scale farmers, across different countries. It is the capabilities to solve these problems and that vary at different levels. Due to limited access to farming resources, smallholder farmers are more likely to farm on poor quality soil and are often plagued by low crop yields [19]. On the other hand, mere provision of free inputs to smallholder farmers attracts unscrupulous players who end up creating black market of the inputs. A farmer that approaches a bank for an inputs loan or a machinery loan may go a long way in carrying out significant production as compared to one who gets invited for free inputs.

Legumes, such as soybean have a high phosphorus (P) requirement for growth and also for nodulation and nitrogen fixation. Low soil phosphorus may contribute to the poor survival of some rhizobial strains [21]. Low phosphorus availability is liable to limit soybean yield on many highly degraded soils in the tropics, even though the external P requirements of soybean are lower than those of some other legumes. It is reported generally that the longer the P is in contact with the soil, the greater the fixation that occurs [12]. If planting is being done on virgin land, inoculation of the seed with *Bradyrhizobium japonicum* should be carried out to enable the crop to fix its own nitrogen through the action of this bacterium in the root nodules [22]. For annual crops such as soybean, P application, 2 weeks after planting is recommended [21].

The flowering stage of soybean requires huge amounts of fertilization for successful seed set. Once the soybean begins to flower, it takes large quantities on nutrients from the soil especially phosphorous and potassium [12, 23]. Abortion of flowers happens a lot in soybean and numerous flowers easily get lost due to limited fertility among other factors. The oversight some farmers make, is to plant soybean after maize and not apply sufficient amounts of phosphorus and potassium hoping there will be sufficient fertility for good yields [23].

5.3 Diseases

Constraints, such as pathogens, pests, and weeds can be classed as biotic factors [24]. On the other hand, plants stressed by too much or too little water or by nutrient imbalances often produce seeds that are abnormal and these are known as abiotic factors. It is recommended for farmers apply fungicide to their soybean seed at planting to improve germination [22]. In the United States, commercial cultivars are marketed as resistant or tolerant to white mold caused by *Sclerotinium rolfsii* which causes sudden death syndrome, *Fusarium solani* f. sp. *Glycines*, brown stem rot *Phialophora gregata* f. sp. Sojae, *Phytophthora* root and stem rot *Phytophthora sojae*, frogeye leaf spot *Cercospora sojina*, stem canker, *Diaporthephaseolorum* var. carlivora, Charcoal rot *Macrophomina phaseolina*, Soybean rust *Phakopsora pachyrhizi*, Soybean mosaic virus a Potyvirus Bean pod mottle virus *A Comovirus*, soybean cyst nematode, *Heterodera glycines*, root know nematode, *Meloidogine arenaria* [25]. Prevalence varies with countries and regions.

5.4 Weed and insect pests

Soybeans are generally less competitive with weeds than other common crop species, which may be one potential limitation associated with including soybeans in a crop rotation. Although soybeans may tolerate early-season weed competition more than maize, it may be important to control weeds prior to the V3–V4 growth stage, 3–4 weeks after emergence to avoid yield reduction [26]. Narrower rows and higher plant populations can increase soybean's competitive ability, but the response is inconsistent and can increase the risk of diseases and soybean lodging [27]. The flowering stage in soybean is critical so you do not need harsh herbicides at this time. One must just make sure all the weed control is done earlier [26, 27].

The most important insect pests of soybean are defoliators or pods feeders; these two groups of insect pests can reduce soybean yield by up to 65% [22]. You do not need insects and bugs at flowering but good insect control as this is the time insects cause most damage by causing wounds to the plant that introduce disease [23]. Pesticides, fungicides and insecticides may be needed on occasion, but are generally not recommended except under certain conditions where an expert has provided guidance on product application [22].

5.5 Crop rotations

Continuous cropping of maize leads to extensive degradation of soil and decrease in crop productivity which endangers household food and nutritional security. Introducing soybean into rotation with maize is a method to diversify diets and nutritional status while reducing abiotic and biotic stresses bringing soil fertility improvement and generating more income for farmers [28]. Several agronomic benefits are associated with the use of soy-maize rotations in the tropics, including increased soil fertility, decreased biotic pressure, and increased maize and soy yields [28]. Diversification and intensification through inclusion of grain legumes in cereal, root, or tuber-based cropping systems represents a key technology in the drive towards the sustainable intensification of agriculture in Sub-Saharan Africa [29].

Soybean can contribute to the nitrogen economy of the soil [28] as the additional nitrogen fixed by soybeans has been found to significantly increase maize yields subsequently planted after soy [29]. Soy-maize rotations build resilience against threats such as Striga (*Striga hermonthica*) [28]. Despite the usefulness of legume-cereal rotations to boost productivity, adoption in Sub-Saharan Africa remains limited [28]. In South Africa, Van der Merwe et al. [30] reported that the increase in production is partly resulting from commercial farmers recognizing the benefits of soybean in crop rotation systems with maize [19].

5.6 Production practices

General principles of good management like crop rotation, planting healthy, vigorous seeds, and selection of soybean varieties may all be important. Berglund and Helms [31] reported that row spacing is a critical determinant of yield in soybean production, because appropriate spacing can ensure effective weed control. Before flowering you also want a plant that can catch huge amounts of solar energy, that can produce and keep the most flowers so as to end up with the most pods. By late planting, the sunlight is much less as the season progresses hence one ends up with small pods and seeds, so adherence to planting dates is important. If one is planting late you may need to use narrower rows giving a heavier population that can catch the sunlight and heat to cushion the stand. Row planting determines the plant population per unit area, and if cultivation practices are not optimized then a low population, that is, wide spacing can adversely influence the total yield of a given area.

5.7 Processing, markets, and other factors

Factors strongly impacting a commercial crop like soybean, such as poor infrastructure, limited access to markets and technical assistance, barriers to acquiring agricultural inputs, pervasive rural poverty, uncertain land tenure, and poor policy enactment can all negatively impact crop productivity in Sub-Saharan Africa [28]. Large corporations have not materially invested in the Sub-Saharan Africa region to cater to either domestic demand or to service other international markets, leaving the market opportunities available for local and regional processors [18].

Intensification of the soybean processing sector is necessary to create demand for production thus reducing on expensive imports [18]. This, however, requires institutional partnerships between governments, the private sectors and development banks to invest in soybean-crushing infrastructure and bio-refineries, and in the reallocation of the recently idle land from traditional crops to alternative cash crops [2].

As the crushing of soybean produces only 18% oil and 78% meal, processing soybean only for oil is expensive for crushers in the absence of a domestic demand for cake. Ethiopia, for instance, due to the lack of crushing infrastructure, exported 53.94 thousand MT of soybean and imported 4.52 thousand MT of soy oil in 2017 [7]. Logistical bottlenecks can also be experienced in countries which have increased production and have limited crushing facilities and farmers in countries such as Argentina have to sometimes stockpile their production and sell it when market conditions improve [5].

5.8 Technology transfer and adoption

Adoption of technologies by farmers in poorer countries requires, unwavering support from government, sufficient government follow up and back-up as well as evaluated results-based management. Extension workers require re-training and re-equipping [32]. Modernization and digitization of platforms is also often necessary to improve efficiency of information transfer. Mere provision of free inputs to farmers may not be effective to bring about the desired transformation of the farming sector as the history of many third world countries proves. Some farmers face poverty cycles that may force them to sell inputs to meet household needs. This way, unscrupulous players get attracted and black markets are promoted. A farmer who approaches a bank for a machinery loan may go a long way in carrying out significant production as compared to one who gets invited for free inputs [32].

6. Country case studies

Three country case studies will be presented of Ghana, a typical "poor African country" which seems to have long term challenges with respect to soybean production, Cambodia and South Africa, both of which are transitioning and are experiencing increased soybean production levels at country level. The three countries will be examined with respect constraints faced, interventions and government support and response and technology adoption levels by farmers.

6.1 Ghana

Ghana like Nigeria are quite old states in Africa. As early as, 1975 and 1977 a major soybean-growing campaign was launched in support of the growing Ghanaian poultry industry which triggered the launch of a major soybean-growing campaign in support of the growing Ghanaian poultry industry [12]. The initial farmer response was high and a considerable increase in production was recorded, but the utilization base was low and knowledge of processing was inadequate [21]. Initiatives that were meant to increase cash income and improve the nutritional status of rural households were therefore prematurely stalled [12, 33].

A number of other factors are identified as attributing to this problem. Technical issues such as fertilizers, herbicides, and pesticides, seem to linger for all farmers from small to large scale, not only in Ghana but in many countries. It's the solution methods and capabilities that vary at different levels. Some of the challenges faced in Ghana were as follows:

- already existent agro-based firms were discouraged from sourcing locally by poor domestic production and poor grain quality. This situation coupled with high import costs literally forced them out of business [12].

- there was a poor adoption of soybean production technologies, resulting in low yields. Many farmers in Ghana shun technologies such as row planting as they do with traditional crops such as sorghum, millets, and bambaranut, resulting in low plant populations and wide gaps which promote increased weed competition. Unlike the traditional crops, soybean cannot be broadcasted randomly which farmers do as a result of lack of manpower and mechanization issues prominent among small-holder farmers in Ghana [12, 33].

- poor pre- and post-harvest techniques where farmers leave their grain at the mercy of the weather, instead of storing it in cool, dry places. Soybean should be harvested when 90% of the pods turn yellow or are dry otherwise shattering of seed occurs, especially in late-planted soybean. When it comes to the actual grain storage, farmers store their soybean seed in airtight polythene bags. However, exposure to sunlight prior to storage induces seed deterioration. The situation is worse for women farmers as they fail to properly handle their crop due to manpower issues [12, 34].

- rapid loss of seed viability in storage as compared to seed of traditional crops such as sorghum, millets, groundnuts, etc. [12].

- poor road networks hamper farmers from linking with their markets thus, attracting smallholder traders who manipulate prices at the farmer's expense. The traders usually lack standardized grading systems which affects pricing [12, 33].

Generally, a large scale commercial farmer with experience is more likely to even out most technical issues and may have lighter issues such as market identification and processing challenges.

6.2 Cambodia

In the past, well before 1994, in Cambodia, soybean was grown for subsistence by most farmers on a small scale, and as supplementary crop for livelihood. However, it has become the main cash crop and the fourth most important crop after rice, maize, and cassava in terms of cultivated area and production due to competitive market prices and demand from consumers [32].

Farmers in Cambodia face a fair share of technical constraints just like any country such as access to agricultural inputs and machinery. Some farmers plant soybean manually by broadcasting using the hand-hoe and only a few use machines for planting. Another major problem is lack of knowledge about pest identification. The soybean sub-sector is hugely immature with limited or no links in the value chain from production to marketing to processing. Domestic soybean seeds are considered by processing companies in local communities to be of poor quality and this leads to low demand and therefore contributes to low prices [32].

Researchers, government sector, private sector, extension agencies, and policy makers need to develop appropriate technologies to enhance soybean production and create an enabling environment of successful cultivation of soybean. Training and re-tooling for extension workers is consistently done to effectively transfer improved soybean technologies to farmer [32]. The government aims to modernize agriculture and increase labor productivity for farmers and in terms of markets, Cambodia aims to carry out digitization of information which will facilitate the formation of value chain platforms through which value chain stakeholders can exchange information, services, and products [35].

The level of technology adoption is very significant due to unwavering support from government [32]. Cambodia's fertilizer usage per hectare of cropland increased from 10.0 kg in 2005 to 33.0 kg in 2018 [35]. Use of pesticides, most of which are imported, has also increased in Cambodia. It is the regulation of their use that still needs to be done for farmers' safety, food safety, and ecosystem health. Cambodian agriculture has experienced a gradual and nationwide mechanization which resulted in replacement of labor with machinery such as tractors, harvesters, power tillers and water pumps bringing significant growth in soybean production alongside other crops [32, 35]. Besides job creation, large scale farms can become information centers for smaller farmers, which is a plus to extension services.

6.3 South Africa

In South Africa large-scale production of soybeans did not begin until the late 1990s. Previously, output hovered below 50,000 tonnes nationwide with acreage below 50,000 ha. The area planted to soybeans has expanded rapidly since then [19]. The soybean sector and industry in South Africa contributes 250 million USD out of the 11.25 billion USD brought in by the whole agriculture [36]. This include sectors carrying out value-addition of the crop as most of the grain has to be processed.

Most farms are commercial while smallholder farms are more predominant in rural areas [11]. As early as 1996 South African farmers still planted less than a 100 thousand hectares but with increased crushing capacity ensuring local demand for soybeans, the active promotion of the benefits of including soybeans into a rotational cropping pattern with other crops. This and management ease brought by genetically modified herbicide-tolerant soybean varieties, more and more farmers choose to plant soybeans in rotation with maize [37].

The department of trade and industry initiated elaborate processes that triggered investments towards new soybean processing plants and improvements in existing ones during the 2012 financial year. In response farmers have committed to produce increasingly high yields of soybeans yearly and the South African Bureau for Food and Agricultural policy [38] projects that there would be an increase in the amount of land set aside for commercial soybean production subsequently [19]. These policy directives elevated soybean as a cash and food crop. In addition, an industrial policy and action plan of 2012/13 to 2014/15 distinguished soybeans as having the potential for creating opportunities for new investments and jobs making South Africa the largest soybean producer in SSA, followed by Zambia, Nigeria, and Uganda [7].

Historically, soybean marketing in South African and other oilseed crops were regulated under an oilseed board initiated in 1937 and revised in 1968. This board was set up primarily to determine the sale prices of oilseeds in the local market. In 1996 the act it was operating under, was replaced by another act which deregulated marketing of agricultural products in the South African agricultural sector leading to the establishment of a council to manage and monitor the government's involvement in the agricultural sector.

This was when soybean producers in South Africa became participants in an international free market environment. In terms of markets, there are many growing and numerous ready markets for soybean in South Africa. Today, some African countries still operate under such restrictive laws which do not improve the true market performance of crop prices thus limiting their producers from becoming global players [39].

7. Future prospects

Soybean has the potential to transform the economy of a country as evidenced by data for countries like South Africa and Cambodia, to name only two countries. According to Kargesa and Reckingac [40], soybean has become one of the most important commodities of trade. This is besides its role in transforming family livelihoods and diets. If all limitations in its production are dealt with and commitment to utilize idle land tracts and adoption and adherence to recommended production techniques is done, it becomes an easily accessible source of protein to an ordinary family. It will take a lot of awareness of its value in Asian diets such as the Chinese diet and culinary industry, where lifestyle diseases have been kept low while maintaining an important balance. Therefore, it is worth any commercial pursuits.

8. Discussion, conclusions, and recommendations

The success of soybean in the top-producing countries is associated with large landmasses with supply of adequate inputs coupled with intensive management and good access to competitive markets.

Africa is a minor player in the soybean industry as African producers supply less than 1% of the world's soybeans due to a persistent yield gap between smallholder farmers and large scale farmers which also occurs among third world and developed countries. Because soybean is not for direct household consumption, it is treated as a secondary crop by subsistence farmers.

If measures are taken to close the yield gaps among other factors by not regarding soybean as a zero inputs crop, as well as increasing scale of production from small to large scale through the utilization of idle land, improve access to inputs and markets, third world countries will improve production.

Technical issues such as access to fertilizers, herbicides, and pesticides, linger for all for farmers from small to large scale farmers, across different countries. It is the capabilities to bring solution that vary at different levels.

Mere provision of free inputs to smallholder farmers attracts unscrupulous players who end up creating black markets of the inputs. A farmer that approaches a bank for a machinery loan may go a long way in carrying out significant production as compared to one who gets invited for free inputs.

Positive transition in soybean production has occurred and is still occurring for countries like South Africa and Cambodia, both in Africa and Asia, respectively. Large scale production should be able to meet domestic demand and excess for exports. In addition to job creation, large scale farms can become information centers for smaller farmers.

Adoption of technologies by farmers in poorer countries backed by sufficient government policies and actions at the same time routing out leakages from shady operations that arise may bring about transition of the soybean sector in African countries.

The soybean sector and industry contributes a quarter of a billion USD to the 11.25 billion USD brought in by the whole agriculture sector in South Africa. This shows that the crop can significantly transform an economy.

The growing feed industry, industrial demand and biodiesel are driving the demand for soybean upwards. The bias towards plant based protein is also expected to benefit the consumption of soybean-based products. Therefore, new soybean frontiers are likely to continuously develop and the Southern African region has an opportunity to tap in, to its own benefit.

Funding

This soybean research project is fully funded by the Research, Development and Postgraduate Studies of the Central University of Technology, Bloemfontein.

Conflict of interest

There are no conflicts of interests regarding this work.

Author details

Moosa M. Sedibe[1], Alina M. Mofokeng[2] and Doreen R. Masvodza[1*]

1 Central University of Technology (CUT), Bloemfontein, South Africa

2 Agriculture Research Council (ARC), Potchefstroom, South Africa

*Address all correspondence to: rmasvodza2011@gmail.com

References

[1] Tukamuhabwa P, Maphosa M. State of Knowledge in Breeding for Resistance to Soybean Rust in the Developing World. Rome, Italy: FAO [A Review Prepared for the Global Partnership Initiative for Plant Breeding Capacity Building (GIPB). FAO Plant Production and Protection Paper 204]. 2012

[2] Debnath D, Babu S. Prospects for sustainable intensification of soybean production in Sub-Saharan Africa. African Journal of Agricultural and Resource Economics. 2020;**15**(4):365-371

[3] Siamabele B. The significance of soybean production in the face of changing climates in Africa. Cogent Food and Agriculture. 2021;7:1

[4] Global Soybean Market Outlook. 2022. Available from: https://www.expert marketresearch.com/reports/soybean-market. [Accessed: November 2022]

[5] Voora V, Larrea C, Bermudez. Global Market Report: Soybeans. International Institute for Sustainable Development Internal Report. 2020. Available from: www.iisi.org. [Accessed: September 2021]

[6] Dutton B. Top 10 Soybean Producing Countries. 2019. Available from: www.cropprophet.com. [Accessed: October 2021]

[7] FAOSTAT. Databases: Soybean Production and Trade Data. 2019. Available from: http://www.fao.org/faostat/en/#data. [Accessed: September 2021]

[8] FAOSTAT. Databases: Soybean Production and Trade Data. 2020. Available from: http://www.fao.org/faostat/en/#data. [Accessed: September 2021]

[9] Grönum CF, van Schalkwyk HD, du Plessis JH. The comparative advantage of dryland soybean production in Brits, North West. Agrekon. 2000;**39**(3):235-243. DOI: 10.1080/03031853.2000.9523575

[10] Goldsmith P. 2018. Farm.Doc Series On: The State of Soybean in Africa. Available from: www.farmdocdaily.illinois.edu

[11] Engelbrecht G, Claassens S, Mienie CMS, Fourie H. South Africa: An Important Soybean Producer in Sub-Saharan Africa and the Quest for Managing Nematode Pests of the Crop. 2020

[12] Mbanya W. Assessment of the constraints in soybean production: A case of Northern Region, Ghana. Journal of Developments in Sustainable Agriculture. 2011;**6**:199-214

[13] Murithi HM, Beed F, Tukamuhabwa P, Thomma BPHJ, Joosten MHAJ. Soybean production in eastern and southern Africa and threat of yield loss due to soybean rust caused by *Phakopsora pachyrhizi*. Plant Pathology. 2015;**65**(2):176-188

[14] Khojely DM, Ibrahim SE, Sapey E, Han T. History, current status, and prospects of soybean production and research in Sub-Saharan Africa. The Crop Journal. 2018;**6**(3):226-235

[15] Opperman C, Varia S. Technical Report: Soybean Value Chain. AECOM International Development. 2011

[16] FAO Commodities and Trade Division, Basic Foodstuffs Service Research Report. The role of soybean in fighting world hunger. In: Paper Presented at the 7th World Soybean Research Conference. Brazil; 2004

[17] Soybean Production Guidelines South Africa. The ARC-Grain Crops Institute and Oil and Protein Development Publication Soybean Rust in Soybean. 2010. Available from: www.nda.agric.za. [Accessed: May 2019]

[18] African Center for Economic Transformation (ACET). The Soybean Agri-Processing Opportunity in Africa. 2016. Available from: Acetforafrica.org [Accessed: September 2022]

[19] Dlamini TS, Tshabalala P, Mutengwa T. Soybeans production in South Africa. Oilseeds and Fats Crops and Lipids. 2014;**21**(2):207-218

[20] Merlos FA, Monzon JP, Mercau JL, Taboada M, Andrade FH, Hall AJ, et al. Potential for crop production increase in Argentina through closure of existing yield gaps. Field Crops Research. 2015;**184**:145-154

[21] Plahar WA. Overview of the Soybean Industry in Ghana: Workshop on Soybean Protein for Human Nutrition and Health, Accra-Ghana. 2006. Available from: http://www.wishh.org/workshops/intl/ghana/ghana06/plahar-06. [Accessed: October 2022]

[22] Heatherly LG, Elmore RW. Managing inputs for peak production. In: Boerma HR, Specht JE, editors. Soybeans: Improvement, Production and Uses. Madison, Wisconsin, USA: Agronomy Monograph 16, American Society of Agronomy, Crop Science Society of America, and Soil Science Society of America; 2004. pp. 451-536

[23] Illinois Soybean Association. Nutrient Management Recommendations for Profitable Soybean Production—A Michigan Perspective. 2020. Available from: Youtube Video. [Accessed: September 2021]

[24] Hartman GL, West ED, Herman TK. Crops that feed the World 2. Soybean worldwide production, use, and constraints caused by pathogens and pests. Food Security. 2011;**3**:5-17

[25] Burton JW, Miranda L. Soybean improvement: Achievements and challenges. Ratarstvo i povrtarstvo. 2013;**50**(2):44-51

[26] Colquhoun J, Boerboom CM, Binning LK, Stoltenberg DE, Norman JM. Common lambsquarters photosynthesis and seed production in three environments. Weed Science. 2001;**49**:334-339

[27] Moechnig M, Clay SA, Deneke D. Management of problem weeds in soybean production. In: Best Management Practices. South Dakota State University Extension. 2019. pp. 34-285. Available from: extension.sdstate.edu

[28] Acevedo-Siaca L, Goldsmith PD. Soy-maize crop rotations in Sub-Saharan Africa: A literature review. International Journal of Agronomy. 2020;**2020**:8833872

[29] Franke AC, van den Brand GJ, Vanlauwe B, Giller KE. Sustainable intensification through rotations with grain legumes in Sub-Saharan Africa: A review. Agriculture, Ecosystems and Environment. 2018;**261**:172-185

[30] Van der Merwe R, Van Biljon A, Hugo A. Current and Potential Usage of Soybean Products as Food in South Africa. University of Free State; 2013. [Abstract 333]

[31] Berglund DR, Helms TC. Soybean Production. 2003. Available from: http://www.ag.ndsu.edu/pubs/plantsci/rowcrops/a250w.htm. [Accessed: April 2021]

[32] Nget R, Aguilar EA, Cruz PCS, Reaño CE, Sanchez PB, Reyes MR, et al.

Overview of farmers' perceptions of current status and constraints to soybean production in Ratanakiri Province of Cambodia. Sustainability. 2021;**13**:4433

[33] Dogbe W, Etwire PM, Martey E, Etwire JC, Baba IY, Siise A. Economics of soybean production: Evidence from Saboba and Chereponi Districts of Northern Region of Ghana. Journal of Agricultural Science. 2013;**5**(12):38-46

[34] Besley T. How do market failures justify interventions in rural credit markets? The World Bank Research Observer 2010;9(1). Available from: http://www.princeton.edu/rpds/papers/ Besley How Do Market Failures Justify Interventions in Rural Credit Markets [Accessed: October 2022]

[35] Asian Development Bank Report Internal Report (ADB). Cambodia Agriculture, Natural Resources, and Rural Development Sector Assessment, Strategy, and Road Map. 2021. Available from: www.adb.org [Accessed: October 2022]

[36] Manthata LS. A competitive analysis of the South African soybean industry [thesis]. University of Pretoria; 2016

[37] Bureau for Food and Agricultural Policy. The potential impact of a breeding and technology levy collection system in South Africa. In: Prepared for the South African Cultivar and Technology Agency (SACTA). 2018

[38] Bureau for Food and Agricultural Policy (BFAP). BFAP Baseline Agricultural Outlook 2013-2022. 2013. Available from: https://www.sagis.org.za/BFAP_2013.pdf. [Accessed: September 2022]

[39] Manthata LS. Competitive Analysis of the South African Soybean Industry. 2018. Available from: http://hdl.handle.net/2263/65911. [Accessed: December 2022]

[40] Kargesa K, Reckingac M. Agro-economic prospects for expanding soybean production beyond its current northerly limit in Europe. European Journal of Agronomy. 2022;**133**:126415

Chapter 5

Production and Utilization of *Lupinus* spp.

Darja Kocjan Ačko and Marko Flajšman

Abstract

The various species of lupin or lupine (*Lupinus* spp.) are classified in the botanical family of legumes (Fabaceae) and in the agronomic crop grouping of grain legumes. Toxic and bitter substances in lupine plants and grain were the reason why it was used in the past mainly to improve soil fertility. With the sustainable focus of the agricultural policy of the European Union, there are real possibilities for sowing and using lupine in the future—and not only bitter varieties, which are suitable for green manure due to their rich foliage, but also selectively bred sweet varieties for grains and herbage, which are a new alternative source of protein (30 to 40%), resistant starch and dietary fiber. Sweet varieties of Mediterranean species of lupine are obtained from seeds that contain almost no alkaloids and therefore have no harmful effects on the health of humans and farm animals. Sowing of sweet lupine varieties provides an opportunity for local processing into soybean-like products. Roasted and ground beans of sweet lupine varieties can serve as an excellent coffee substitute.

Keywords: white lupine, blue lupine, yellow lupine, food, feed

1. Introduction

The genus *Lupinus* includes around 600 species, of which 200 are more important annual, biennial, and perennial species. Mediterranean species are used as economically important lupines for improving soil fertility, for human consumption, and livestock feed: white lupine (*Lupinus albus* L.), blue lupine (*Lupinus angustifolius* L.), and yellow lupine (*Lupinus luteus* L.) [1–4].

The Andean lupine (*Lupinus mutabilis* Sweet) is cultivated among more than 100 American species, for now, limited to local production and consumption, and contains at least 10% more protein in the grain than the Mediterranean species [5]. The many-leaved or large-leaved lupine (*Lupinus polyphyllus* Lindl.) also originates in America; more specifically, its natural habitats are in the western parts of North America, from Alaska to northern California. As an ornamental plant, it has spread from Canada all over the world. Many hybrid cultivars are popular perennials in gardens, from where their seeds spread into the natural environment, where lupine plants displace native herbaceous species, such as wolf's bane, devil's claw, and lady orchid. Wild lupine reduces biodiversity, changes the original flora and fauna, and is therefore on the list of non-native invasive plants in the European Union and other countries around the world. Ecologists promote the removal of whole plants by uprooting and regular mowing before they flower or produce seeds.

Based on their origin, time of domestication, and use in the Old World, Mediterranean species of lupine are called Old World lupine species, while American species are called New World lupine species. Archeological findings indicate that the current cultivated lupine species were domesticated thousands of years ago, while the results of molecular genetic studies show that lupine species in the Old World developed earlier [1–3, 6–8].

With the cultivation and use of herbage and seeds, various names had developed throughout history. The name lupine is derived from the Latin word lupus, meaning wolf [1]. In Roman times, the plant was named after wolves that roamed the hilly areas of its natural habitats. This led to common names spread among European nations: *volčjak*, *volčec*, *volčji bob,* and *volčji fižol* (note: *volk* means "wolf" in Slovenian). Names for the plant that were associated with coffee, such as wild coffee, tall coffee, and Turkish coffee, came about much later when people realized that roasted lupine seed split into two parts that resembled a coffee bean. Roasted and ground lupine beans were used in Europe as a substitute for real coffee, especially during World War One and World War Two, when the import of coffee beans (*Coffea arabica* L.), the plant that grows in tropical and subtropical areas of the world, was restricted.

2. Morphological traits of Mediterranean species

All three Mediterranean species of lupine have common morphological, biological, and physiological characteristics, as well as their own distinctive features [2, 9–13]. Lupine has a strong and well-developed spindle-shaped root, which is capable of excellent penetration into compacted soil, to a depth of 1.5 meters, sometimes even more than 2 meters deep. Side roots spread out from the main root, with many root tubers or nodules forming when the plant's flowers.

The herbaceous stem of the lupine is 50 to 150 cm high, robust, firm and upright, covered with fine, soft, and silvery hairs. Because the stem does not become prostrate during cultivation, lupine can be used as good support for cereals and other legumes. In the past, it was sown together with rye, rapeseed and white mustard, pea, spring pea, and vetch. Single-stemmed plants, without side branches, have a terminal or determinate growth, while plants with side branches form an indeterminate type, which in some varieties has a bushy appearance.

The long-petiolate leaves of all lupine species are finger-shaped, palmately lobed, usually consisting of 5 to 9 ovate-oval leaflets, but may have even more leaflets. A lupine flower consists of five fused sepals and five petals. The petals form the typical shape of a papilionaceous (butterfly-like) flower. The names of Mediterranean species are based on the color of their petals (white, blue, and yellow), but some varieties have multi-colored flowers. Blue, pink, and crimson shades predominate in Andean and many-leafed lupine. In a bisexual flower, there is a pistil with a superior carpel and ten fused stamens, which distinguishes lupine from other legumes, which have nine fused stamens and one solitary stamen. In white and blue lupines, the flowers are self-pollinating, while the yellow lupine is partially allogamous [9].

Because unwanted pollination must not occur when selectively breeding new varieties and producing lupine seed-producing crops, isolation between different crops is required. For white and blue lupines, which are almost self-pollinating, a distance of

Species	Seed shape and color	Thousand seed weight (g)
White lupine	round, flattened, wavy seed up to one centimeter in diameter, white to creamy color	220 to 530
Yellow lupine	medium-sized oval seed, yellow-brown to creamy with a speckled pattern on the seed coat	110 to 165
Blue lupine	smaller reniform seed, light to dark brown with smaller spots	105 to 210
Andean lupine	round, bulging seed with a diameter of up to one centimeter, white, gray, black or green-yellow color	200 to 380
Many-leaved lupine	very small oval to reniform seed, gray to black color	12 to 30

Table 1.
Shape, color, and thousand seed weight of seeds of cultivated species of lupine (Lupinus *spp.*).

200 meters between crops is sufficient, whereas the allogamous yellow lupine, which is pollinated by insects, requires a distance of 500 m. The American many-leaved lupine is also an allogamous entomophilous species.

The papilionaceous flowers at the top of the main stem or at the ends of the side branches are grouped into flat and erect raceme inflorescences. Toward the end of flowering, when the top flowers open, the lower fertilized flowers have already formed pods. A young green pod turns yellow over time and turns brown and woody as it becomes mature. It contains 3 to 10 seeds of different shapes and sizes. The white lupine has the longest and widest pods, up to 12 cm long. It contains up to 10 round, slightly flattened, rounded and wavy seeds, white, gray-white to creamy colored, with a diameter of about 1 cm. The yellow and blue lupine have shorter pods, the number of seeds they contain is lower (4 to 8), and the seeds are smaller. In terms of shape, the yellow lupine has oval seeds, while the blue lupine has reniform (kidney-shaped) seeds. Yellow lupine seeds are yellow-brown to ochre with spots on the seed coat, while blue lupine seeds are light to dark brown with larger to smaller spots. The thousand seed weights of the seeds of Mediterranean lupine species can range from 100 to 500 g.

Compared to the white lupine, the South American Andean lupine has similar-sized seeds with a thousand seed weight of 200 to 380 g, enclosed in a black, white, or gray-brown to green-yellow seed coat. The gray-brown to black seeds of the many-leaved lupine are very small with a thousand seed weight of 12 to 30 g (**Table 1**).

The internal structure of lupine seeds is similar to other legumes [9, 11, 12]. Almost everything that is contained in the seed (grain) inside the seed coat is a young plant. A young plant needs reserve materials to start growing upon germination. With the development of the first green leaves, the plant begins to produce organic substances through photosynthesis and is no longer dependent on the reserve materials accumulated in the leaves. Similar to soybeans and beans, lupine germination is above ground or epigeal. During germination, both cotyledons rise up with the stem and appear from the soil.

3. Cultivation prevalence depending on intended crop usage

Considering the scale of cultivation throughout the world, lupine is an almost unknown grain legume. The Mediterranean species of lupine, for which sowing data is collected in producing countries, occupy less than one million hectares of land, which ranks it ninth among dry grain legumes after soybeans, beans, peanuts, chickpeas, cowpea, peas, lentils, and broad beans [14] (**Table 2**). In recent years, over half of lupine is produced in Australia, where blue lupine is being cultivated on 95% of the land. Sweet varieties of blue lupine are successfully replacing imported soybean meal in cattle feed [15, 16]. The average yield of lupine grains in the world in 2020 was 1.2 t/ha [14].

Interest in lupines for human consumption and livestock feed is also present in Europe, where all three Mediterranean species are cultivated. Sweet varieties of white lupine are mainly cultivated in southern Europe (in Portugal, Spain, and Southern France), where it thrives best. Sweet varieties of yellow lupine are cultivated in Northern Europe, Belarus, and Ukraine, and on a small scale in Southern France and Madeira. The main European producers of sweet blue lupine varieties are Germany, Poland, and the Netherlands. Compared to yellow and white lupine, blue lupine is more suitable for slightly heavier soils and is less sensitive to low soil and air temperatures.

Of the 222,220 hectares of lupine fields cultivated for dry grain in the European Union in 2020, most fields were in Poland (170,540 ha), whereas the number of fields was much lower in Germany (22,300 ha) and Greece (13,400 ha). In 2022, lupine was sown in France, Lithuania, Spain, and the Czech Republic on 5840 hectares to 1910 hectares, and between 570 and 80 hectares of lupine were in Italy, Slovakia, Austria, Hungary, Latvia, and Romania ha [14]. The average yield by country was 1 to 2 t/ha. There is no statistical data on the cultivation of old bitter lupine varieties for green manure (for mulch or churning) and new sweet varieties for fodder herbage, hay, and silage.

Compared to the association of soybean-producing countries in the Danube Soya Association (Dunau Soja) and occasional EU agricultural policy support for soybean production, the incentives for the production and use of lupine are much lower. Nevertheless, individual researchers and experts as well as local growers, processors, and users do not hide their enthusiasm for the properties of lupine as they discover the possibilities of its versatile use, noticing benefits for the soil, in human consumption, and livestock feed ha [2, 4, 17].

Grain legumes for dry grain	Surface (ha)	Yield (t)	Yield (t/ha)
Soybean (*Glycine max* (L.) Merr.)	126,951,517	353,463,735	2.8
Common bean (*Phaseolus vulgaris* L.)	34,801,567	27,545,942	0.8
Peanut (*Arachys hypogea* L.)	31,568,626	53,638,932	1.7
Chickpea (*Cicer arietinum* L.)	14,841,941	15,083,971	1.0
Cowpea *(Vigna unguiculata (L.) Walp.)*	15,056,435	8,901,644	0.6
Pea (*Pisum sativum* L.)	7,190,442	14,642,466	2.0
Lentil (*Lens culinaris* Medik.)	5,009,933	6,537,581	1.3
Broad bean (*Vicia faba* L.)	2,671,497	5,669,185	2.1
Lupine (*Lupinus* spp.)	**888,507**	**1.046.70**	**1.2**

Table 2.
*Lupine (*Lupinus *spp.) among the world's most widespread grain legumes in 2020, land size (ha), and grain yield (t and t/ha) [14].*

DOI: http://dx.doi.org/10.5772/intechopen.110227

4. Ameliorative, fertilizing and phytosanitary importance of lupine

When it was first domesticated millennia ago, lupine was already recognized as a plant that increases grain yields. The ancient Egyptians, ancient Greeks, and Romans have sowed lupine, specifically in otherwise mono-cultural production of wheat and barley. From its original homeland in the Mediterranean, North Africa, and the Middle East, lupine was spread to the interior of Europe during the time of the Roman Empire. Historical sources most often mention white lupine, although people in the past sowed and used also blue and yellow lupine. All three still occur as self-sown today in areas of their original habitats; however, in the modern era, cultivation in the interior of Europe has caused them to spread to natural habitats, meadows, among bushes, rocks, and roadsides [2].

Farmers realized that it is an undemanding plant that has a great influence on soil fertility. A saying arose in Central Europe in the eighteenth and nineteenth centuries: "If wheat is the queen, the lupine is the king of the wheat." All three best-known species of lupine were spread throughout Europe: white, blue, and yellow. On sandy and acidic soils, farmers were most impressed with the yellow lupine, which they named the miracle lupine. A combination of yellow lupine and rye worked very well. For green manure, a mixture of blue and white lupine was sown, and white lupine was called the backbone of green manure because of its good foliage. This involves mowing during flowering, mulching, and churning of herbage or burying cut herbage (plowing in) in order to increase soil fertility, as humus and nutrients are created over time from decaying organic matter [2].

In the twentieth century, scientific explanations were formed for the ameliorative, fertilizing, and phytosanitary importance of lupine cultivation in garden and agricultural rotation, as well as sowing in vineyards, fig plantations, southern and other fruits, which are still in use in some parts of southern Europe today [18]. With loosening, the water and air regime of soil increase the availability of nutrients, especially phosphorus. The exceptional regenerative effect of lupine on degraded and abandoned land, depleted by intensive agriculture, has been proven. Lupine makes such land usable once again. Although farmers used the fertilizing effect of lupine long ago, the process of biological nitrogen fixation was only explained in the nineteenth century [19]. After species-specific bacteria *Rhizobium lupini* and *Bradyrhizobium lupini* free-living in the soil find lupine roots, tubular growths, structures or nodules form on the roots about 20 days after sowing. Bacteria that live and reproduce in these nodules bind nitrogen from the air between the roots and convert it into the ammonium form [19–21]. Over time, these nodules increase in mass and can grow to the size of a hazelnut, which is larger than in other grain legumes [22–24]. Lupine uses 60 to 80% of nitrogen for the synthesis of its own proteins, and the bacteria get their life-sustaining carbohydrates from lupine plants. The amount of biologically obtained nitrogen with lupine is up to 100 kg/ha and is usually higher than in other annual grain legumes [25]. It depends on the lupine species and the duration of the growing season. Blue lupine has been found to fixate the most nitrogen [18, 22]. A crop that stays in the field for a longer period of time (the main crop) is more productive than a second crop, and autumn cooling of the soil can prevent the fixation process during the second crop.

Research results also indicate the great phytosanitary importance of lupine crops in suppressing weeds, pathogens, and pests and reducing their occurrence [16, 17, 19, 26].

5. Grain and herbage alkaloid poisoning

The ancient Greeks named lupine thermos, which means warm (hot), and warns of the bitter substances in the grain. Because of its bitter taste, lupine grain never became a commonplace dietary item in ancient times but was conditionally edible when properly prepared. Despite its bitter taste, lupine grains appeared in the human diet from time to time, especially during periods of famine when other foods were unavailable. Most cases of poisoning occurred among the poor, who gathered grain from the fields in times of scarcity, and—similar to dry beans and peas—soaked it in water, boiled it, and consumed it. However, several hours of soaking were not enough. The first signs of poisoning were a burning sensation and dry mouth, vomiting, and general malaise. Ingestion of large amounts of toxic substances caused tremors, problems with thinking, speech, movement of arms and legs, and other nervous system disorders until death by respiratory paralysis and cardiac arrest [2].

Soaking lupine grains in salt water or seawater for a few days, draining the water and rinsing the grains under running water, and cooking them until soft, made it possible to consume the grains without poisoning. This improved the flavor of the dish, especially if lupine was cooked together with grains of other legumes and cereals, and if spices were added to the dish. Only with the development of science have scientists identified the bitter substances in the grain as tannins, saponins, and quinolizidine alkaloids, the most common of which are albin, angustifolin, lupinin, lupanin, lupidin, and sparteine [25, 27].

In the past, lupine poisoning also occurred in farm animals. Grazing on sites with lupine plants and using grains or herbage as livestock feed often proved fatal for pregnant animals, resulting in frequent abortions of the embryo at the start of pregnancy, premature births, degenerative developmental disorders of the skeleton in offspring, and stillbirths. Based on experience in animal husbandry, poisonous lupine grain was also used in the planned abortion of human embryos; the most abortifacient substance was later determined to be sparteine.

Mycotoxins (phomopsins), decomposition products secreted by fungi, especially Diaporthe toxica and Diaporthe woodii, can also be the cause of poisoning when livestock are fed with infected plants. Signs of poisoning are loss of appetite, jaundice, and, in cases of severe poisoning, death due to liver failure. In the past, grazing on mature bitter grains or feeding with herbage and fresh ripe lupine grains have been shown to be particularly dangerous to small ruminants, sheep, and goats [8]. Tannins and saponins can also cause digestive problems and reproductive disorders if consumed in excessive amounts. Livestock poisoning due to various lupinotoxins was named lupinosis.

6. Sweet varieties of lupine were discovered at the beginning of the twentieth century

From the domestication of wild plants until the middle of the twentieth century, the variety of lupine cultivated contained a lot of bitter substances in grain and herbage [1]. With the discovery of natural mutants—plants that were not able to accumulate alkaloids in grains and herbage—a new possibility of lupine use in human consumption and livestock feed was discovered. In early 1930, German breeders used a recessive mutation of the bitter lupine to develop varieties with a much lower alkaloid content and named them sweet varieties (Weiße Süßlupine). The "Pflugs

Gela," "Pflugs Ultra" and other varieties proved to have tastier and more easily digestible grain but did not attract much interest in cultivation and use at that time. Industrialization and specialization of agriculture slowed their adoption of agriculture. Only with the development of new sustainable methods of agriculture since the end of the twentieth century, which require natural means for maintaining and improving soil fertility and provision of high-value protein foods to consumers, did the need to include sweet lupine in agriculture become more realistic and sensible [4, 25].

An important characteristic of such varieties is not the sweet taste of grains and herbage, but the lower content of toxic alkaloids and other bitter substances, such as tannins and saponins. Compared to bitter varieties, which have up to 6% alkaloids in their grain, the grain and herbage of sweet varieties contain hardly any alkaloids, or only in trace amounts, with a content of 0.001 to 0.06%. The permitted alkaloid content in grain depends on the respective national legislation. In some countries, the maximum permitted alkaloid content is 0.02 g per 100 g. Experts are not yet in agreement on the amount of alkaloids that has no harmful effects on human and livestock health [6, 8].

Most of the sweet varieties of blue lupine for grain and herbage feed are selectively bred in Australia. Selective breeding of all types of lupine aimed at obtaining sweet varieties also takes place in the European Union, mainly in countries where the cultivation of individual species is somewhat more widespread.

6.1 Sweet lupine varieties: New source of protein for human consumption

Compared to legume species that have 20–30% protein content in the grain, the grain of Mediterranean lupine species of lupine has at least 10% more protein with an excellent amino acid composition that contains almost all essential amino acids (lysine, leucine, phenylalanine, tryptophan, threonine, isoleucine, histidine, and valine [4, 28, 29]. This means that lupine is comparable to soybean, the world's most important protein legume. Similar to soybean, proteins in lupine are composed of water-insoluble globulins (about 90%) and water-soluble albumins (about 10%). As there are no prolamins and glutelins in the grain, gluten is not formed, so the grain ground into flour is suitable for anyone who cannot consume wheat products [29–31].

Lupine contains less carbohydrates (around 40%) than most legumes (around 65%). The predominant carbohydrate is dietary fiber (about 30%), about 10% is resistant starch (amylose), while starch content is very low, that is, from 3 to 8% [32]. Insoluble cellulose and hemicellulose are the predominant fibers, followed by soluble oligosaccharides, which stimulate the reproduction of bifidobacteria in the intestine and have a beneficial effect on improving the immune system on the one hand, but on the other, undigested oligosaccharides in the large intestine undergo microbial fermentation, producing CO_2, H_2, and methane, thus causing bloating and flatulence. Because of bloating and flatulence, the public has a generally negative opinion of a legume diet [4].

The grain of blue and yellow lupine contains 2 to 6% fat, while the grain of white lupine contains up to 10% fat, and there are also differences between varieties (**Table 3**). Because lupine contains less fat than soybean (around 20%), it is easier to avoid fatty and high-calorie meals with lupine dishes. The lupine seed oil has an extremely favorable fatty acid composition, with a predominance of monounsaturated fatty acids and an appropriate ratio of ω-6 to ω-3 fatty acids, so it is not surprising that one of the objectives of the selective breeding of white lupine is to increase the share of fat above 10% [4].

Species	Protein content (%)	Fat content (%)
White lupine	35 to 40	up to 10
Yellow lupine	35 to 40	2 to 6
Blue lupine	28 to 35	2 to 6
Andean lupine *	35 to 50	15 to 25

**In terms of protein content, Andean lupine grains exceed soybean and Mediterranean lupine species by at least 10%.*

Table 3.
Protein (%) and fat (%) conltent in the grain of different types of lupine.

Lupine (3 to 4%) and soybean (around 5%) are also quite close in terms of mineral content and composition. Potassium, manganese, magnesium, calcium, iron, and phosphorus are the predominant minerals in lupine grain, while zinc, chromium, cobalt, nickel, copper, and lead are present in smaller amounts. The sodium content is low, which meets the guidelines for lower salt intake.

Lupine grain contains many bioactive substances (polyphenols, flavonoids, isoflavones, glucosinolates, phytoestrogens, phytosterols, squalene, terpenoids, carotenoids, and others) that are also found in soybeans. Antioxidants include: carotenoids, mainly α- and β-carotene, lutein, and zeaxanthin, with some carotenoids being converted in the liver into retinol or vitamin A. Lupine is a good source of B group vitamins, with folate, thiamine, and riboflavin being the most predominant. Lupine and soybean grains also contain isoflavones, which play an important role in the prevention of osteoporosis, cardiovascular diseases, and hot flushes during menopause, in lowering cholesterol and preventing the development of breast, cervical, and prostate cancer. The predominant isoflavone in lupine is genistein. Bitter varieties of lupine are richer in some compounds than sweet varieties [4, 33].

Lupine grains contain antinutrients (glycosides, enzyme inhibitors, lectins, oxalates, phytates, saponins, tannins, and alkaloids), which are non-nutritional substances known for their negative effects on the human organism, although they also have positive effects. For example, with improper preparation of food using a grain of bitter varieties, the amount of alkaloids in consumed food can prove fatal; however, trace alkaloids can promote appetite [8, 34].

Fortunately, the negative effect of non-nutritional substances in the diet can be prevented by choosing sweet lupine varieties, by properly preparing food, which begins with soaking the grain and draining the water, followed by cooking, roasting, and baking, or by using various techniques of microbiological processing of the grain into curd, cheese, and various sauces. When cooking, lupine grains do not become soft but retain a firm inner texture.

If you are not used to dietary fiber, lupine should be introduced into your diet gradually and in smaller quantities. Follow the rules for preparing dry grains of legumes for cooking and consider your diet. Bloating is caused not only by legumes and the substances they contain, but also by quick eating, swallowing food without chewing the grain completely, and also talking, as a result of which we swallow a lot of air with our food [35].

7. Foods prepared with lupine

Cooked lupine grains can be eaten in a salad with onions or pickled in brine or vinegar. It is used in spoon dishes, such as minestrone and pasta. Cooked and mashed grains can be livened up with spices and chopped vegetables for a spread on wholegrain bread. The taste of whole-cooked lupine beans in a salad is reminiscent of beans, while roasted and baked grains are reminiscent of nuts. Roasted lupine grains are suitable as a salty or sweet snack. Roasted and ground grains are used as a substitute for real coffee, which, unlike real coffee, does not contain caffeine. Lupine coffee has an excellent aroma and flavor, which depends on the temperature and method of roasting. The aroma and flavor have been impressing coffee lovers, who are promoting lupine coffee to new consumers. Cafés in Germany, which have recently started serving lupine coffee, are an example worth emulating. Lupine flakes, which are produced from rolled grain, match cereals in muesli and cereals for breakfast or other meals.

Various semi-finished products and products can be produced from lupine grains during artisanal or industrial processing [4, 8, 28]. The basic semi-finished product is flour, which is the raw material used for various bakery products, confectionery, and the thickening of dishes. Lupine bread is a special type of bread, with 15 to 20% of lupine flour added to wheat flour, which has been proven to improve the bread's shelf life, keeping it fresh for longer. Globulin proteins can be prepared as fibrous, creamy, and spreadable products similar in appearance to meat and milk of animal origin, and can replace similar soy products. The creamy composition of flour is an excellent binder when added to ground animal meat for fresh products, such as ćevapčići (grilled minced meat), hot dogs, salami, and for dry meat products (sausages), which are therefore cheaper. In products for vegans and vegetarians, flour is the basis for the production of substitutes for milk and meat of animal origin [4].

Production of protein concentrates and isolates and dietary fiber isolates, which can be added to cereal flour for bread, pasta, sweets, snacks, and beverages, as well as to meat of animal origin, is more technically complex. The neutral taste of the protein isolate from lupine combines perfectly with various types of animal meat, without any after-taste being detected in the products.

Microbiological processing of lupine grains produces many products (curd, cheese, and sauce), which are difficult to attribute to lupine because of their appearance. Soybean curd, known as tofu, is called *lopino* when made from lupine. Similar to soybean, these products have higher nutritional value, better sensory properties, and longer shelf life [8].

Because lupine grain contains almost no normal starch but contains resistant starch, it breaks down slower. The slowly degradable starch regulates blood sugar, and prolongs the time of satiety, thereby reducing the need for quantitatively abundant meals and snacks, which contributes to reducing obesity or maintaining healthy body weight. Resistant starch and dietary fiber also prevent the development of cardiovascular disease and diseases of the large intestine [4, 36].

Sweet lupine grains can be prepared traditionally in modern cuisine: boiled, roasted, and baked. Roasted and salted lupine beans are a popular street snack or a beer and wine snack in the Mediterranean, Middle East, and India [8].

In Latin America, where bitter Andean lupines are grown (the locals call it *tarwi*, *chocho*, or *lupino*), and in some places in the Mediterranean, the Middle East, and India, where grains of bitter lupine varieties are still used for traditional dishes, dishes are prepared or processed with the help of well-established grain debittering procedures [5]. Lupine grains are first soaked in salt water for a few days, and then rinsed under running water for a long time. Cooked grains are preserved by pickling in brine or vinegar, as is common for olives or pickles. The grains are edible either with or without the husk, which is sometimes removed before pickling. Locals are used to removing the husk by rubbing the lupine grain between their index finger and thumb.

In Portugal and Spain, the roasted grain, called *tremoços* (Portuguese) and *altramuces* (Spanish), is a popular snack while drinking beer and wine. In Egypt, lupine is known by its Arabic name *termes*, used for roasted and salted grain sold by street vendors [8].

7.1 Lupine allergenicity

Lupine is categorized as an allergen, so it must be listed as an ingredient on the food label according to the EU Directive (2007/68/EU). An allergy occurs as an immune system responds to lupine proteins. An allergic reaction is often triggered by structurally similar antigens of soybean, peanut, broad beans, or nuts. After consuming sweet varieties of lupine, some sensitive people experience rashes, inflammation of the eyes, and even breathing problems that can lead to anaphylactic shock. Particularly people with allergies should pay more attention to unpackaged lupine products, such as bread, cakes, pizzas, pasta, and ice cream [8]. It is better to avoid street food than to seek medical help, where physicians can help with anti-inflammatory drugs—antihistamines, if there is still time.

7.2 Incentives for use of lupine for human consumption

The market for lupine for human consumption is currently small, but experts believe that lupine has great potential for human consumption. Lupine products are an excellent replacement for various sweet, salty, or fatty carbohydrate snacks. In the food industry, when developing dishes from sweet varieties of lupine, the emphasis is on fermented products, which are similar to soybean products in terms of taste, nutrition, and digestibility. Lupine products are an alternative to soybean for people who either do not like soybean or are afraid that it is genetically modified. Although genetic technology has already been used in the selective breeding of lupine, no GM (genetically modified) varieties of lupine are currently in production [8].

In order to promote the use of lupine for human consumption, it is necessary to raise awareness among consumers, as it is a very promising food. Consumers need to be made aware that excessive consumption of animal meat has a negative impact on the environment and health. With the help of cooking courses, it is possible to present how lupine can be used in food and to explain how lupine, other grain legumes and cereal porridges can be used at home to prepare delicious meals. At the same time, we should raise awareness and connect all the links of the supply chain for lupine in the local environment, which affects shorter transportation and therefore a smaller carbon footprint that would result from remote cultivation. Cooperation between all stakeholders in the chain of cultivation, processing, and marketing of lupine is the only way to ensure that our good intentions are realized and observed in food [4, 17].

8. Lupine grain processing into nonfood products

Proteins in the form of globulin in lupine grain also allow industrial processing into nonfood products, from plastics to man-made fibers for fabrics and ropes. Similar to soybean, it is possible to industrially treat globulin using chemical reagents and biological enzymes and to process it into fibers. Antibiotics, anti-inflammatory, and UV protection agents are added during the spinning process. The produced fibers are mixed with cashmere fibers, silk, cotton, bamboo, and elastane fibers for fabrics for underwear, bedding, shirts, evening dresses, and children's and sports clothes.

The higher fat content and the favorable fat composition in white lupine attracted some selective breeders to cultivate varieties with a fat percentage above 10%. In addition to cooking oil, there are also opportunities for producing nonfood products, such as soap, paints, and varnishes. In South America, where Andean lupine is grown, which contains 15 to 25% fat, it is traditionally processed into cooking oil, soap, and paints. Breeders believe that varieties with a higher proportion of fat are promising for the local population and beyond.

8.1 Importance of sweet lupine varieties for livestock feed

Selective breeding of lupine has made the grain of newer sweet varieties of all three lupine species suitable for livestock feed without the need for heat treatment [37]. Compared to soybean, lupine grain does not contain trypsin, hemagglutinins, and urease inhibitors [38]. Lupine grain also contains less fat than soybean (20%), in which the main feed for cattle is a low-fat meal (1 to 3% fat) obtained by extracting fats from the grain with the help of hot steam, solvents, and solvent extractions.

Compared to white lupine grain, which contains about 10% fat, blue and yellow lupine grain contains 2 to 6% fat. When preparing livestock meals with grains, care should be taken not to exceed the daily amount of 5% of raw fat per kg of dry matter for cattle feed; therefore, sweet varieties of yellow and blue lupine are preferred in livestock feed [38–40].

Although grain of sweet lupine varieties is also suitable for human consumption, for now, its importance is greater in animal husbandry. The beginnings of the cultivation of sweet blue lupine varieties for animal husbandry were in Germany in the first half of the twentieth century. A lot of experience with this kind of livestock feed (for cattle, small ruminants, poultry, and pigs) has been gained in recent decades in Australia, where half of the world's lupine-producing fields are used to grow blue lupine. In recent years, Australian cattle farmers have successfully substituted fresh, crushed, or ground sweet blue lupine grain for soybean meal.

The usefulness of sweet lupine varieties in animal husbandry is supported by results of scientific research, which confirm the beneficial effect of lupine feed on appetite and growth in all species and categories of livestock [41]. Livestock farmers also feed whole plants to cattle and small ruminants, either as fresh herbage, hay, or silage alone or in a mixture with other plants. Protein utilization from lupine grain and herbage is almost 90% and 70–80%, respectively.

The world's main source of protein of plant origin in animal husbandry is soybeans, of which 70% must be imported to meet all the needs of the European Union. Because lupine is quite similar to soybean in terms of protein composition, it is worth considering replacing soybean meal with lupine protein in animal husbandry. Sweet lupine varieties have the potential of protein feed from local fields.

9. Lupine varieties with at least some bitter substances and new options of use for bitter varieties

Producers of sweet lupine varieties have observed that crops and grain in storage are more susceptible to diseases and pests that were not present in older bitter varieties. Researchers have confirmed that the cause for these observations is the absence of alkaloids in herbage and grain. Alkaloids in old bitter varieties inhibit the reproduction of bacteria and fungi, repel pests and herbivorous wild animals from the crops, and prevent the germination of various weeds [34].

For green manure, it is increasingly recommended to churn in or lay lupine mulch between rows when growing other agricultural plants, as it has a beneficial effect on soil and plant health. For this purpose, bitter white lupine varieties with rich foliage are preferred because of their abundant crop.

Varieties of all species of bitter lupine, particularly blue lupine with a higher alkaloid content in the grain and herbage, are being studied by scientists as raw material for the production of biotic preparations for plant protection [34]. Plant protection products include biostimulants that use extracts of bitter lupine varieties to improve the rooting of cultivated plants, reduce the occurrence of fungal diseases and repel pests, which, together with other protective measures, contributes to increased quality and quantity of the crop [42]. **Figure 1** presents the deviation between bitter and sweet varieties according to the intended use.

Despite the advantages of sweet variety feeds, which contain almost no alkaloids and other bitter substances (tannins and saponins), studies have shown that a low content that is not harmful to health has a beneficial effect on the appetite and health of livestock, particularly on the reduction of external parasites that linger on the skin and hair, as well as internal parasites (endoparasites), especially intestinal parasites.

A goal in developing new sweet varieties is to determine the amount of alkaloids in herbage and grain that has no harmful effects on livestock health. Some believe that the limit value for alkaloid content in herbage and grain should be higher than the existing value permitted by current legislation. This indicates the possibilities for growing varieties whose grain contains almost no alkaloids, while herbage would be rich in alkaloids and other bitter substances, which would reduce the occurrence of diseases during growth and development, and repel pests and herbivorous wild animals. Straw with a high bitter substance content after grain harvest can be a source for obtaining extracts for natural pesticides, as well as for traditional applications, such as mulching and incorporation into the soil.

Among the varieties of blue or narrow-leaved lupine (Lupinus angustifolius L.), sweet varieties are distinguished from bitter ones in Australia by using the term blue lupine for sweet varieties and narrow-leaved lupine for bitter varieties. Globally, the name blue lupine is used for both bitter and sweet varieties; as Australians explain, such use of names makes accurate communication easier when purchasing seed, developing and using production technologies, and defining crop used for grain or herbage.

Bitter lupine varieties	Sweet lupine varieties
Bitter varieties produce more leaf mass and are more suitable for green manure (for mulching and incorporation). Herbage or grain extracts can be a source of compounds for the production of biotic plant protection agents. The use of lupine tea in organic farming reduces weeds and occurrence of fungal diseases and repels pests.	Sweet varieties produce less leaf mass, while the grain, which contains almost no alkaloids and other bitter substances, is suitable for human consumption or livestock feed, without fear of poisoning.

Figure 1.
Bitter and sweet varieties according to the intended use.

10. Agrotechnical instructions for growing lupine

All three Mediterranean species of white lupine (*Lupinus albus* L.), blue or narrow-leaved lupine (*L. angustifolius* L.), and yellow lupine (*Lupinus luteus* L.) have common characteristics and distinctive differences that producers must take into account [3, 21, 43].

10.1 Soil pH can determine the success of cultivation

Lupine species have different requirements regarding soil type; the yellow lupine thrives best on light sandy soils, while white and blue lupines grow best on medium sandy loam to loamy sand soils; the blue lupine tolerates slightly heavier soils. Heavy, poorly drained soils are unsuitable for lupine cultivation. When choosing a field for a specific lupine species (white, blue, and yellow), the soil pH is an important indicator: acidic sites with a pH of 4.5 are still suitable for yellow lupine; however, slightly acidic to alkaline soils with a pH of 6.5 to 7.8 is more suitable for blue and white lupine, with white lupine tolerating more calcium in the soil (**Table 4**).

10.2 Basic tillage and fertilization

After choosing the species and variety of lupine for a particular soil, the soil must be properly tilled according to the type of soil and growing conditions; for spring sowing, traditional tillage with autumn plowing is more common. Shallow tillage with a plow and cultivator is sufficient for sowing lupine stubble crops, but conservation tillage without plowing is becoming increasingly widespread. With abundant weeds, traditional tilling is a better choice, especially in grain production.

Although lupine is a legume that acquires nitrogen during growth and development, nitrogen fixation will only take place under suitable growing conditions, that is, at a soil temperature of at least 8°C, sufficiently moist soil, if there is sufficient Ca, P, Fe, Mo, and B in the ground. Phosphorus in the soil increases nitrogen-fixing capacity and contributes to flowering, while potassium increases tolerance to disease and drought. Phosphorus and potassium peaks are not necessary [44]. In conventional tilling, pre-sowing fertilization with around 40 kg of nitrogen/ha is recommended, but many experts believe nitrogen fertilization is unnecessary with optimal nutrient concentration in the soil. Too much available nitrogen in the soil inhibits biological fixation by *Rhizobium* and *Bradyrhizobium lupini* bacteria [21, 24, 25, 45].

In organic production of lupine, well-rotted and composted farmyard manure (15 to 30 t/ha) is suitable for basic fertilization, which is suitable for autumn fertilization. There will also be much less problems with weeds when sowing lupine after potatoes, as long as the weeds have not spread with sowing seeds or fresh farmyard manure.

Species	Soil type	Recommended soil pH
White lupine	light sandy loam to medium soil	6.5 to 7.8
Blue lupine	sandy loam to medium soil, with sufficient moisture	6.0 to 6.8
Yellow lupine	light, sandy soil, dry locations	4.5 to 6.8

Table 4.
Differences between lupine species in terms of soil type and soil pH.

If lupine is in the rotation after cereals and rapeseed, the stale seedbed technique can be used with one to three sweeps or harrows before sowing. This kills weeds at the small seedling stage, which can greatly reduce the seed supply of weeds in the soil.

The intensification and specialization of farming led to problems of narrow crop rotation (more diseases, pests, and weeds and less humus in the soil). Conventional producers have become accustomed to mineral fertilizers that work quickly, almost immediately. However, when deciding on a new paradigm of sustainable agriculture, the possibilities for sowing green manure crops reveal themselves.

Regarding the importance of sowing crops for green manure and incorporation, there is a claim made in Slovenian specialized literature: “What you give to the earth, you get back with interest.” Farmers at that time sowed a mixture of white and blue lupine on the stubble of cereal crops.

When sufficiently densely sowed, the abundant foliage of lupine maintains soil moisture, and reduces soil erosion and weeds. Due to too fast mineralization in summer, stubble catch crops are best suited for green manure crops for incorporation when the primary crop is harvested at the end of the growing season when growth is stopped by cold and frost.

The modern process of preparing a lupine crop for incorporation is rolling, followed by mowing with the repeated cutting of plants with a disc harrow and plowing. For the faster decomposition of herbage, compost or slurry is applied, as well as mineral nitrogen in conventional cultivation.

10.3 Time and method of sowing

Blue lupine is sown in March, or at the end of February in regions with a mild climate. The optimal time for sowing yellow and white lupine is the first half of April. In colder locations in cold years, it is better to wait until May, just like with soybeans. Sowing of stubble lupine crops should be done as soon as possible after harvesting the main crop.

Lupine sowing depth depends on the size of the seeds and the type of soil. White lupine can be sown at the greatest depth, yellow at medium depth, and blue lupine at the shallowest depth. Sowing on heavier soils should be shallower than on lighter soil. Due to the different thickness of seeds and soil properties, the amount of seed for sowing lupine ranges from 70 to 250 kg per hectare. The amount of seed for sowing is calculated using data for thousand seed weight, germination, and purity. With a certified seed of sweet varieties, it is necessary to adhere to the recommendations of the breeder and the seed dealer, to set up the sowing machine accordingly, and to check the coverage at the time of sowing.

Dense sowing of lupine for herbage and grain is carried out with a grain seeder for compact sowing. Sowing with a seeder for row spacing is suitable for white lupine in non-determinant varieties, where it is possible to till the soil before the development of side branches and ground cover. On sandy soils and in dry conditions, rolling is recommended, especially for sowing stubble crops. This increases the germination and emergence of seedlings. Sparse sowing for grain requires 40 to 50 germinating seeds per m2, whereas spaced sowing at an inter-row spacing of 25 to 40 cm and intra-row spacing of 5 to 10 cm, and cultivation for herbage requires double the number of germinating seeds, specifically 80 to 100 germinating seeds per m2. Dense sowing is carried out at an inter-row spacing of 15 cm and intra-row spacing of 2.5 to 10 cm. When sowing at greater inter-row spacing, the development of cover of the inter-row space is slower, and the greater spacing between rows enables mechanical treatment with a finger hoe until the ground cover develops (**Table 5**).

DOI: http://dx.doi.org/10.5772/intechopen.110227

Species	Number of seeds per m^2	Amount of sowing seed (kg/ha)
White lupine	60 to 70	180 to 240
Blue or narrow-leaved lupine	90 to 100	140 to 160
Yellow lupine	70 to 80	120 to 140

Table 5.
Sowing density of lupine and amount of seed for sowing.

If the seed for sowing is certified, it has varietal purity, is healthy, undamaged, has a sufficiently large thousand seed weight, and high germination and purity. Standard seed purity and germination for lupine are at least 90%. Seeds for organic production must not be disinfected with conventional synthetic agents, but can be disinfected before sowing in a warm water bath at a temperature of up to 50°C or in a warm herbal bath for only a few minutes, after which they must be thoroughly dried at a temperature of up to 40°C. If soaked in a table salt solution, seeds can be sorted by removing unhealthy and damaged seeds that float to the surface, while healthy, heavier seeds sink.

If the soil becomes crusted before the emergence of seedlings, the crust must be crushed, either with a mesh or some other light harrow. When adjusting the depth, be careful not to set the wedges too deep, especially if the seeds are already germinating.

10.4 Similarities and differences between species in terms of requirements for successful growth and development

Lupine species differ in terms of plant height. The yellow lupine is the smallest (about 50 cm), the blue lupine is medium tall (50 to 120 cm), and the height of the white lupine ranges from 80 to 150 cm (**Table 6**). Compared to broad beans and peas, lupines do not require support and do not tend to become prostrate. Extremely tall varieties can become prostrate, especially after storms and downpours during the ripening period, when the weight of pods and grains increases significantly. Plant height is affected by growing conditions, soil type, and soil pH, nutrient concentrations in the soil and fertilization, seeding density, and lighting [12].

The growing period of lupine depends on the species and variety; the blue lupine has the shortest time from sowing to seed maturity (90 to 110 days), the yellow lupine has a slightly longer growing period (100 to 130 days), and the white lupine has the longest growing period, that is, 140 to 180 days (**Table 6**). Lupine is most often sown in spring. Exceptions are regions with mild winters, where lupine sown in autumn can withstand the winter perfectly, and the grain yield is usually higher than when lupine is sown in spring. Lupine sown in spring stays on the field for a longer time, so it is grown as a main crop; if sown after grain or early potatoes, it is used as a catch crop.

Species	Time of sowing	Duration of growing period	Plant height (cm)
Blue lupine	March	90 to 110 days	50 to 120
Yellow lupine	April	100 to 130 days	around 50
White lupine	April	140 to 180 days	80 to 150

Table 6.
Differences between lupine species in terms of the time of sowing, length of growing period, and plant height.

Regardless of the time of sowing, winter cereals, grasses or grass mixtures, potatoes, rapeseed, field, and garden vegetables are the best-preceding crops in rotation. Bulb vegetables, such as garlic, onions, shallots, and leeks, should be avoided when rotating crops.

10.5 Ways to reduce crop weed and damage due to diseases and pests

The foundation of crop protection against weeds, disease agents, and pests is a properly composed and sufficiently long crop rotation [3, 16, 26] A suitable time until resowing in the same field is at least 4 years. Healthy seeds, a field with as few weeds as possible, sowing at the optimal time, and in a way that corresponds to the species and variety and the intended use of the crop, all play a preventive role in plant protection. Bands of bitter lupine around crops of other cultivated plants have been shown to deter pests and wild animals. The positive effect of bitter substances of plants incorporated into the soil-on-soil health has also been confirmed.

Reducing weeds by hoeing around young plants is only possible with greater inter-row spacing, otherwise, young crops are combed one to three times at weekly intervals. A comb harrow can be used to thin out crops that are too dense. There is a growing number of machines, tools, and know-how available for mechanical measures, among the newer ones, there is also the option of burning weeds. It is important that all agrotechnical measures are carried out precisely.

Although sufficiently dense sowing of lupine is beneficial because of less weed, the density must be adjusted to the species and variety, depending on the intended use of the crop. When growing grain with greater inter-row spacing, we must not miss the opportunity for hoeing.

Protection of lupine is based on a rotation and on varieties that are tolerant to specific pathogens. Lupine is susceptible to infections by various pathogens, such as *Erysiphe*, *Fusarium*, *Rhizoctonia*, *Pythium*, *Colletotrichum,* and *Uromyces*. They most often appear and spread when the soil is too moist and the sowing is too dense.

Low soil moisture, sparse sowing, sowing of healthy seeds, seed baths, and removal of infected plants are some of the measures to reduce infections. Compared to natural means, when reducing the occurrence of diseases includes several measures, the use of fungicides and insecticides is more effective. If you notice twisting and curling of the leaves, lice, and thrips, which carry viral diseases, have certainly reproduced excessively, and thrips can cause damage to the epidermis by sucking.

10.6 Herbage and grain harvest

Lupine yield ranges from 20 to 60 t of herbage and from 1.5 to 6 t of grain per hectare. It depends on the species, variety, growing conditions, and technology, that is, agricultural techniques and agrotechnical measures [9, 46, 47]. Ripe lupine pods of newer varieties usually do not open, while overripe pods burst much less than in other grain legumes, so seed losses at harvest are mainly due to improper combine harvester settings. Combine harvester adjustments include changing the mesh, and reducing operating speed and drum rotation speed. Harvesting is done when the grain is firm and resistant to pressure, that is, at a grain moisture content of 15 to 20%. Grain is stored at a moisture content of 12 to 14%. Lupine for hay is first mowed and dried; for silage, it is harvested by a forage harvester for corn when side shoots start flowering; it should be ensilaged alone or mixed with corn or sunflower.

11. Conclusions

Lupine has a positive effect on improving and maintaining soil fertility. Its ameliorating and fertilizing effect on the soil has been proven, as well as its phytosanitary importance in crop rotation in reducing the incidence of diseases and pests. Although sweet lupin varieties were discovered at the beginning of the twentieth century, new paradigms of sustainability offer them an opportunity in the production of food for humans and livestock. The substitution of soy protein is particularly emphasized. The grains of all three Mediterranean lupin species contain a similar amount of protein and have a similar amino acid composition to soybeans, and the grain has less fat than soybeans. As a food source, it is gluten-free, contains almost no starch but resistant starch, and is high in fiber, some minerals, and bioactive compounds. In the modern diet, sweet lupine beans can be prepared by cooking, pickling, roasting, or baking. Through various processes, products similar to soybean can be obtained from the grain: flour, fibrous proteins, protein isolate, milk and meat substitutes, and various sauces through fermentation. Processing focuses on the special properties of the proteins, such as creaminess, lubricity, and fiber. The market for lupin for human consumption is currently small, but researchers believe it has great potential. Lupin can be used to improve the composition of daily meals or even replace a predominantly meat-based diet with a plant-based one. For blue or narrow-leaved lupin is most commonly used for feeding livestock, either as a vegetable or as a grain, which has a better protein yield than soybeans. The main producer of lupins, Australia, is an example of a successful substitute for soybean feed.

Acknowledgements

The chapter preparation was partly supported by Research Program P4-0077 of the Slovenian Research Agency.

Author details

Darja Kocjan Ačko and Marko Flajšman*
Biotechnical Faculty, Department of Agronomy, University of Ljubljana, Ljubljana, Slovenia

*Address all correspondence to: marko.flajsman@bf.uni-lj.si

References

[1] Kurlovich BS. Lupins: Geography, classification, genetic resoirces and breeding. OY International North Express, Kurlovich B.S. (ur.), St. Petersburg, Rusija: Intan; 2002. 468 str.

[2] Gladstones JS. Distribution, origin, taxonomy and importance. In: Gladstones JS, Atkins CA, Hamblin J, editors. Lupins as Crop Plants. Biology, Production and Utilization. Wallingford: CAB International; 2007. pp. 1-39

[3] French B, Shea G, Buirchell B. Introduction and history. In: White P, French B, McLarty A, editors. V: Producing lupins. South Perth: Department of Agriculture and Food; 2008. pp. 11-18. http://archive.agric.wa.gov.au/objtwr/imported_assets/content/fcp/lp/lup/lupins/lupin%20bulletin%20v10-lr.pdf

[4] Lucas MM, Stoddard FL, Annicchiarico P, Frias J, Martinez-Villaluenga C, Sussmann D, et al. The future of lupin as a protein crop in Europe. Frontiers in Plant Science. 2015;**6**:705. DOI:10.3389/fpls.2015.00705

[5] Gulisano A, Alves S, Martins JN, Trindade LM. Genetics and breeding of Lupinus mutabilis: An emerging protein crop. Frontiers in Plant Science. 2019;**10**:1385. https://www.frontiersin.org/ articles/10.3389/fpls.2019.01385/full

[6] Buirchell BJ, Cowling WA. Genetic resources in Lupins. In: Gladstones JS, Atkins CA, Hamblin J, editors. Lupins as Crop Plants. Biology, Production and Utilization. Wallingford: CAB International; 2007. pp. 41-66

[7] Wolko B, Naganowska B, Nelson MN, Clements J, Yang H. Lupins. In: Kole C, editor. V: Wild Crop Relatives: Genomic and Breeding Resurces, Legume Crops and Forages. Berlin, Heidelberg, New York: Springer; 2011. pp. 153-208

[8] Petterson DS. Composition and food uses of Lupins. In: Gladstones JS, Atkins CA, Hamblin J, editors. Lupins as Crop Plants. Biology, Production and Utilization. Wallingford: CAB International; 2007. pp. 353-384

[9] Clapham WM, Elbert-May D. Influence of population on white lupin morphology and yield. Canadian Journal of Plant Science. 1989;**69**: 161-170

[10] Craig AA, Smith PMC, Sanjiv G, Jones MGK, Caligari PDS. Genetics, cytology and biotechnology. V: Lupins as a Crop Plant: Biology, Production and Utilization. Gladstones JS, Atkins C, Hamblin J. (ur.). Wallingford, CAB International: pp. 81-86

[11] Hertel K. Vegetative growth. In: Walker J, Hertel K, Parker P, Edwards J, editors. V: Lupins Growth and Development. New South Wales: NSW Department of Industry and Investment; 2011. pp. 31-42

[12] Walker J, Hertel K, Parker P, Edwards J. Lupins Growth and Development. New South Wales, NSW: Department of Industry and Investment; 2011. p. 84. https://www.dpi.nsw.gov.au/__data/assets/pdf_file/0006/516183/Procrop-lupin-growth-and-development.pdf

[13] Georgieva NA, Kosev VI, Genov NG, Butnariu M. Morphological and biological characteristics of white lupine cultivars (Lupinus albus L.). Romanian Agricultural Research. 2018;**35**:109-119

[14] Faostat. Food and Agriculture Organization of the United Nations Statistics Division. 2022. https://www.fao.org/faostat/en/#home [Accessed: December 18, 2022]

[15] Cox B. Marketing and trade. In: Gladstones JS, Atkins CA, Hamblin J, editors. Lupins as Crop Plants. Biology, Production and Utilization. Wallingford: CAB International; 2007. pp. 437-454

[16] Pannell DJ. Economic assessment of the role and value of Lupins in the farming system. In: Gladstones JS, Atkins CA, Hamblin J, editors. Lupins as Crop Plants. Biology, Production and Utilization. Wallingford: CAB International; 2007. pp. 339-351

[17] Dergan T, Ivanovska A, Kocjančič T, Iannetta PPM, Debeljak M. 'Multi-SWOT' multi-stakeholder-based sustainability assessment methodology: Applied to improve Slovenian legume-based Agri-food chains. Sustainability. 2022;**14**:1-26. DOI: 10.3390/su142215374

[18] Longnecker N, Brennan R, Robson A. Lupin nutrition. In: Gladstones JS, Atkins CA, Hamblin J, editors. Lupins as Crop Plants. Biology, Production and Utilization. Wallingford: CAB International; 2007. pp. 121-148

[19] Hennig E. 1997. The Secrets of Fertile Soils. OLV Organischer Landbau Verlag Kurt Walter Lau. Xanten: 202 str.

[20] Sharma S, Aneja MK, Mayer J, Munch JC, Schloter M. Characterization of bacterial community structure in rhizosphere soil of grain legumes. Microbial Ecology. 2005;**49**(3):407-415

[21] Pate JS, Emery RJN, Atkins CA. Transport Physiologiy and partitioning. In: Gladstones JS, Atkins CA, Hamblin J, editors. Lupins as Crop Plants. Biology, Production and Utilization. Wallingford: CAB International; 2007. pp. 181-226

[22] Howieson JG, Fillery IRP, Legocki AB, Sikorski MM, Stepkowski T, Minchin FR, et al. Nodulation, nitrogen fixation and nitrogen balance. In: Gladstones JS, Atkins CA, Hamblin J, editors. Lupins as Crop Plants. Biology, Production and Utilization. Wallingford: CAB International; 2007. pp. 149-180

[23] Muraveev AA, Naumkin VN, Naumkin LA, Lukashevich MI. Productivity of white lupine seeds after using an inoculation, fertilizers and plant growth regulators. Forage Production. 2012;**8**:23-27

[24] Naumkin VN, Kurenskaya OJ, Murawev AA, Kryukov AN. White lupin efficiency at different levels of mineral nutrition. Legume Crops. 2015;**4**(16):61-68

[25] Martin JH, Waldren RP, Stamp DL. Principles of Field Crop Production. Upper Saddle River, New Jersey, Columbus, Ohio: Pearson Prentice Hall; 2006. p. 954

[26] Sweetingham MW, Jones RAC, Brown AGP. Diseases and pests. In: Gladstones JS, Atkins CA, Hamblin J, editors. Lupins as Crop Plants. Biology, Production and Utilization. Wallingford: CAB International; 2007. pp. 263-289

[27] Allen JG. Toxins and Lupinosis. In: Gladstones JS, Atkins CA, Hamblin J, editors. Lupins as Crop Plants. Biology, Production and Utilization. Wallingford: CAB International; 2007. pp. 411-435

[28] Sizenko EI, Lisitsin AB, Rastyapina AV. Nutritional value of lupine and use of its products. All about meat. 2004;**4**:34-40

[29] Lara-Rivera AH, Ruiz-Lopez MA, Rodriguez-Macias R, Soto-Velasco C, Garcia-López PM, Barrientos-Ramirez L, et al. Grain yield, and chemical and

protein composition of Lupinus angustifolius varieties grown in Mexico. Revista Internacional de Botánica Experimental. 2017;**86**:89-96

[30] Kohajdová Z, Karovičová J, Schmidt Š. Lupin composition and possible use in bakery - a review. Czech Journal of Food Sciences. 2011;**29**(3):203-211

[31] Pereira A, Ramos F, Sanches SA. Lupin (Lupinus albus L.) seeds: Balancing the good and the bad and addressing future challenges. Molecules. 2022;**27**:8557. DOI: 10.3390/molecules27238557

[32] Aranda P, Dostalova J, Frias J, Lopez-Jurando M, Kozlowska H, Pokorny J, et al. Carbohydrates in grain legume seeds. In: Hedley CL, editor. Improving Nutritional Quality and Agronomic Characteristics. Wallingford: CABI Publishing; 2001. pp. 61-87

[33] Vollmannova A, Lidikova J, Musilova J, Snirc M, Bojnanska T, Urminska D, et al. White Lupin as a promising source of antioxidant Phenolics for functional food production. Journal of Food Quality. 2021;**2021**:1-11. DOI: 10.1155/2021/5512236

[34] Frick KM, Kamphuis LG, Siddique KHM, Singh KB, Foley RC. Quinolizidine alkaloid biosynthesis in Lupins and prospects for grain quality improvement. Frontiers in Plant Science. 2017;**8**:87. DOI: 10.3389/fpls.2017.00087

[35] Iqbal A, Khalil IA, Ateeq N, Khan MS. Nutritional quality of important food legumes. Food Chemistry. 2006;**97**:331-335

[36] Flight I, Clifton P. Cereal grains and legumes in the prevention of coronary heart disease and stroke: A review of the literature. European Journal of Clinical Nutrition. 2006;**60**:1145-1159

[37] Lukashewich MI, Sviridenko TV. Directions and results of breeding white lupine. Forage production. 2012;**5**:22-24. DOI: 633.367.3:631.524/.527

[38] van Barneveld RJ. Understanding the nutritional chemistry of lupin (Lupinus spp.) seed to improve livestock production efficiency. Nutrition Research Reviews. 1999;**12**:203-230

[39] Edwards AC, van Barneveld RJ. Lupins for livestock and fish. In: Gladstones JS, Atkins CA, Hamblin J, editors. Lupins as Crop Plants. Biology, Production and Utilization. Wallingford: CAB International; 2007. pp. 385-409

[40] Gataulina GG, Medvedeva NV, Shtele AL, Tsigutkin AS. Growth, development, yield and feeding value of varieties of white lupine (Lupinus albus L.) in RGAU-ICCA. Izvestiya Timiryazev Agricultural Academy. 2013;**6**:12-30

[41] Abraham EM, Ganopoulos I, Madesis P, Mavromatis A, Mylona P, Nianiou-Obeidat I, et al. The use of Lupin as a source of protein in animal feeding: Genomic tools and breeding approaches. International Journal of Molecular Sciences. 2019;**20**(4):851. DOI: 10.3390/ijms20040851

[42] Mazur VA, Mazur KV, Pantsyreva HV. Influence of the tehnological aspects growing on quality composition of seed white lupine (Lupinus albus L.) in the Forest steppe of Uraine. Ukrainian. Journal of Ecology. 2019;**9**(1):50-55

[43] Römer P. Lupinen-Verwertung und Anbau. Rastatt, Gesellschaft zur Förderung der Lupine. 2007;**37**. http://lelf.brandenburg.de/media_fast/4055/lupine07.15564210.pdf

[44] Dracup M, Turner NC, Tang C, Reader M, Palta J. Responses to abiotic stresses. In: Gladstones JS, Atkins CA, Hamblin J, editors. Lupins as Crop Plants. Biology, Production and Utilization. Wallingfod: CAB International; 2007. pp. 227-262

[45] Naumkin VN, Naumkin LA, Mesheryakov OD, Artyuhov AI, Lukashevich MI, Ageeva PA. Prospects of cultivation of lupine in the central Chernozemski region. Agriculture. 2012;**1**:27-29

[46] Faluyi MA, Zhang F, Leibovitch S, Smith DL. White Lupin growth, yield, and yield components in eastern Canada: Influence of management factors. Agronomy Journal. 1997;**89**(5):781-788

[47] Zamora-Natera JF, Hernandez IZ, Villalvazo A, Macias RR, Perez ES, Garcia PM. Performance of blue lupin (Lupinus angustifolius L.) cultivars on acid soils of Jalisco, Mexico. Academia Journal of agricultural Research. 2017;**5**(10):300-305. DOI: 10.15413/ajar.2015.0176

Chapter 6

White Clover (*Trifolium repens* L.) Benefits in Grazed Pastures and Potential Improvements

John R. Caradus, Marissa Roldan, Christine Voisey and Derek R. Woodfield

Abstract

White clover has been, and continues to be, a valuable component of grazed pastures through improving feed quality and nutritive value, improving seasonal dry matter distribution, and providing biologically fixed nitrogen that benefits not only white clover itself but also the surrounding plants. The contribution of white clover to sustainability and environmental goals is a growing focus of breeding programs. The use of genome mapping and genotyping by sequencing to determine genetic variation and population structure in clover improvement programs needs to be expanded to improve breeding efficiencies. Seed yields also need to be improved while maintaining the selected agronomic performance traits to ensure that commercial cultivars remain cost-effective with other crops and land uses. Beneficial traits not available within the white clover genome may be provided through genetic modification and gene editing, particularly traits that contribute towards addressing challenges associated with animal nutrition and health, water quality and climate change. The inherent benefits of white clover as well as the potential for including additional beneficial traits will be described.

Keywords: biologically fixed nitrogen, breeding, environment, genetic modification, nutritive value

1. Introduction

White clover (*Trifolium repens* L.) is a critical component of grazed pastures in most temperate areas of the world [1]. The value of white clover in mixed species grazed pastures is due to its contribution towards improving feed quality and nutritive value, complementary seasonal dry matter distribution, and the provision of biologically fixed nitrogen (**Figure 1**). A meta-analysis demonstrated that including white clover in perennial ryegrass swards maintained or increased milk solids yield at lower stocking rates and lower N application rates [2]. This can lead to economic benefit and improved profitability of pastoral farming systems. White clover plant breeding programs have sought to increase dry matter yield, improve feed quality, improve persistence, or a combination of these. However, with changing management

Figure 1.
White clover in a mixed sward, a highly nutritious component of multi-species grassland pastures.

systems, resource constraints, environmental imperatives, and climate variability continued improvement will be required. New genomic and breeding techniques provide an opportunity to achieve new and better outcomes and will ensure that white clover continues to be a species of value and importance in grazed temperate pastures. The aim here is to describe the origin of white clover, its domestication, overview breeding objectives, describe the known advantages of white clover, and then discuss future improvements that will be required, and how they can be achieved, to ensure white clover continues to deliver benefit.

2. Origin

White clover is an allotetraploid (2n = 4x = 32), originating from hybridisation of two diploid *Trifolium* species [3]. As an amphidiploid, white clover has the full diploid set of chromosomes from each parent species [4]. The identity of those two ancestral species was purported to be *T. nigrescens* and *T. uniflorum* [5], or *T. nigrescens* and *T. occidentale* [6]. However, the most likely ancestral species based on DNA sequence analyses, molecular cytogenetics, interspecific hybridization are a diploid alpine species (*T. pallescens*) and a diploid coastal species (*T. occidentale*), which probably occurred during the last major glaciations 13,000–130,000 years ago [7–9]. F1 hybrids between *T. pallescens* and *T. occidentale* have been created using embryo rescue which produced a significant frequency of unreduced gametes, indicating this as the likely mode of polyploidisation, and these hybrids were themselves inter-fertile with white clover [8]. The increased genetic diversity created by allopolyploidisation can confer enhanced fitness, phenotypic plasticity, and adaptability, and has been correlated with survival in stressful environments [9].

White clover originated from multiple hybridisation events in Mediterranean glacial refugia characterised by fertile soils, good soil moisture, and the presence of grazing animals which conceivably led to its spread through Europe and into western Asia and North Africa [9–11].

3. Domestication

White clover is a perennial stoloniferous plant which can also seed prolifically. It is the most important pasture legume in many temperate parts of the world, particularly where defoliation is through grazing. Domestication of white clover occurred at least 400 years ago in the Netherlands and spread globally with European colonisation [12]. The wide habitat tolerance of white clover has ensured its success in temperate [13], Mediterranean [14] and some subtropical regions [15].

Trait inheritance for white clover is disomic where chromosome pairing during meiosis is similar to that of nonhomologous pairs of chromosomes in diploids [16]. White clover has a strong gametophytic self-incompatibility mechanism such that only a small proportion of plants in a population are self-compatible [17]. The outcrossing and disomic inheritance of white clover results in populations that are a heterogeneous mixture of heterozygous individuals [11].

3.1 Types of white clover

White clover cultivars and ecotypes have been categorised largely on leaf size as Small, Intermediate, Large and Ladino types [1, 18]. Cyanogenesis, the production of hydrogen cyanide in damaged leaves [19], has been another trait used to classify white clover. Plants can quantitatively vary from having high levels to no expression (acyanogenic types) of hydrogen cyanide. While both Ladino and Large categories of white clover are large-leaved, Ladino types are characterised by being completely acyanogenic [18, 20]). Large leaved types generally have moderate to high cyanogenesis, and Small and Intermediate types may display low to high cyanogenesis [18].

Ladino types of white clover all originate from the Po Valley, particularly in the area of southern Lombardy close to the town of Lodi [21] in northern Italy [20]. This large leaved acyanogenic type of clover is believed to have developed during the fifteenth and sixteenth centuries with white clover grown under a management system involving mowing to feed an intensive dairy system supporting Parmesan cheese production [22]. Ladino types were widely adopted in North America where the strong, erect growth proved popular [10].

Significant relationships between yield of white clover populations in perennial ryegrass (*Lolium perenne*) swards and shoot morphology and cyanogenesis traits have been observed [18, 23]. Of note were significant ($P < 0.05$) negative correlations between leaf size and stolon growing point number of −0.66 and −0.46, in years one and two respectively after planting; positive correlations between leaf size and clover percentage content of +0.73 and +0.25, in years one and two respectively after planting; and interestingly in year one, a negative correlation between stolon growing point density and clover percentage content of −0.55, but in year two a positive correlation of +0.41 [23].

3.2 Breeding objectives

Plant breeding of white clover has occurred in most countries with temperate environments. Traditionally, plant breeding has sought to improve on-farm productivity, primarily through increased DM yield, improved feed quality, improved persistence, or a combination of these [24]. This has led to successful outcomes for both yield and clover percentage content in a grass sward [25]. Breeding programs have also been undertaken seeking improvements in resistance to pests and diseases, tolerance of drought, aluminium toxic soils, and improved yield at low levels of soil phosphorus.

3.2.1 Yield and combining ability with grass

The negative association between yield potential and persistence of white clover [26] has led to breeding programs seeking to break this relationship resulting in high yielding and persistent cultivars [27].

A study comparing 20 cloned genotypes from each of 15 white clover cultivars in three different grass swards (*L. perenne*, *Festuca arundinacea* and *Agrostis capillaris*) that were intermittently grazed by sheep over 18 months from planting showed that, despite not detecting differences in the effect of grass species on particular white clover cultivars, there was a strong difference in the spread of genotypes within each cultivar and that there may be a differential response to grasses at an individual genotype level [28]. This provides scope for improving competitive ability and reinforces the importance of selecting white clover under grass competition rather than as spaced white clover plants growing in monoculture. Competition effects of grasses maybe stronger under grazing than cutting, and competition effects become severe when grasses shade stolons [29].

3.2.2 Persistence

Persistence can be adversely affected by grazing management, diseases and pests, competition from other species, deficiencies and toxicities of nutrients and climatic factors [26]. As a stoloniferous species white clover depends on its taproot only in its seedling stage, with the taproot lasting less than 18-months from establishment [30]. The nodal root systems then maintain the remaining plant parts. Rooting frequency of nodes is positively correlated with stolon branching frequency [31]. However, it is the combination of the timing of death of the seminal tap root and the development of stolons that determines the persistence of white clover rather than the absolute survival of the seminal taproot [32].

Selection for increased stolon development while maintaining leaf size is seen as the key to improving both yield and persistence of white clover selections [30]. In general, leaf size along with plant height, both positively related to yield at least initially [33], are negatively correlated with stolon growing point density [18] which is intuitively associated with vegetative persistence [34].

In pasture systems using nitrogen from both white clover biological nitrogen fixation and from nitrogen fertiliser, pasture management can maintain clover content and as a result, pasture nutritive quality. For example, when up to 200 kg N ha^{-1} yr^{-1} of nitrogen fertiliser is used on dairy pastures, clover content can be maintained by ensuring additional pasture is fully utilised, particularly in spring [35] so that the grass component does not shade the clover and put it at a competitive disadvantage.

3.2.3 Seed production

Monitoring seed production potential of white clover cultivars is crucial in commercial delivery of any agronomically superior cultivar. White clover seed production yield is a product of inflorescence density and yield per inflorescence [36]. However, each node is only capable of producing either a flower or a stolon branch [37] so increased yield per inflorescence is a preferred strategy for large leaved cultivars with fewer nodes per unit area [36]. Vigorous and continued flowering results in plants being less persistent vegetatively [37]. While inflorescence density and seed yield per inflorescence are under independent genetic control and can be utilised to increase seed yield of new white clover cultivars [36]. Increases in seed yield are mostly associated with increases in inflorescence density (inflorescences/m^2), and to a lesser extent with increased seed yield/inflorescence [38]. However, importantly seed yield can be achieved while maintaining desirable morphological features and improving the uniformity of the cultivars.

3.2.4 Plant morphology

The success of white clover as a perennial legume in grazed swards is largely reliant on its ability to spread vegetatively through profusely branching stolons (**Figure 2**). Selections have been made within both a large and a small leaved cultivar of white clover for high and low proportions of nodal branches, long and short internodes, and large and small leaf size [23]. Heritability estimates were higher for leaflet size and internode length than for proportion of nodes branching, indicating that increasing shoot density and therefore persistence should focus on selection for reduced internode length rather

Figure 2.
White clover with a part of the canopy removed to expose the stolon network which allows the plant to persist, spread and vegetatively replicate.

than increased proportion of nodes branching. Indeed, developing white clover cultivars with higher stolon growing point densities at a particular leaf size should improve persistence while maintaining the greater yield potential [27, 39].

3.2.5 Phenotypic plasticity

Phenotypic plasticity describes the ability, or not, of plants to respond to their environment by making changes to their morphology and physiology [40, 41]. 'Differential phenotypic plasticity' is the extent to which phenotypic plasticity occurs with a species [42]. White clover grows in a wide range of environments and has a high level of phenotypic plasticity, a trait common to many clonal species [43, 44]. Using soil phosphorus level as the environmental variable, all plant characters of white clover measured exhibited plasticity with yield-related characters in general being more plastic than characters associated with plant morphology [42]. Of the morphological characteristics measured internode length and leaf size were the most plastic. The large variation observed for phenotypic plasticity indicated that breeding for an increase or decrease in plasticity of plant traits in white cover is achievable. Plasticity of plant traits has been identified as important in the yield of white clover during adaptation to environmental and seasonal fluctuations [45].

3.2.6 Pest and disease resistance

In many environments high cyanogenesis is associated with greater persistence than acyanogenic clovers [26]. Cyanogenic white clover plants are avoided by slugs and/or snails [46, 47], voles (*Arvicola terrestris*) [48], and larvae of alfalfa weevils (*Hypera postica*) [49]. However, cyanogenic expression while slowing symptom expression of pepper spot caused by *Stemphylium sarciniforme* did not provide long term resistance [50].

Several invertebrate pests can seriously affect white clover production and concomitantly nitrogen fixation. In New Zealand pastures this includes slugs (*Deroceras recticulatum*), clover flea (*Sminthurus viridus*), grass grub (*Costelytra giveni*), porina (*Wiseana* spp.), clover weevil (*Sitona obsoletus*), black field cricket (*Teleogryllus commodus*) and root nematodes such as clover cyst (*Heterodera trifolii*) and root-knot (*Meloidogyne hapla*) [51–53]. Simply removing nematode effects using nematicides has shown increases of 40% for annual white clover yield and 57% for nitrogen fixed [54, 55]. Selection for resistance to root feeding insects and nematodes has been challenging. While variation has been observed under controlled conditions for resistance/tolerance to nematodes [56, 57], and insect pests such as grass grub (*Costelytra zealandica*) [58], none have resulted in commercial releases due to the recessive genetic control of clover cyst and root-knot nematode resistance.

3.2.7 Abiotic tolerances

White clover plants adapted to cold environments have little to no cyanogenic expression [59–61]. Heritability for tolerance to frost in white clover is high, ranging from 0.75 to 0.93 [62], as it is for many other species such as wheat [63] and rice [64]. During hardening, prior to exposure to frost, increases occur for dry matter content, soluble carbohydrates, sucrose and proline levels in stolons [65].

Drought can have significant effects on clover persistence, with the quantum of impact associated with grazing management [66, 67]. Under set stocking with sheep, loss of stolon dry weight was much lower than for plants managed under rotational grazing, where stolon dry weight decreased by 75–90%, and white clover content in the sward reduced from 15 to 2%. Selections for improved tolerance to drought in white clover has had marginal success. White clover is a shallow rooted creeping legume where seedling taproots and nodal root size is positively correlated with leaf size [30]. Selection for specific root characteristics has improved yield and persistence in drought prone environments. For example, white clover populations developed by divergent selection for taproot diameter and for root weight ratio (proportion root weight to total plant weight), when assessed under grazing in a drought-prone environment and in a controlled-environment study, respectively, demonstrated that selection for medium leaf size and large taproot diameter gave yields 70% better in moist conditions and 35% better under dry conditions than that of the standard cultivar, Grasslands Huia [68]. Selection for increased root weight ratio was also effective in improving growth and survival in drought prone environments. Including ecotypes collected from drought-prone sites has been part of the development of cultivars in Australia, New Zealand and USA for heat and drought affected environments [69–71].

White clover is a species that requires high levels of soil phosphorus for optimal yields, particularly when grown in competition with grasses [72, 73]. Differences in response to added phosphorus among white clover genotypes has been shown in controlled environments [74–78], but this has not been effectively transferred to benefits in grazed pastures [79]. Selection for increased root hair length in white clover has been achieved [80] but when used in a field environment any benefit related to phosphorus uptake is negated by mycorrhizal infection in low phosphorus soils [81]. While mycorrhizal infection is important for white clover growth and survival in low phosphorus soils, selection for clovers able to develop more effective relationships with mycorrhiza has not yet been achievable [82].

Similarly for aluminium tolerance in acid soils, differences between white clover cultivars in controlled environments can be shown but these do not necessarily result in differences in field trials [83].

3.2.8 Introgression using interspecific hybridisation

To increase genetic variation in white clover concerted attempts have been made to create interspecific hybrids with 11 related *Trifolium* species, notably *T. nigrescens*, *T. uniflorum*, *T. occidentale*, *T. pallescens*, and *T. ambiguum* [84, 85]. These species range from annuals to long-lived, hardy perennials, some with adaptations to stressful environments, providing new traits for breeding more resilient cultivars of white clover for seasonally dry, infertile grassland environments. However, to date only one cultivar derived from interspecific hybridisation has been commercially released. Named Aberlasting, this cultivar was derived from crosses between *T. repens* and *T. ambiguum*. Initial results suggested enhanced persistence under grazing, possibly due to the presence of rhizomes in the hybrids [86], although other agronomic trials have not shown expected benefits [87]. Adequate seed production remains a major hurdle for successful commercialisation of *Trifolium* hybrids [88, 89].

4. Benefits of white clover

White clover has been the go-to legume in grazed pastures because of its ability to withstand defoliation and compete with companion species, but also due to being able to effectively fix nitrogen, have a high nutritive value, provide complementary seasonal yield with companion grasses, and improve on-farm profitability. Combining white clover with not just grasses but also forage herbs such as chicory (*Cichorum intybus*) and plantain (*Plantago lanceolata*) can contribute additional micro- and macro-minerals to livestock diets [90]. It has been proposed, with some evidence, that for white clover to make any significant contribution to the nitrogen economy and feed quality of a pasture it should make up at least 30% total dry matter [91]. White clover is a component of most diverse pasture mixes and one that tends to dominate over time due to the loss of herbs and other shorter-lived species [90]. The inclusion of herbs such as plantain with biological nitrification inhibition may help further reduce N emissions in diverse pastures [92].

4.1 Nitrogen fixation

White clover has an affinity for *Rhizobium leguminosarum* bv. *trifolii*, and this nitrogen-fixing symbiosis can produce on average 80–100 kg N/ha/year (range 10–270 kg N/ha/year) in grazed permanent clover/grass pastures in temperate regions of the world [93, 94]. Compared with white clover monocultures, grass competition has been shown to markedly increase the proportion of clover nitrogen derived from symbiotic nitrogen fixation [95]. This phenomenon is the result of strong competitiveness by ryegrass for soil nitrogen such that white clover in the clover-ryegrass mixtures becomes more dependent on symbiotic nitrogen fixation than when grown in monoculture [96].

Severe defoliation can cause rapid degradation of leghaemoglobin in nodules resulting in decreased nitrogen fixation capacity [97]. However, less severe defoliation may preferentially influence symbiotic nitrogen fixation, as opposed to the uptake of mineral nitrogen from the soil [96]. This observation led to the conclusion that symbiotic nitrogen fixation does not limit the supply of nitrogen to clover and hence its growth. Therefore, symbiotic nitrogen fixation in white clover is regulated more by the demand for nitrogen rather than by the availability of carbohydrate reserves in the plant.

The application of nitrogen fertiliser also reduces the level of biologically fixed nitrogen from clover. In a mixed grass-clover sward grazed by sheep the application of up to 390 kg N ha^{-1} yr^{-1} (applied at 30 kg N ha^{-1} after each grazing) has been shown to decrease annual nitrogen fixation by nearly 60% [98]. Similarly, in a mixed grass-clover sward grazed by dairy cows the application of 400 kg N ha^{-1} yr^{-1} (applied at approximately 40 kg N ha^{-1} after each grazing) decreased annual nitrogen fixation from 154 kg N ha^{-1} yr^{-1} when no nitrogen was added to 39 to 53 kg N ha^{-1} yr^{-1} [99]. In a UK study, it was determined that under intensive grazing, the maximum applied N rate that optimised herbage yield while having minimal effects on white clover content and nitrogen fixation rates was 60–120 kg N ha^{-1} [100].

Low temperatures also have a detrimental effect on biological nitrogen fixation. In a controlled environment study higher shoot temperatures (23°C vs. 13°C day temperatures) resulted in increased nitrogen fixed irrespective of whether or not root temperature was increased in parallel [101]. Low root temperature (5°C) however did result in a lower proportion of nitrogen derived from biological nitrogen fixation.

Grass-legume swards containing white clover produce higher grass and total sward yield than mixtures containing red clover, alfalfa or birdsfoot trefoil [102]. This is potentially due to the higher N fixation and a faster release of N from roots of white clover than alfalfa. Louarn et al. [103] reported 60% less transfer of N fixed by alfalfa to the associated grasses than white clover despite the alfalfa having twice the biomass of the white clover.

4.2 Nutritive value

Forage legumes are generally considered to be of higher nutritive value than grasses due to a higher intake, a higher ratio of protein/energy absorbed [104–108] and higher digestibility [109]. Dry matter intake has been shown to be at its greatest when white clover is about 60% of the feed mixture consumed [110]. Increased intakes of clover with higher nutritive value are the main contributing factors leading to increased milk yields [111] and lamb growth rates [112] associated with high clover diets. Mixtures of clover and forage herbs such as chicory (*Cichorium intybus*) and plantain (*Plantago lanceolata*) resulted in higher growth rates of sheep and cattle particularly during summer and autumn compared with ryegrass/white clover pastures due to the higher nutritive value [113]. Herb and clover mixes, while having a similar crude protein content compared with ryegrass/white clover pastures, have lower fibre content and higher organic matter digestibility and metabolisable energy levels.

Compared with a concentrate diet offered *ad libitum* lambs fed a cocksfoot (*Dactylis glomerata*) and white clover pasture mix resulted in carcasses with less fat and more protein [114]. However, comparison of lambs fed either white clover or perennial ryegrass found that clover-fed lambs had 40% greater slaughter weights but also had higher amounts of fat resulting from the greater production of rumen-reticulum volatile fatty acids [115]. A lower stocking rate associated with lambs grazing grass/clover compared with grass fertilised with 190 kg N ha^{-1} was compensated for by higher live-weight gain and carcass weight without changes in fatty acid composition of carcass tissues [116]. However, polyunsaturated fatty acid concentrations are often higher in white clover than alfalfa (*Medicago sativa*) and grasses [117]. Higher liveweight gain and earlier slaughter of lambs grazing clover-dominant swards tend to outweigh any fatness disadvantages relative to ryegrass-dominant pastures due to high feed conversion efficiency [118].

Methods to select for improved nutritive value of white clover have been developed [119]. This could allow the identification of germplasm with proteins that are relatively insoluble and resistant to rumen degradation leading to increased levels of amino acids that are available for absorption from the intestine.

4.3 Seasonal yield

Asynchronous seasonal biomass production of components in mixed species pastures has been related to increased yield [120] and yield stability [121] of sown grasslands. However, a study comparing perennial ryegrass pure stands and eight populations of white clover either in pure stands or in mixture with perennial ryegrass over three years at three sites concluded that it was doubtful if genetic variability of seasonal growth patterns within white clover can be used to increase the performance of clover-ryegrass mixtures [122].

4.4 Economic benefits

The inclusion of *Trifolium* species in grazed grass swards has been demonstrated to improve both productivity and profitability compared with grass-only swards for both sheep and dairy production systems [2, 123, 124]. Introduction of more persistent white clovers into south-eastern USA pastures added US$86/ha through increased cattle liveweight gain and reduced N fertiliser requirements [125]. In New Zealand the annual financial contribution of white clover through fixed nitrogen, forage yield, seed production and honey production was estimated to be NZ$3.095 billion [126]. The contribution of white cover to New Zealand's direct and dependent industry Gross Domestic Product has been estimated to be NZ$2.35 billion in 2015/16 [127] when milk solid payout was about NZ$4.40 per kg milk solids whereas now that is closer to NZ$9 per kg milk solids [128]. The inclusion of white clover in low-fertility hill country pasture in New Zealand has been modelled to result in a 17% increase in spring and summer forage consumption generating a 32% greater cattle carcass weight production per ha and leading to a 49% improvement in farm system profit [129]. This represents a positive net present value of over NZ$360,000 for the original investment in white clover establishment into existing pastures.

5. Future improvements

Future breeding aims need to align with increasing environmental challenges and the regulations imposed on farming operations such as limits of nitrogen fertiliser use, protection of waterways, identification of plants that will mitigate against or be adapted to predicted climate change, and the effect this will have on plant performance, species requirements, and the resulting changes that will happen in farm systems [24].

5.1 Breeding techniques

5.1.1 Genomics and trait mapping

Genome mapping and genotyping by sequencing to determine genetic variation and population structure in clover improvement programs provide the opportunity to improve breeding efficiencies [130–135]. However, there are limited examples of successes despite gene markers being identified for seed yield [136, 137], or drought tolerance using quercetin glycoside accumulation gene markers [138].

Genomic selection utilises DNA markers and trait data to estimate the breeding value and kinship of genotypes without having to phenotype them. In white clover Ehoche et al. [133] demonstrated the potential of genomic selection to be at least double the rate of genetic gain for DM yield in white clover compared with a conventional half-sib breeding scheme. Once validated in the field, this can shorten the breeding cycle and improve efficiency of breeding for many multigenic traits by enabling access to within family variation. The lack of access to within-family genetic variation has been identified as a major reason for the poor genetic gain in forages [139].

A potential setback to the implementation of genomic selection is the increase in net inbreeding per year as the reduction in generation interval decreases genetic variance faster [140]. Phenotypic selection typically takes 3 years or more to perform one cycle of selection, while two cycles per year can be completed with genomic selection. Breeding schemes for white clover aim to increase the frequency of desirable alleles in a population while maintaining heterozygosity. Consequently, breeders are faced with a dilemma of increasing genetic gain by selection whilst preserving or even increasing genetic diversity. Practically, this problem can be ameliorated by initiating selections in populations with high genetic diversity, or simultaneously running pre-breeding activities so that new genetic variability can be introduced as a plateau in the response to selection is reached [140, 141].

5.1.2 Genetic modification and gene editing

Beneficial traits not available within the white clover genome may be provided through genetic modification and gene editing. Initial genetic modification of white clover sought to improve insect resistance [142, 143] and virus resistance [144, 145]. Breeding strategies for developing genetically modified white clover cultivars have been considered [146]. However, traits that contribute towards addressing challenges associated with animal nutrition and health, water quality, drought tolerance and climate change have become increasingly important [147–149].

5.2 Environmental benefits

Pastoral agriculture has been criticised for exacerbating both air and water issues through methane production from ruminants contributing to increasing greenhouse gas levels, and through nitrogen movement to waterways [150–153]. White clover as a high protein component of grazed pasture contributes to this concern but it also has the opportunity to provide solutions. One study has laid to rest the concern that biological nitrogen fixation might exacerbate N_2O emissions, this appears to be more influenced by soil carbon content and surplus nitrogen levels [154].

Reducing emissions of the methane from ruminants grazing pastures is a serious research target in some countries. An example of this is the utilisation of plant secondary compounds such as condensed tannins. Condensed tannins are found in the leaves of several forage legumes, but not to any significant extent in white clover. They are known to bind proteins, protecting them from degradation in the rumen where methane producing-microbes are active [155, 156]. White clover synthesises condensed tannins, which occurs naturally in the flowers, and in trichomes on the under-surface of leaves [157]. A recent advance, using a molecular biology approach, has identified a transcription factor or master switch that can 'turn on' the condensed tannin pathway present in white clover leaves, and with the appropriate promoters allows biologically significant levels of condensed tannin expression in leaf tissue [148, 158, 159]. *In vitro* tests have demonstrated that the condensed tannins produced in white clover leaves can bind to protein at pH 6.5, as found in the rumen, and then release them at pH 2.0, the pH in the abomasum This suggests that protein protection in the rumen is possible, and that when released in the acidic abomasum, these proteins will be digested into essential amino acids for absorption in the small intestine of the animal [160, 161]. These studies also demonstrated that these condensed tannins could reduce methane production by up to 15% in the first 6 hours of incubation in rumen fluid under laboratory conditions (**Figure 3**). While the use of genetically modified organisms in many jurisdictions is regulated, this development has the potential to improve environmental, animal health and animal productivity outcomes from grazed pasture systems.

5.3 Persistence, yield and competitive ability

Although past breeding programs have been successful in selecting for persistence and yield [25, 69], future programs will continue to focus on these traits, particularly in mixed species swards and under grazing [24]. The use of grass competition and grazing in selection trials has been important in identifying persistent and high yielding cultivars particularly when grown in stressed environments [26, 39, 162]. This has resulted in the production of cultivars such as Durana [69], Trophy [70], and

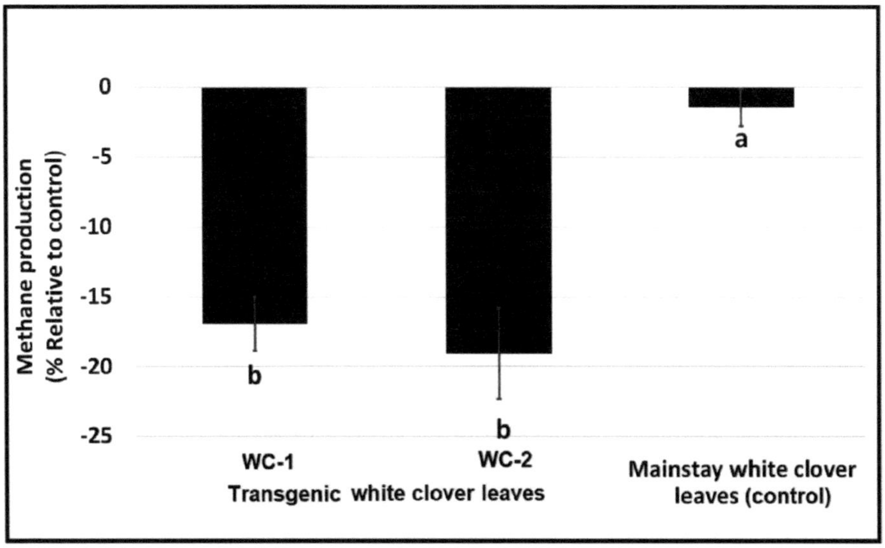

Figure 3.
Effect of condensed tannins in white clover leaves (WC-1 and WC-2) on methane production after 6 hours of incubation in rumen fluid in vitro, compared with untransformed control (white clover cv Mainstay). Means that do not share a letter are significantly different at $p < 0.01$ using Tukey's multiple comparison test. Graph redrawn as part of data published in Roldan et al. [160].

Tribute [163]. The challenge for breeders is to identify effective screening and selection processes, sourcing new genetic variation and integrating genotyping by sequencing to link important traits to gene markers to improve selection efficiencies.

5.4 Microbial associations

5.4.1 Rhizobium symbiosis

The provision of effective rhizobium strains, along with novel seed-coating technology that extends shelf life, can led to increased symbiotic capacity in white clover [164]. Selecting rhizobium strains that are competitive with naturalised rhizobia strains to ensure both their persistence in the soil and superior nodule occupancy is key [165]. A better understanding of the genes associated with ensuring a competitive and effective symbiosis would be beneficial [166]. Spill-over benefits of rhizobium have been demonstrated, with the white clover *Rhizobium* strain TA1 conferring tolerance against Cd toxicity, an impurity in phosphate fertilisers which may have toxic effects on both plant growth and rhizobia activity [167]. Whether variation in nitrogen fixation capacity by genotypes within populations of white clover can be exploited for more effective symbiotic outcomes is yet to be determined [168].

5.4.2 Mycorrhiza

Synergistic effects between arbuscular mycorrhiza and rhizobium strains has shown increased nitrogen acquisition by white clover, as well as increased shoot and root growth, and increased amino acids levels in roots [169]. Mycorrhiza, such as *Glomus mosseae,* have been shown to extend the soil phosphorus depletion zone to nearly 12 cm compared with non-mycorrhizal white clover roots which may extend to 1 cm [170]. However, mycorrhizae are only effective at low soil phosphorus levels [171–173]. There is some evidence that mycorrhiza may not only aid uptake of phosphorus, but also may enhance growth and drought tolerance of white clover [174]. It is unlikely however that mycorrhiza are a route for transfer of nitrogen between white clover and grasses [175].

5.4.3 Bioprotectants

Microbial bioprotectants can enhance plant growth, improve nutrient uptake, and suppress disease and pests [176–178]. Inoculation with plant growth-promoting rhizobacter (e.g. *Bacillus aryabhattai* and *Azotobacter vinelandii*) along with effective *Rhizobium* strains has been shown to significantly increase nitrogenase activity plus potassium, calcium, and magnesium contents in shoots when grown in phosphorus deficient soils [179]. Use of bioprotectants, other than *Rhizobium*, to improve white clover growth and persistence is a research area requiring attention [179].

5.5 Use as a cover crop

Perennial legumes such as white clover have been used as cover crops for improving soil properties, increasing future crop production, and positively impacting environmental aspects of any farming operation [180]. For example, mixtures of white clover and perennial ryegrass have been successfully used as a living mulch to achieve high yields, with sufficient irrigation and additional fertilisation, while increasing the inputs of nitrogen through biological nitrogen fixation into the entire cropping system [181]. Consistent yields in maize on unfertilised soil where white clover had previously been used as a living mulch, was shown to be the result of effective mycorrhizal fungus colonisation leading to improved phosphorus uptake by maize [182, 183].

6. Conclusion and future perspectives

White clover will continue to be a crucial component of grazed pastures in the temperate world, particularly as consumer demands for improved environmental and animal welfare outcomes in agricultural production systems become more strident. Use of new molecular and genomic methodologies for more effective and efficient selection of beneficial traits will remain a priority. Reliance on legume-based swards resulting in reduced inorganic nitrogen use will become increasingly important in reducing nutrient runoff into waterways and nitrous oxide emissions. Including traits into white clover that reduce both methane emissions and nitrogen losses can be achieved through genetic modification. Traits such as leaf expression of condensed tannins in forage can simultaneously deliver to these environmental goals, plus enhance animal health by reducing bloat, and increase production of meat, milk and fibre. The challenge then will be balancing the perceived risk of using genetic modification against the benefits of improving the environmental footprint of livestock farming and animal health and productivity. In addition, enhancements in white clover performance using microbial technologies may create more sustainable farming outcomes through reduced synthetic fertiliser and pesticidal inputs.

Conflict of interest

John Caradus and Derek Woodfield are employed by organisations that breed and own the intellectual property associated with some white clover cultivars mentioned in this review. Christine Voisey and Marissa Roldan are involved in the condensed tannin expression research outlined above.

Author details

John R. Caradus[1*], Marissa Roldan[2], Christine Voisey[2] and Derek R. Woodfield[3]

1 Grasslanz Technology Ltd., Palmerston North, New Zealand

2 AgResearch, Palmerston North, New Zealand

3 PGG Wrightson Seeds Ltd., Palmerston North, New Zealand

*Address all correspondence to: john.caradus@grasslanz.com

References

[1] Caradus JR. Genetic diversity within white clover (*Trifolium repens* L.). Proceedings of Agronomy Society of New Zealand. 1994;**24**:1-6

[2] Dineen M, Delaby L, Gilliland T, McCarthy B. Meta-analysis of the effect of white clover inclusion in perennial ryegrass swards on milk production. Journal of Dairy Science. 2018;**101**(2):1804-1816. Epub 2017/11/28. DOI: 10.3168/jds.2017-12586

[3] Ansari HA, Ellison NW, Reader SM, Badaeva ED, Friebe B, Miller TE, et al. Molecular cytogenetic organization of 5S and 18S-26S rDNA loci in White clover (*Trifolium repens* L.) and related species. Annals of Botany. 1999;**83**(3):199-206. DOI: 10.1006/anbo.1998.0806

[4] Attwood SS, Hill HD. The regularity of meiosis in microsporocytes of *Trifolium repens*. American Journal of Botany. 1940;**27**(9):730-735. DOI: 10.1002/j.1537-2197.1940.tb10943.x

[5] Badr A, Sayed-Ahmed H, El-Shanshouri A, Watson IE. Ancestors of white clover (*Trifolium repens* L.), as revealed by isozyme polymorphisms. Theoretical and Applied Genetics. 2002;**106**(1):143-148. Epub 2003/02/13. DOI: 10.1007/s00122-002-1010-5

[6] Williams WM, Ansari HA, Hussain SW, Ellison NW, Williamson ML, Verry IM. Hybridization and introgression between two diploid wild relatives of White clover, *Trifolium nigrescens* Viv. and *T. occidentale* coombe. Crop Science. 2008;**48**(1):139-148. DOI: 10.2135/cropsci2007.05.0295

[7] Ellison NW, Liston A, Steiner JJ, Williams WM, Taylor NL. Molecular phylogenetics of the clover genus (Trifolium--Leguminosae). Molecular Phylogenetics and Evolution. 2006;**39**(3):688-705. Epub 2006/02/18. DOI: 10.1016/j.ympev.2006.01.004

[8] Williams WM, Ellison NW, Ansari HA, Verry IM, Hussain SW. Experimental evidence for the ancestry of allotetraploid Trifolium repens and creation of synthetic forms with value for plant breeding. BMC Plant Biology. 2012;**12**:55. DOI: 10.1186/1471-2229-12-55

[9] Griffiths AG, Moraga R, Tausen M, Gupta V, Bilton TP, Campbell MA, et al. Breaking free: The genomics of allopolyploidy-facilitated niche expansion in white clover. The Plant Cell. 2019;**31**(7):1466-1487. Epub 2019/04/27. DOI: 10.1105/tpc.18.00606

[10] Gibson PB, Cope WA. White Clover. Clover Science and Technology; 1985. pp. 471-490

[11] Williams WM. Adaptive variation. In: Baker MJ, Williams WM, editors. White Clover. Wallingford, UK: CAB Int; 1987. pp. 299-321

[12] Zeven AC. Four hundred years of cultivation of Dutch white clover landraces. Euphytica. 1991;**54**(1):93-99. DOI: 10.1007/BF00145635

[13] Brougham RW, Ball PR, Williams WM. The ecology and management of white clover based pastures. In: Wilson R, editor. Plant Relations in Pastures. Australia: CSIRO; 1978. pp. 309-324

[14] Davies EW, Young NR. The characteristics of European, Mediterranean and other populations of white clover (*Trifolium repens* L.). Euphytica. 1967;**16**(3):330-340. DOI: 10.1007/BF00028939

[15] O'Brien AD, editor. White clover (*Trifolium repens* L.) in a subtropical environment on the east coast of Australia. In: Proceedings 11th International Grasslands Congress. Australia: Surfers Paradise; 1970

[16] Williams WM, Mason KM, Williamson ML. Genetic analysis of shikimate dehydrogenase allozymes in *Trifolium repens* L. Theoretical and Applied Genetics. 1998;**96**(6):859-868. DOI: 10.1007/s001220050813

[17] Thomas RG. Reproductive development. In: Lancahsire JA, editor. White Clover. Wallingford: CAB International; 1987. pp. 63-123

[18] Caradus JR, MacKay AC, Woodfield DR, van den Bosch J, Wewala S. Classification of a world collection of white clover cultivars. Euphytica. 1989;**42**(1-2):183-196. DOI: 10.1007/BF00042631

[19] Till I. Variability of expression of cyanogenesis in white clover (*Trifolium repens* L.). Heredity. 1987;**59**(2):265-271. DOI: 10.1038/hdy.1987.122

[20] Annicchiarico P, Ruisi P, Di Miceli G, Pecetti L. Morpho-physiological and adaptive variation of Italian germplasm of sulla (*Hedysarum coronarium* L.). crop and pasture. Science. 2014;**65**(2):206-213. DOI: 10.1071/CP13342

[21] Sansone A. Il ladino. Biblioteca Agraria Ottavi. Italy: Casale Monferrato; 1905

[22] Haussmann G. Il suolo d'Italia nella storia. Storia d'Italia I I caratteri originali. Torino, Italy: Einaudi; 1972

[23] Caradus JR, MacKay AC, editors. Selection for stolon branching and internode length in white clover. In: Proceedings 9th Australian Plant Breeding Conference; 27 June-1 July 1988. Wagga Wagga: Agricultural Research Institute; 1988

[24] Caradus J, Bouton J, Brummer C, Faville M, George R, Hume D, et al., editors. Plant breeding for resilient pastures. In: Resilient Pasture Symposium, Grassland Research and Practice Series. Vol. 17. Karapiro, New Zealand: New Zealand Grassland Association; 2021. pp. 247-268. DOI: 10.33584/rps.17.2021.3441

[25] Woodfield DR, Caradus JR. Genetic improvement in white clover representing six decades of plant breeding. Crop Science. 1994;**34**(5):1205-1213. DOI: 10.2135/cropsci1994.0011183X003400050011x

[26] Caradus JR, Williams WM, editors. Breeding for legume persistence in New Zealand. 'Persistence of forage legumes' Proceedings of a Trilateral Workshop, Honolulu, Hawaii; 17-22 July 1988; Madison, Wisconsin. USA: American Society of Agronomy; 1989

[27] Caradus JR, Clifford PTP, Chapman DF, Cousins GR, Williams WM, Miller JE. Breeding and description of 'Grasslands Sustain', a medium-large-leaved white clover (*Trifolium repens* L.) cultivar. New Zealand Journal of Agricultural Research. 1997;**40**(1):1-7. DOI: 10.1080/00288233.1997.9513224

[28] Campbell BD, Caradus JR, Given MDJ, Karsten HD, Berthelsen HB, Williamson DY. Variation in the spread of white clover plants growing in competition with different grasses. Proceedings of the Agronomy Society of New Zealand. 1994;**24**:43-46

[29] Jackman RH, Mouat MCH. Competition between grass and clover for phosphate. I. Effect of browntop (*Agrostis tenuis* Sibth) on white clover (*Trifolium*

repens L.) growth and nitrogen fixation. New Zealand Journal of Agricultural Research. 1972;**15**(4):653-666. DOI: 10.1080/00288233.1972.10421622

[30] Caradus JR. The structure and function of white clover root systems. In: Brady NC, editor. Advances in Agronomy. Vol. 43: Academic Press; 1990. pp. 1-46. DOI: 10.1016/S0065-2113(08)60475-7

[31] Chapman DF. Growth and demography of *Trifolium repens* Stolons in Grazed Hill pastures. Journal of Applied Ecology. 1983;**20**(2):597-608. DOI: 10.2307/2403529

[32] Janssen PWL, Hoekstra NJ, van der Schoot JR, van Eekeren N. White clover (*Trifolium repens*) population dynamics are partly dependent on timing of seminal taproot death. Grass and Forage Science. 2022:1-11. DOI: 10.1111/gfs.12598

[33] Brock JL, Tilbrook JC. Effect of cultivar of white clover on plant morphology during the establishment of mixed pastures under sheep grazing. New Zealand Journal of Agricultural Research. 2000;**43**(3):335-343. DOI: 10.1080/00288233.2000.9513432

[34] Gibson PB, Beinhart G, Halpin JE, Hollowell EA. Selection and evaluation of white clover clones. I. Basis for selection and a comparison of two methods of propagation for advanced evaluations. Crop Science. 1963;**3**(1):83-86. DOI: 10.2135/cropsci1963.0011183X000300010025x

[35] Harris SL, Clark DA. Effect of high rates of nitrogen fertiliser on white clover growth, morphology, and nitrogen fixation activity in grazed dairy pasture in northern New Zealand. New Zealand Journal of Agricultural Research. 1996;**39**(1):149-158. DOI: 10.1080/00288233.1996.9513173

[36] Woodfield DR, Baird IJ, PTP C. Genetic control of white clover seed yield potential. Proceedings of the New Zealand Grassland Association. 2004;**66**:111-117. DOI: 10.33584/jnzg.2004.66.2567

[37] Thomas RG. Growth of the white clover plant in relation to seed production. In: Lancashire JA, editor. Herbage Seed Production. Vol. 1. Lincoln, New Zealand: Grassland Research and Practice Series; 1979. pp. 56-63. DOI: 10.33584/rps.1.1979.3286

[38] Widdup KHW, Woodfield DR, Baird IJ, Clifford PTP. Response to selection for seed yield in six white clover cultivars. Proceedings of the New Zealand Grassland Association. 2004;**66**:103-110. DOI: 10.33584/jnzg.2004.66.2566

[39] Woodfield DR, Caradus JR. Factors affecting white clover persistence in New Zealand pastures. Proceedings of the New Zealand Grassland Association. 1996;**58**:229-235. DOI: 10.33584/jnzg.1996.58.2196

[40] Bradshaw AD. Evolutionary significance of phenotypic plasticity in plants. In: Caspari EW, Thoday JM, editors. Advances in Genetics. Vol. 13. Academic Press; 1965. pp. 115-155. DOI: 10.1016/S0065-2660(08)60048-6

[41] West-Eberhard MJ. Phenotypic plasticity and the origins of diversity. Annual Review of Ecology and Systematics. 1989;**20**(1):249-278. DOI: 10.1146/annurev.es.20.110189.001341

[42] Caradus JR, Hay MJM, Mackay AD, Thomas VJ, Dunlop J, Lambert MG, et al. Variation within white clover (*Trifolium repens* L.) for phenotypic plasticity of morphological and yield related characters, induced by phosphorus supply. New Phytologist. 1993;**123**(1):175-184. DOI: 10.1111/j.1469-8137.1993.tb04543.x

[43] Hill J. Plasticity of White Clover Growth in Competition with Perennial Ryegrass. Aberystwyth, UK: University College of Wales; 1977

[44] Horikawa Y. Plastic allocation of photosynthetic product in white clover (*Trifolium repens* L.). Journal of Japanese Society of Grasslands Science. 1986;**32**:225-234

[45] Nölke I, Tonn B, Isselstein J. Seasonal plasticity is more important than population variability in effects on white clover architecture and productivity. Annals of Botany. 2021;**128**(1):73-82. Epub 2021/03/14. DOI: 10.1093/aob/mcab040

[46] Crawford-Sidebotham TJ. The role of slugs and snails in the maintenance of the cyanogenesis polymorphisms of *Lotus corniculatus* and *Trifolium repens*. Heredity. 1972;**28**(3):405-411. DOI: 10.1038/hdy.1972.52

[47] Dirzo R, Harper JL. Experimental studies on slug-plant interactions: IV. The performance of cyanogenic and *Acyanogenic morphs* of *Trifolium repens* in the field. Journal of Ecology. 1982;**70**(1):119-138. DOI: 10.2307/2259868

[48] Saucy F, Studer J, Aerni V, Schneiter B. Preference for acyanogenic white clover (*Trifolium repens*) in the vole Arvicola terrestris: I. Experiments with two varieties. Journal of Chemical Ecology. 1999;**25**(6):1441-1454. DOI: 10.1023/A:1020943313142

[49] Ellsbury MM, Pederson GA, Fairbrother TE. Resistance to foliar-feeding hyperine weevils (Coleoptera: Curculionidae) in cyanogenic white clover. Journal of Economic Entomology. 1992;**85**(6):2467-2472. DOI: 10.1093/jee/85.6.2467

[50] Wilkinson HT, Millar RL. Cyanogenic potential of *Trifolium repens* L. in relation to pepper spot caused by *Stemphylium sarciniforme*. Canadian Journal of Botany. 1978;**56**(20):2491-2496. DOI: 10.1139/b78-300

[51] Goldson SL, Rowarth JS, Caradus JR. The impact of invasive invertebrate pests in pastoral agriculture: A review. New Zealand Journal of Agricultural Research. 2005;**48**(4):401-415. DOI: 10.1080/00288233.2005.9513673

[52] Gerard P, Ferguson C, Van Amsterdam S. Comparison of New Zealand perennial clovers for resilience against common pasture pests. New Zealand Plant Protection. 2017;**70**:241-249. DOI: 10.30843/nzpp.2017.70.57

[53] Ferguson CM, Barratt BIP, Bell N, Goldson SL, Hardwick S, Jackson M, et al. Quantifying the economic cost of invertebrate pests to New Zealand's pastoral industry. New Zealand Journal of Agricultural Research. 2019;**62**(3):255-315. DOI: 10.1080/00288233.2018.1478860

[54] Watson RN, Yeates GW, Littler RA, Steele KW. Responses in nitrogen fixation and herbage production following pesticide applications on temperate pastures. Proceedings of the Australasian Conference on Grassland Invertebrate Ecology. 1985;**4**:103-113

[55] Watson RN, Mercer CF. Pasture nematodes: The major scourge of white clover. Proceedings of the New Zealand Grassland Association. 2000;**62**:195-199

[56] Watson RN, Bell NL, Neville FJ, Aalders LT, Rohan TC. Breeding white clover for tolerance to nematodes: Overview of process and progress. Proceedings of the New Zealand Grassland Association. 2007;**69**:193-196. DOI: 10.33584/jnzg.2007.69.2661

[57] Mercer CF, Watson RN, Woodfield DR. Performance of

nematode-resistant white clover in field trials. Proceedings of the New Zealand Grassland Association. 2005;**67**:29-34

[58] Van den Bosch J, Caradus JR, Lane GA, Gaynor DL, Dymock JJ. Screening white clover for resistance to grass grub in a controlled environment. New Zealand Journal of Agricultural Research. 1995;**38**(3):329-336. DOI: 10.1080/00288233.1995.9513134

[59] Daday H. Gene frequencies in wild populations of *Trifolium repens* L. I. Distribution by latitude. Heredity. 1954;**8**(3):61-78. DOI: 10.1038/hdy.1954.40

[60] Daday H. Gene frequencies in wild populations of *Trifolium repens* L. II. Distribution by altitude. Heredity. 1954;**8**:377-384. DOI: 10.1038/hdy.1954.40

[61] Caradus JR, Mackay AC, Bosch JVD, Greer DH, Wewala GS. Intraspecific variation for frost hardiness in white clover. The Journal of Agricultural Science. 1989;**112**(2):151-157. Epub 2009/03/27. DOI: 10.1017/S002185960008504X

[62] Caradus JR, Forde MB, Wewala S, Mackay AC. Description and classification of a white clover (*Trifolium repens* l.) germplasm collection from southwest europe. New Zealand Journal of Agricultural Research. 1990;**33**(3):367-375. DOI: 10.1080/00288233.1990.10428433

[63] Sutka J. Genetic studies of frost resistance in wheat. Theoretical and Applied Genetics. 1981;**59**(3):145-152. Epub 1981/03/01. DOI: 10.1007/bf00264968

[64] Yang SC. Studies on the relationship between seedling tolerance to low temperature and glabrous hull in long-grain *indica* rice. Journal of Agricultural Research of China. 1982;**31**:102-107

[65] R⊘snes K, Junttila O, Ernstsen A, Sandli N. Development of cold tolerance in White clover (*Trifolium repens* L.) in relation to carbohydrate and free amino acid content. Acta Agriculturae Scandinavica, Section B—Soil and Plant Science. 1993;**43**(3):151-155. DOI: 10.1080/09064719309411233

[66] Brock J, Caradus J. Influence of grazing management and drought on white clover population performance and genotypic frequency. In: Woodfield D, editor. White Clover: New Zealand's Competitive Edge Grassland Association Grassland Research and Practice. 1995. pp. 79-82

[67] Lane LA, Ayres JF, Lovett JV. The pastoral significance, adaptive characteristics, and grazing value of white clover (*Trifolium repens* L.) in dryland environments in Australia: A review. Australian Journal of Experimental Agriculture. 2000;**40**(7):1033-1046. DOI: 10.1071/EA99141

[68] Caradus JR, Woodfield DR. Genetic control of adaptive root characteristics in white clover. Plant and Soil. 1998;**200**(1):63-69. DOI: 10.1023/A:1004296707631

[69] Bouton JH, Woodfield DR, Hoveland CS, McCann MA, Caradus JR. Enhanced survival and animal performance from ecotype derived white clover cultivars. Crop Science. 2005;**45**(4):1596-1602. DOI: 10.2135/cropsci2004.0335

[70] Ayres JF, Caradus JR, Murison RD, Lane LA, Woodfield DR. Grasslands trophy: A new white clover ('*Trifolium repens* L.') cultivar with tolerance of summer moisture stress. Australian Journal of Experimental Agriculture. 2007;**47**(1):110-115. DOI: 10.1071/EA04029

[71] Jahufer MZZ, Ford JL, Widdup KH, Harris C, Cousins G, Ayres JF, et al. Improving white clover for Australasia. Crop and Pasture Science. 2012;**63**(9):739-745. DOI: 10.1071/CP12142

[72] Jackman RH, Mouat MCH. Competition between grass and clover for phosphate. II. Effect of root activity, efficiency of response to phosphate,and soil moisture. New Zealand Journal of Agricultural Research. 1972;**15**(4):667-675. DOI: 10.1080/00288233.1972.10421623

[73] Caradus J. Distinguishing between grass and legume species for efficiency of phosphorus use. New Zealand Journal of Agricultural Research. 1980;**23**(1):75-81. DOI: 10.1080/00288233.1980.10417847

[74] Mackay AD, Caradus JR. White clover cultivar responses to phosphate fertilisers of differing solubility. Proceedings New Zealand Grassland Association. 1988;**49**:151-156. DOI: 10.33584/jnzg.1988.49.1845

[75] Mackay AD, Caradus JR, Dunlop J, Wewala GS, MCH M, Lambert MG, et al., editors. Response to phosphorus of a world collection of white clover cultivars. In: Proceedings 3rd International Symposium on Genetic Aspects of Plant Mineral Nutrition 19-24 June 1988. Braunschweig, F.R.G; 1990

[76] Dunlop J, Lambert MG, Van Den Bosch J, Caradus JR, Hart AL, Wewala GS, et al. A programme to breed a cultivar of *Trifolium repens* L. for more efficient use of phosphate. In: El Bassam N, Dambroth M, Loughman BC, editors. Genetic Aspects of Plant Mineral Nutrition. Dordrecht: Springer Netherlands; 1990. p. 547-552.

[77] Caradus JR, Mackay AD, Wewala S, Dunlop J, Hart A, Van Den Bosch J, et al. Inheritance of phosphorus response in white clover (*Trifolium repens* L.). Plant and Soil. 1992;**146**(1):199-208. DOI: 10.1007/BF00012013

[78] Caradus JR. Selection for improved adaptation of white clover to low phosphorus and acid soils. Euphytica. 1994;**77**(3):243-250. DOI: 10.1007/BF02262637

[79] Caradus JR, Dunn A. Adaptation to low fertility hill country in New Zealand of white clover lines selected for differences in response to phosphorus. New Zealand Journal of Agricultural Research. 2000;**43**(1):63-69. DOI: 10.1080/00288233.2000.9513409

[80] Caradus JR. Selection for root hair length in white clover (*Trifolium repens* L.). Euphytica. 1979;**28**(2):489-494. DOI: 10.1007/BF00056609

[81] Caradus JR. Genetic differences in the length of root hairs in white clover and their effect on phosphorus uptake. In: Scaife A, editor. Plant Nutrition Proceedings of 9th International Plant Nutrition. Plant Nutrition. England: Colloquium, Warwick University; 1982. pp. 84-88

[82] Crush JR, Caradus JR. Effect of mycorrhizas on growth of some white clovers. New Zealand Journal of AgriculturalResearch.1980;**23**(2):233-237. DOI: 10.1080/00288233.1980.10430791

[83] Caradus JR, Crush JR, Ouyang L, Fraser W. Evaluation of aluminium-tolerant white clover (*Trifolium repens*) selections on East Otago upland soils. New Zealand Journal of Agricultural Research. 2001;**44**(2-3):141-150. DOI: 10.1080/00288233.2001.9513470

[84] Williams WM, Hussain SW. Development of a breeding strategy for interspecific hybrids between Caucasian clover and white clover.

New Zealand Journal of Agricultural Research. 2008;**51**(2):115-126. DOI: 10.1080/00288230809510441

[85] Williams WM. *Trifolium* interspecific hybridisation: Widening the white clover gene pool. Crop and Pasture Science. 2014;**65**(11):1091-1106. DOI: 10.1071/CP13294

[86] Lloyd DC, Vale JE, Sizer-Coverdale EM, Marshall AH, editors. Interspecific hybridisation of white clover and Caucasian clover confers grazing tolerance. Grassland resources for extensive farming systems in marginal lands: major drivers and future scenarios. In: Proceedings of the 19th Symposium of the European Grassland Federation; 7-10 May 2017; Alghero, Italy. 2017

[87] Gerard PJ, Aalders LT, Hardwick S, Wilson DJ. Investigation into the contrasting production of eight perennial clover cultivars in the first two years at field sites in in Waikato and Canterbury. New Zealand Journal of Agricultural Research. 2022;**65**(4-5):271-289. DOI: 10.1080/00288233.2020.1775657

[88] Widdup KH, Hussain SW, Williams WM, Lowther WL, Pryor HN, Sutherland BL. The development and plant characteristics of interspecific hybrids between white and caucasian clover. In: Moot DJ, editor. Legumes for Dryland Pastures. 11. NZ Grassland Association Research and Practice Series: Lincoln University; 2003. pp. 143-148

[89] Naeem M, Verry IM, Kemp PD, Millner JP, Williams WM. Comparing mating designs to restore seed production of interspecific hybrids between *Trifolium repens* (white clover) and *Trifolium uniflorum*. Plant Breeding. 2017;**136**(3):420-426. DOI: 10.1111/pbr.12481

[90] Jaramillo DM, Sheridan H, Soder K, Dubeux JCB. Enhancing the sustainability of temperate pasture systems through more diverse swards. Agronomy. 2021;**11**(10):1912. DOI: 10.3390/agronomy11101912

[91] Stewart TA. Utilising clover in grass based animal production systems. Occasional Symposium of the British Grassland Society. 1984;**16**:93-103

[92] Carlton AJ, Cameron KC, Di HJ, Edwards GR, Clough TJ. Nitrate leaching losses are lower from ryegrass/white clover forages containing plantain than from ryegrass/white clover forages under different irrigation. New Zealand Journal of Agricultural Research. 2019;**62**(2):150-172. DOI: 10.1080/00288233.2018.1461659

[93] Hoglund J, Crush J, Brock J, Ball R, Carran R. Nitrogen fixation in pasture. New Zealand Journal of Experimental Agriculture. 1979;**7**:45-51

[94] Ledgard SF. Nitrogen cycling in low input legume-based agriculture, with emphasis on legume/grass pastures. Plant and Soil. 2001;**228**(1):43-59. DOI: https://link.springer.com/article/10.1023/A:1004810620983

[95] Nesheim L, Boller BC. Nitrogen fixation by white clover when competing with grasses at moderately low temperatures. Plant and Soil. 1991;**133**(1):47-56. DOI: 10.1007/BF00011898

[96] Seresinhe T, Hartwig UA, Kessler W, Nosberger J. Symbiotic nitrogen fixation of white clover in a mixed sward is not limited by height of repeated cutting. Journal of Agronomy and Crop Science. 1994;**172**(4):279-288. DOI: 10.1111/j.1439-037X.1994.tb00179.x

[97] Chu ACP, Robertson AG. The effects of shading and defoliation on nodulation and nitrogen fixation by white clover.

Plant and Soil. 1974;**41**(3):509-519. DOI: 10.1007/BF02185812

[98] Ledgard SF, Sprosen MS, Steele KW. Nitrogen fixation by nine white clover cultivars in grazed pasture, as affected by nitrogen fertilization. Plant and Soil. 1996;**178**(2):193-203. DOI: 10.1007/BF00011583

[99] Ledgard SF, Sprosen MS, Penno JW, Rajendram GS. Nitrogen fixation by white clover in pastures grazed by dairy cows: Temporal variation and effects of nitrogen fertilization. Plant and Soil. 2001;**229**(2):177-187. DOI: 10.1023/A:1004833804002

[100] Enriquez-Hidalgo D, Gilliland TJ, Hennessy D. Herbage and nitrogen yields, fixation and transfer by white clover to companion grasses in grazed swards under different rates of nitrogen fertilization. Grass and Forage Science. 2016;**71**(4):559-574. DOI: 10.1111/gfs.12201

[101] Kessler W, Boller BC, Nösberger J. Distinct influence of root and shoot temperature on nitrogen fixation by white clover. Annals of Botany. 1990;**65**(3):341-346. DOI: 10.1093/oxfordjournals.aob.a087942

[102] Gierus M, Kleen J, Loges R, Taube F. Forage legume species determine the nutritional quality of binary mixtures with perennial ryegrass in the first production year. Animal Feed Science and Technology. 2012;**172**(3):150-161. DOI: 10.1016/j.anifeedsci.2011.12.026

[103] Louarn G, Pereira-Lopès E, Fustec J, Mary B, Voisin A-S, de Faccio Carvalho PC, et al. The amounts and dynamics of nitrogen transfer to grasses differ in alfalfa and white clover-based grass-legume mixtures as a result of rooting strategies and rhizodeposit quality. Plant and Soil. 2015;**389**(1):289-305. DOI: 10.1007/s11104-014-2354-8

[104] Ulyatt MJ, Lancashire JA, Jones WT. The nutritive value of legumes. Proceedings of the New Zealand Grassland Association. 1976;**38**:107-118. DOI: 10.33584/jnzg.1976.38.1475

[105] Rogers GL, Porter RHD, Robinson IB. Comparison of perennial ryegrass and white cloverfor milk production. In: Proceedings Conference "Dairy Production from Pasture". New Zealand Society of Animal Production; 1982. pp. 213-214

[106] Gibb MJ, Treacher TT. The performance of weaned lambs offered diets containing different proportions of fresh perennial ryegrass and white clover. Animal Science. 1984;**39**(3):413-420. Epub 2010/09/02. DOI: 10.1017/S0003356100032141

[107] Dewhurst RJ, Delaby L, Moloney A, Boland T, Lewis E. Nutritive value of forage legumes used for grazing and silage. Irish Journal of Agricultural and Food Research. 2009;**48**(2):167-187. DOI: https://www.jstor.org/stable/20720367

[108] Guy C, Hennessy D, Gilliland TJ, Coughlan F, McClearn B, Dineen M, et al. Comparison of perennial ryegrass, *Lolium perenne* L., ploidy and white clover, *Trifolium repens* L., inclusion for herbage production, utilization and nutritive value. Grass and Forage Science. 2018;**73**(4):865-877. DOI: 10.1111/gfs.12366

[109] Brink GE, Sanderson MA, Casler MD. Grass and legume effects on nutritive value of complex forage mixtures. Crop Science. 2015;**55**(3):1329-1337. DOI: 10.2135/cropsci2014.09.0666

[110] Harris SL, Auldist MJ, Clark DA, Jansen EBL. Effects of white clover

content in the diet on herbage intake, milk production and milk composition of New Zealand dairy cows housed indoors. Journal of Dairy Research. 1998;**65**(3):389-400. DOI: 10.1017/S0022029998002969

[111] Harris S, Clark D, Jansen E. Optimum white clover content for milk production: New Zealand Society of Animal Production; 1997. 169-71 p.

[112] Papadopoulos YA, Charmley E, McRae KB, Farid A, Price MA. Addition of white clover to orchardgrass pasture improves the performance of grazing lambs, but not herbage production. Canadian Journal of Animal Science. 2001;**81**(4):517-523. DOI: 10.4141/a97-061

[113] Cranston L, Kenyon PR, Morris ST, Kemp PD. A review of the use of chicory, plantain, red clover and white clover in a sward mix for increased sheep and beef production. Journal of New Zealand Grasslands. 2015;**77**:89-94. DOI: 10.33584/jnzg.2015.77.475

[114] Turner KE, Belesky DP, Fedders JM, Solomon MB. Autumn-grazed Orchardgrass-White clover pasture: Nutritive value of herbage and lamb performance. Journal of Production Agriculture. 1998;**11**(1):85-91. DOI: 10.2134/jpa1998.0085

[115] Cramer DA, Barton RA, Shorland FB, Czochanska Z. A comparison of the effects of white clover (*Trifolium repens*) and of perennial ryegrass (*Lolium perenne*) on fat composition and flavour of lamb. The Journal of Agricultural Science. 1967;**69**(3):367-373. Epub 2009/03/27. DOI: 10.1017/S0021859600019031

[116] Vipond JE, Swift G, Noble RC, Horgan G. Effects of clover in the diet of grazed lambs on production and carcass composition. Animal Science. 1993;**57**(2):253-261. Epub 2010/09/02. DOI: 10.1017/S0003356100006863

[117] Boufaïed H, Chouinard PY, Tremblay GF, Petit HV, Michaud R, Bélanger G. Fatty acids in forages. I. Factors affecting concentrations. Canadian Journal of Animal Science. 2003;**83**(3):501-511. DOI: 10.4141/a02-098

[118] Scales GH. Carcass fatness in lambs grazing various forages at different rates of liveweight gain. New Zealand Journal of Agricultural Research. 1993;**36**(2):243-251. DOI: 10.1080/00288233.1993.10417760

[119] Waghorn G, Caradus JR. Screening white clover cultivars for improved nutritive value—development of a method. Proceedings of the New Zealand Grassland Association. 1994;**56**:49-53. DOI: 10.33584/jnzg.1994.56.2117

[120] Husse S, Huguenin-Elie O, Buchmann N, Lüscher A. Larger yields of mixtures than monocultures of cultivated grassland species match with asynchrony in shoot growth among species but not with increased light interception. Field Crops Research. 2016;**194**:1-11. DOI: 10.1016/j.fcr.2016.04.021

[121] Prieto I, Violle C, Barre P, Durand JL, Ghesquiere M, Litrico I. Complementary effects of species and genetic diversity on productivity and stability of sown grasslands. Nat Plants. 2015;**1**(4):15033. Epub 2015/01/01. DOI: 10.1038/nplants.2015.33

[122] Tonn B, Koops D, Schweneker D, Heshmati S, Feuerstein U, Isselstein J. Temporal synchrony of white clover populations with perennial ryegrass affects yield and yield stability of grass-clover mixtures. In: Proceedings

of the Joint 20th Symposium of the European Grassland Federation and the 33rd Meeting of the EUCARPIA Section 'Fodder Crops and Amenity Grasses' Zürich, Switzerland 24-27 June 2019. Vol. 24. The Netherlands: Wageningen Academic Publishers; 2019. pp. 81-83

[123] Egan M, Lynch MB, Hennessy D. Including white clover in nitrogen fertilized perennial ryegrass swards: Effects on dry matter intake and milk production of spring calving dairy cows. The Journal of Agricultural Science. 2017;**155**(4):657-668. Epub 2016/11/28. DOI: 10.1017/S0021859616000952

[124] McClearn B, Shalloo L, Gilliland TJ, Coughlan F, McCarthy B. An economic comparison of pasture-based production systems differing in sward type and cow genotype. Journal of Dairy Science. 2020;**103**(5):4455-4465. DOI: 10.3168/jds.2019-17552

[125] Bouton J. The economic benefits of forage improvement in the United States. Euphytica. 2007;**154**(3):263-270. DOI: 10.1007/s10681-006-9220-6

[126] Caradus JR, Woodfield DR, Stewart AV. Overview and vision for white clover. In: Woodfield D, editor. White Clover: New Zealand's Competitive Edge. NZ Grassland Association Grassland Research and Practice Series 6:1-6 6. New Zealand: Lincoln University; 1995

[127] Nixon C. How valuable is that plant species? Application of a method for enumerating the contribution of selected plant species to New Zealand's GDP. NZIER report to the Ministry for Primary Industries. MPI Technical Paper No: 2016/62. 2016:227

[128] Dairy industry payout history. https://www.interest.co.nz/rural-data/dairy-industry-payout-history [Internet]. Available from: https://www.interest.co.nz/rural-data/dairy-industry-payout-history [Accessed: 2 December 2022]

[129] Dodd M, Tozer K, Vogeler I, Greenfield R, Stevens D, Rhodes T, et al. Quantifying the value proposition for white clover persistence on a New Zealand summer-dry hill-country farm. Journal of New Zealand Grasslands. 2020;**82**:199-209. DOI: 10.33584/jnzg.2020.82.2973

[130] Woodfield DR, Brummer EC, editors. Integrating Molecular Techniques to Maximise the Genetic Potential of Forage Legumes. Molecular Breeding of Forage Crops. Dordrecht: Springer Netherlands; 2001

[131] Jahufer MZZ, Cooper M, Ayres JF, Bray RA. Identification of research to improve the efficiency of breeding strategies for white clover in Australia—A review. Australian Journal of Agricultural Research. 2002;**53**(3):239-257. DOI: 10.1071/ar01110

[132] Zhang Y, Sledge MK, Bouton JH. Genome mapping of white clover (*Trifolium repens* L.) and comparative analysis within the Trifolieae using cross-species SSR markers. Theoretical and Applied Genetics. 2007;**114**(8):1367-1378. DOI: 10.1007/s00122-007-0523-3

[133] Ehoche GAS, Larking A, Jauregui R, Cousins G, O'Connor J, Jahufer Z, et al. Developing genomic selection for dry matter yield in white clover. Journal of New Zealand Grasslands. 2021;**83**:79-90. DOI: 10.33584/jnzg.2021.83.3502

[134] Ehoche OG. Assessing the potential of genomic selection to improve yield and persistence in white clover: a thesis presented in the partial

fulfilment of the requirements for the degree of Doctor of Philosophy (PhD) in Plant Biology at Massey University, Manawatu, New Zealand [Doctoral]: Massey University; 2020

[135] Lukjanová E, Řepková J. Chromosome and genome diversity in the genus Trifolium (Fabaceae). Plants (Basel). 2021;**10**(11). Article ID: 2518. Epub 2021/11/28. DOI: 10.3390/plants10112518

[136] Barrett BA, Baird IJ, Woodfield DR. A QTL analysis of White clover seed production. Crop Science. 2005;**45**(5):1844-1850. DOI: 10.2135/cropsci2004.0679

[137] Barrett BA, Baird IJ, Woodfield DR. Genetic tools for increased white clover seed production. Proceedings of the New Zealand Grassland Association. 2004;**66**:119-126

[138] Ballizany WL. Novel markers for drought resistance in white clover [doctoral dissertation]. Lincoln University; 2011

[139] Casler MD, Brummer EC. Theoretical expected genetic gains for among-and-within-family selection methods in perennial forage crops. Crop Science. 2008;**48**(3):890-902. DOI: 10.2135/cropsci2007.09.0499

[140] Goddard ME, Hayes BJ. Genomic selection. Journal of Animal Breeding Genetics. 2007;**124**:323-330

[141] Knight R. Quantitative genetics, statistics and plant breeding. In: A 'Course Manual in Plant Breeding'. Australia: Australian Vice-Chancellors' Commitee; 1979

[142] Voisey CR, White DWR, Dudas B, Appleby RD, Ealing PM, Scott AG. Agrobacterium-mediated transformation of white clover using direct shoot organogenesis. Plant Cell Reports. 1994;**13**(6):309-314. DOI: 10.1007/bf00232627

[143] McManus MT, Laing WA, Watson LM, Markwick N, Voisey CR, White DWR. Expression of the soybean (Kunitz) trypsin inhibitor in leaves of white clover (*Trifolium repens* L.). Plant Science. 2005;**168**(5):1211-1220. DOI: 10.1016/j.plantsci.2004.12.020

[144] Panter S, Chu PG, Ludlow E, Garrett R, Kalla R, Jahufer MZZ, et al. Molecular breeding of transgenic white clover (*Trifolium repens* L.) with field resistance to Alfalfa mosaic virus through the expression of its coat protein gene. Transgenic Research. 2012;**21**(3):619-632. DOI: 10.1007/s11248-011-9557-z

[145] Ludlow EJ, Mouradov A, Spangenberg GC. Post-transcriptional gene silencing as an efficient tool for engineering resistance to white clover mosaic virus in white clover (*Trifolium repens*). Journal of Plant Physiology. 2009;**166**(14):1557-1567. Epub 2009/08/08. DOI: 10.1016/j.jplph.2009.07.001

[146] Woodfield DR, White DWR. Breeding strategies for developing transgenic white clover cultivars. In: Woodfield DR, editor. White Clover: New Zealand's Competitive Edge. 6. NZ Grassland Association Grassland Research and Practice Series: Lincoln University New Zealand; 1995. pp. 125-130

[147] Ma XF, Wright E, Ge Y, Bell J, Xi Y, Bouton JH, et al. Improving phosphorus acquisition of white clover (*Trifolium repens* L.) by transgenic expression of plant-derived phytase and acid phosphatase genes. Plant Science. 2009;**176**(4):479-488. DOI: 10.1016/j.plantsci.2009.01.001

[148] Hancock KR, Collette V, Fraser K, Greig M, Xue H, Richardson K, et al. Expression of the R2R3-MYB transcription factor TaMYB14 from *Trifolium arvense* activates proanthocyanidin biosynthesis in the legumes *Trifolium repens* and *Medicago sativa*. Plant Physiology. 2012;**159**(3):1204-1220. DOI: 10.1104/pp.112.195420

[149] Jiang Q, Zhang J-Y, Guo X, Bedair M, Sumner L, Bouton J, et al. Improvement of drought tolerance in white clover (*Trifolium repens*) by transgenic expression of a transcription factor gene WXP1. Functional Plant Biology. 2010;**37**(2):157-165. DOI: 10.1071/FP09177

[150] Bibbee A. Green Growth and Climate Change Policies in New Zealand OECD Economics Department Working Papers. Vol. 893. 36 p. Paris [Internet]: OECD Publishing; 2011. DOI: 10.1787/5kg51mc6k98r-en

[151] Muller A, Jawtusch J, Gattinger A. Mitigating Greenhouse Gases in Agriculture. Research Institute of Organic Agriculture; 2011. p. 88

[152] Garnett T, Godde C, Muller A, Röös E, Smith P, de Boer IJM, et al. Grazed and Confused? Ruminating on Cattle, Grazing Systems, Methane, Nitrous Oxide, the Soil Carbon Sequestration Question – and What It All Means for Greenhouse Gas Emissions. Food Climate Research Network (FCRN). Environmental Change Institute, University of Oxford; 2017. p. 127

[153] Harrison MT, Cullen BR, Mayberry DE, Cowie AL, Bilotto F, Badgery WB, et al. Carbon myopia: The urgent need for integrated social, economic and environmental action in the livestock sector. Global Change Biology. 2021;**27**:5726-5761. DOI: 10.1111/gcb.15816

[154] Reinsch T, Malisch C, Loges R, Taube F. Nitrous oxide emissions from grass–clover swards as influenced by sward age and biological nitrogen fixation. Grass and Forage Science. 2020;**75**(4):372-384. DOI: 10.1111/gfs.12496

[155] Waghorn GC, Ulyatt MJ, John A, Fisher MT. The effect of condensed tannins on the site of digestion of amino acids and other nutrients in sheep fed on lotus *Corniculatus* L. British Journal of Nutrition. 1987;**57**(1):115-126. DOI: 10.1079/BJN19870015

[156] Waghorn G. Beneficial and detrimental effects of dietary condensed tannins for sustainable sheep and goat production—Progress and challenges. Animal Feed Science and Technology. 2008;**147**(1-3):116-139

[157] Woodfield D, McNabb W, Kennedy L, Cousins G, Caradus J, editors. Floral and Foliar Tannin Content in White Clover. Proceedings of the Fifteenth Trifolium Conference; 1998; Madison, Wisconsin 1998

[158] Hancock K, Collette V, Chapman E, Hanson K, Temple S, Moraga R, et al. Progress towards developing bloat-safe legumes for the farming industry. Crop and Pasture Science. 2014;**65**(11):1107-1113. DOI: 10.1071/CP13308

[159] Woodfield DR, Roldan MB, Voisey CR, Cousins GR, Caradus JR. Improving environmental benefits of white clover through condensed tannin expression. Journal of New Zealand Grasslands. 2019;**81**:195-202. DOI: 10.33584/jnzg.2019.81.382

[160] Roldan MB, Cousins G, Muetzel S, Zeller WE, Fraser K, Salminen J-P, et al. Condensed tannins in White clover (*Trifolium repens*) foliar tissues expressing the transcription factor TaMYB14-1 bind to forage protein

and reduce ammonia and methane emissions in vitro. Frontiers in Plant Science. 2022;**12**. Article ID: 777354. DOI: 10.3389/fpls.2021.777354

[161] Caradus JR, Voisey CR, Cousin GR, Kaur R, Woodfield DR, Blanc A, et al. The hunt for the "holy grail": Condensed tannins in the perennial forage legume white clover (*Trifolium repens* L.). Grass and Forage Science. 2022;**77**(2):111-123. DOI: 10.1111/gfs.12567

[162] Widdup KH, Ford JL, Cousins GR, Woodfield DR, Caradus JR, Barrett BA. A comparison of New Zealand and overseas white clover cultivars under grazing in New Zealand. Journal of New Zealand Grasslands. 2015;**77**:51-56. DOI: 10.33584/jnzg.2015.77.483

[163] Woodfield DR, Clifford PTP, Baird IJ, Cousins GR, Miller JE, Widdup KH, et al. Grasslands tribute: A multi-purpose white clover for Australasia. Proceedings of the New Zealand Grassland Association. 2003;**65**:157-162. DOI: 10.33584/jnzg.2003.65.2488

[164] Shi S, Villamizar L, Gerard E, Ronson C, Wakelin S, Ballard R, et al. Increasing biological nitrogen fixation by white clover-rhizobia symbiosis. Journal of NZ Grasslands. 2019;**81**:231-234. DOI: 10.33584/jnzg.2019.81.380

[165] Irisarri P, Cardozo G, Tartaglia C, Reyno R, Gutiérrez P, Lattanzi FA, et al. Selection of competitive and efficient rhizobia strains for white clover. Frontiers in Microbiology. 2019;**10**(768). DOI: 10.3389/fmicb.2019.00768

[166] Ferguson S, Major AS, Sullivan JT, Bourke SD, Kelly SJ, Perry BJ, et al. Rhizobium leguminosarum bv. Trifolii NodD2 enhances competitive nodule colonization in the clover-Rhizobium Symbiosis. Applied and Environmental Microbiology. 2020;**86**(18):e01268-e01220. DOI: 10.1128/AEM.01268-20

[167] Young SD, van Koten C, Gray CW, Cavanagh JAE, Wakelin SA. Symbiosis between *Rhizobium leguminosarum* bv. *trifolii* strain TA1 and a white clover cultivar benefits clover tolerance to cadmium toxicity. New Zealand Journal of Agricultural Research. 2020;**63**(3):353-364. DOI: 10.1080/00288233.2019.1680394

[168] Weith SK, Jahufer MZZ, Hofmann RW, Anderson CB, Luo D, Ehoche OG, et al. Quantitative genetic analysis reveals potential to breed for improved white clover growth in symbiosis with nitrogen-fixing Rhizobium bacteria. Frontiers in Plant Science. 2022;**13**:953400. Epub 2022/10/11. DOI: 10.3389/fpls.2022.953400

[169] Xie MM, Zou YN, Wu QS, Zhang ZZ, Kuča K. Single or dual inoculation of arbuscular mycorrhizal fungi and rhizobia regulates plant growth and nitrogen acquisition in white clover. Plant, Soil and Environment. 2020;**66**(6):287-294. DOI: 10.17221/234/2020-PSE

[170] Li X-L, George E, Marschner H. Extension of the phosphorus depletion zone in VA-mycorrhizal white clover in a calcareous soil. Plant and Soil. 1991;**136**(1):41-48. DOI: 10.1007/BF02465218

[171] Baylis GTS. Experiments on the ecological significance of phycomycetous mycorrhizas. New Phytologist. 1967;**66**(2):231-243. DOI: 10.1111/j.1469-8137.1967.tb06001.x

[172] Mosse B. Plant growth responses to vesicular-arbuscular mycorrhizas IV. In soil given additional phosphate. New Phytologist. 1973;**72**(1):127-136. DOI: 10.1111/j.1469-8137.1973.tb02017.x

[173] Hall IR. Effects of endomycorrhizas on the competitive ability of white clover. New Zealand Journal of Agricultural Research. 1978;**21**(3):509-515. DOI: 10.1080/00288233.1978.10427441

[174] Tuo X-Q, He L, Zou Y-N. Alleviation of drought stress in white clover after inoculation with arbuscular mycorrhizal fungi. Notulae Botanicae Horti Agrobotanici Cluj-Napoca. 2017;**45**(1):220-224. DOI: 10.15835/nbha45110709

[175] Rogers JB, Scott Laidlaw A, Christie P. The role of arbuscular mycorrhizal fungi in the transfer of nutrients between white clover and perennial ryegrass. Chemosphere. 2001;**42**(2):153-159. DOI: 10.1016/S0045-6535(00)00120-X

[176] Janarthanam L. Bioprotectant with multifunctional microorganisms: A new dimension in plant protection. Journal of Biopesticides. 2013;**6**(2):219-230

[177] Pole A, Srivastava A, Zakeel MCM, Sharma VK, Suyal DC, Singh AK, et al. 12—Role of microbial biotechnology for strain improvement for agricultural sustainability. In: Soni R, Suyal DC, Yadav AN, Goel R, editors. Trends of Applied Microbiology for Sustainable Economy. Academic Press; 2022. pp. 285-317

[178] Sharma B, Kumawat KC. Functional diversity of microbes in rhizosphere: A key player for soil health conservation under changing climatic conditions. In: Vaishnav A, Arya SS, Choudhary DK, editors. Plant Stress Mitigators: Action and Application. Singapore: Springer Nature Singapore; 2022. pp. 469-493

[179] Matse DT, Huang C-H, Huang Y-M, Yen M-Y. Effects of coinoculation of Rhizobium with plant growth promoting rhizobacteria on the nitrogen fixation and nutrient uptake of Trifolium repens in low phosphorus soil. Journal of Plant Nutrition. 2020;**43**(5):739-752. DOI: 10.1080/01904167.2019.1702205

[180] Martin G, Durand J-L, Duru M, Gastal F, Julier B, Litrico I, et al. Role of ley pastures in tomorrow's cropping systems. A review. Agronomy for Sustainable Development. 2020;**40**(3):17. DOI: 10.1007/s13593-020-00620-9

[181] Stein S, Hartung J, Möller K, Zikeli S. The effects of leguminous living mulch intercropping and its growth management on organic cabbage yield and biological nitrogen fixation. Agronomy. 2022;**12**(5):1009. DOI: 10.3390/agronomy12051009

[182] Deguchi S, Uozumi S, Touno E, Kaneko M, Tawaraya K. Arbuscular mycorrhizal colonization increases phosphorus uptake and growth of corn in a white clover living mulch system. Soil Science and Plant Nutrition. 2012;**58**(2):169-172. DOI: 10.1080/00380768.2012.662697

[183] Deguchi S, Shimazaki Y, Uozumi S, Tawaraya K, Kawamoto H, Tanaka O. White clover living mulch increases the yield of silage corn via arbuscular mycorrhizal fungus colonization. Plant and Soil. 2007;**291**(1):291-299. DOI: 10.1007/s11104-007-9194-8

Chapter 7

Digestibility of Proteins in Legumes

Stephanie A. Misquitta, Deepika N. Kshirsagar, Pooja R. Dange, Vikram G. Choudhari and Mukund M. Kabra

Abstract

Legume proteins have recently attracted interest from the food industry. Indeed, they are economical and have good nutritional and functional attributes. In addition to being important for growth and maintenance, they also provide antioxidant peptides, and are hence gaining importance for these additional health benefits. The nutritional benefits of leguminous seeds, are linked to the digestibility of the proteins into peptides and amino acids. Seed proteins have a complex structure. Coexisting with these proteins in the seed matrix, are other components that interfere with protein digestibility. Among them, are the antinutritional factors (ANFs), like trypsin inhibitors, which are also significant in animal nutrition. Thus, improving access to legume proteins, often depends on the removal of these inhibitors. Therefore, this chapter focuses on the factors affecting the efficient digestion of proteins, with emphasis on ANFs and methods to eliminate them. Enzymatic treatment is an effective method to solve the problems encountered. Exogenous enzymes, act as digestive aids and help improve protein digestibility *in vivo*, where digestion is impaired due to insufficient digestive enzymes. Enzymes provide an environment-friendly alternative to energy-intensive processes in the food industry. Complete digestion of legumes will prevent wastage and enhance food security, besides contributing to sustainability.

Keywords: protein digestibility, antinutritional factors, trypsin inhibitors, enzymes, proteases

1. Introduction

The origin of legumes in the diet of human beings, dates back to ancient times. The discovery of what is believed to be a pigeonpea in an Egyptian tomb, lead us to believe that lentils were used as food thousands of years ago. What was part of the diet of the ancient Aztec, Inca, Greek, Egyptian and Indian Vedic cultures, continues to hold importance even in today's modern world. For centuries now, legumes have been consumed by people all over the world. Globally, grain legumes occupied 81 million ha with production of more than 92 million tonnes. Major grain legume producing countries are India, China, Myanmar, Canada, Australia, Brazil, Argentina, USA and Russia [1]. Among the legumes consumed by humans, soyabean is by far the most widely used. Referred to as "poor man's food", pulses and beans are part of the staple diet among the low-income population, as they are used as a main source of protein, instead of animal meat, which has traditionally been more expensive and not as easily available. They have emerged as effective tools in the fight against global malnourishment. Most health organizations recommend consuming vegetable protein on a regular basis, as it has been shown to lower blood cholesterol levels, the risk of coronary heart disease, and diabetes [2]. According to Dietary guidelines for Americans, U.S. Department of Agriculture, and U.S. Department of Health and Services, legumes should be included several times a week, in the diet.

Apart from being used as a protein source for the diet, legumes have other health benefits that are only now being realized. However, the digestibility of plant seed proteins is low, as compared to animal proteins. Hence it is important to understand the factors influencing the complete breakdown of proteins into their constituent components, so that remedial measures can be undertaken to maximize their use in food or in food applications.

2. Health benefits of legumes

The nutritional value of legumes was recognized in ancient cultures. Fava beans were used in recipes, in what is claimed to be the oldest cookbook during the Roman civilization. For human nutrition, approximately 20 leguminous species are employed as dry grains. Among the legumes used, the most common one is soyabean, followed by lentil, chickpea, and cowpea, with soyabean being the most important, due to its high protein content (**Table 1**).

Sr. no	Legumes	Crude protein % (w/w)	Reference
1.	Soyabean	38	[3, 4]
2.	Lentil	26	[5]
3.	Chickpea	22	[3, 5]
4.	Cowpea	25	[6]

Table 1.
Crude protein content of commonly used legumes.

In comparison to animal protein sources, legume seeds are high in dietary fiber, which is good for gut health [7]. They possess high nutritional value. Legumes are rich sources of good quality proteins, calories, certain minerals, fibers, vitamins and are cholesterol free. Thus, legumes have the potential to increase the nutritional quality of foods, and hence, efforts are underway for their integration into novel food preparations with improved nutritional and functional qualities [8].

Proteins or peptides derived from legumes have played a significant role, beyond simply providing amino acids for growth and tissue repair. The role of legume proteins in the general growth and maintenance of living organisms is well documented. However, little is known about the beneficial effects of peptides derived from legumes.

2.1 Antioxidant property of peptides

Bioactive peptides are amino acid sequences, that exert beneficial effects in the body to improve human health beyond their nutritional values [9, 10]. These peptides can have antioxidative, antimicrobial, anticarcinogenic, or anti-inflammatory activities, based on their sequence and size. The antioxidant activity can be defined as metal chelating or radical scavenging properties, which have a direct or indirect impact on the inhibition of free radical generation. Intake of such bioactive peptides can minimize the risk of chronic diseases [11, 12].

Environment-friendly processes like enzymatic hydrolysis are preferred to chemical hydrolysis as it results in bioactive peptides [13, 14]. The most frequently used commercial proteolytic enzymes are papain, pancreatin, trypsin, chymotrypsin, and bromelain. The high antioxidant activity of soy hydrolysate obtained after proteolytic digestion has been well documented earlier [15]. In a recent study, an enzyme formulation, PepzymeAG has been shown, to not only improve the digestion of pea protein, but also result in peptides with antioxidant and antidiabetic properties [16]. Peptides are therefore gaining importance and their use is expanding, in nutraceuticals and pharmaceuticals products.

Antioxidant properties of peptides can be assessed by different methods viz. DPPH (2,2-diphenyl-1-picrylhydrazyl), ABTS (2,2′-azino-bis(3-ethylbenzothiazoline-6-sulfonate) etc. Purification and identification of specific peptides and/or amino acids with antioxidant activities are needed to expand their application in the food and pharmaceutical industries.

3. Digestion of proteins into amino acids

Proteins cannot be absorbed by the digestive tract as is. Several proteolytic enzymes are at play in the digestive system of mammals. In the acidic condition of the stomach, pepsin has optimum activity. The pancreas secrete proteolytic enzymes, like trypsin and chymotrypsin, which function at a higher pH of 8–9. Due to the action of these proteolytic enzymes, proteins are digested into oligopeptides and then amino acids (**Figure 1**). The amino acids available are of great importance in nutrition.

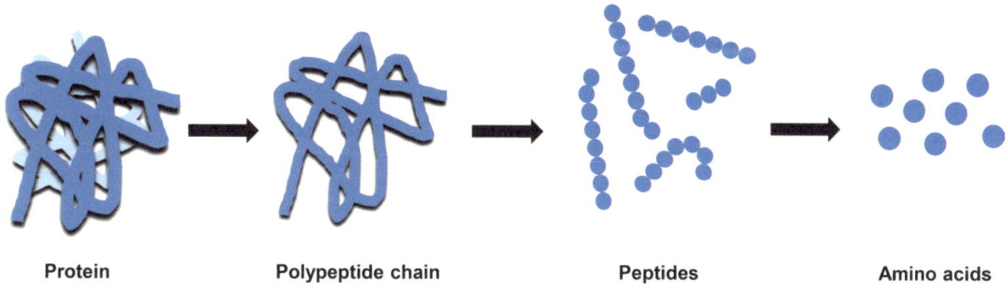

Figure 1.
Digestion of proteins into peptides and amino acids.

3.1 Essential amino acids

An essential amino acid, or indispensable amino acid, is an amino acid that cannot be synthesized from scratch by the organism fast enough to supply its demand, and must therefore come from the diet. The essential amino acids (EAAs), (e.g., arginine, methionine, lysine, leucine, isoleucine, tryptophan, valine, threonine, phenylalanine, and histidine) cannot be produced endogenously, so 10–20 mg/kg body weight of each must be obtained in the diet each day from consumed protein [17]. Moreover, dietary protein sources must provide the whole range of EAAs since proteins deficient in one or more EAAs generate an unpleasant eating response, resulting in a

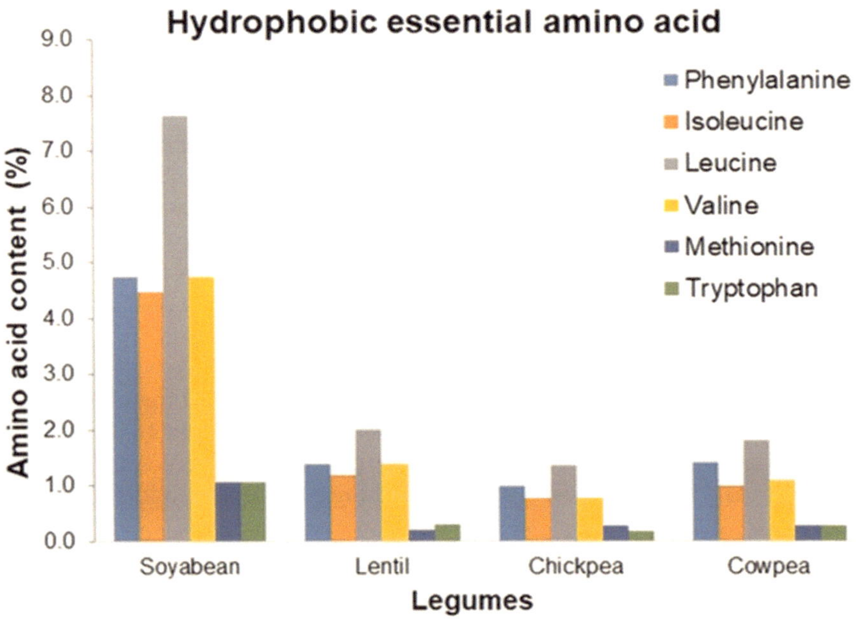

Figure 2.
Hydrophobic essential amino acid profile in different legumes.

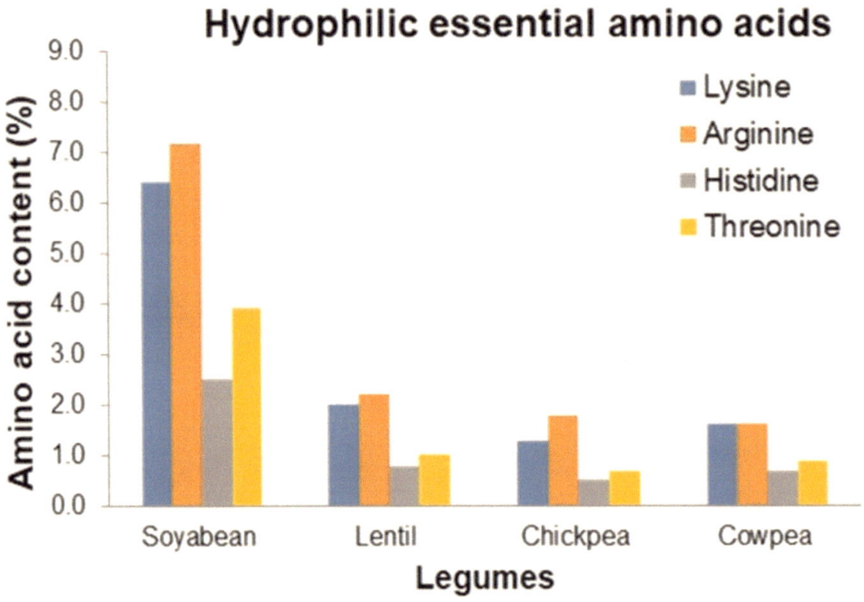

Figure 3.
Hydrophilic essential amino acid profile in different legumes.

considerable decline in diet consumption. **Figures 2** and **3** illustrate all the hydrophobic and hydrophilic essential amino acids, present in easily accessible legumes such as soyabean, chickpea, cow pea, and lentils.

The following percent of their contents in soyabean grain are documented in the reference literature: Leucine is approximately 7.6% of crude protein and lysine is about 6.3% of crude protein whereas valine, isoleucine and phenylalanine are around 4.7% each, of crude protein [18]. When compared to animal proteins, soyabean protein has a lower amount of sulfur containing amino acids. Legume proteins, with the exception of soyabean (*Glycine max*), are considered incomplete due to a lack of key sulfur-containing amino acids (methionine and cysteine). To compensate for this deficiency, legume proteins are supplemented with cereal proteins, which are low in lysine but high in methionine and cysteine [3].

3.2 Protein digestibility evaluation method

Although legume-derived proteins are nutritionally adequate, their protein quality and digestibility remain an issue [19]. WHO recommends that in order to support optimal health and growth, humans should consume high quality proteins [20]. Protein quality is the ability of dietary proteins to fulfill the metabolic needs of the body, thus quality matrices are governed by the content of limiting amino acids in food and their digestibility [21]. Limiting amino acids are those amino acids that do not meet the minimal requirement of the body and need to be included in a diet.

Different regulatory bodies across the world (US-FDA, Canadian food inspection agency) use protein quality information to determine 'Protein Digestibility'. From a consumer point of view, protein quality claims can influence the perception of health benefits of the product. Therefore, nowadays, commercial protein powders often provide protein content claims in the form of a digestibility score.

Protein digestibility can be defined as the fraction of protein that is available for absorption after it is ingested. It is a measure of the bioavailability of the protein. High digestibility is dependent on the hydrolysis of peptide bonds that are characteristic of proteins. The digestibility of plant proteins is lower (<80%) than animal proteins (≥90%) [22]. A joint FAO/WHO (Food and Agricultural organization/ World Health Organization) expert consultation committee proposed the first method for protein quality evaluation in 1990, the Protein digestibility-corrected amino acid score (PDCAAS).

$$\text{PDCAAS\%} = \frac{(\text{mg of first limiting amino acid in 1 g test protein})}{(\text{mg of the same amino acid in 1 g reference protein})} \times \text{TD} \times 100$$

Here, true digestibility (TD) $= \frac{I-F-Fk}{I}$

I = protein intake of rats fed Test diet

F = protein excreted in feces of rats fed Test diet

Fk = protein excreted of rats fed protein-free diet.

However, in 2011, FAO/WHO made a recommendation that the new protein quality measure (digestible indispensable amino acid score; DIAAS) replace the old PDCAAS.

$$\text{DIAAS\%} = \frac{(\text{mg of digestable dietary indispensable amino acid in 1 g of the dietary protein})}{(\text{mg of the same dietary indispensable amino acid in 1 g of the reference protein})} \times 100$$

There are many reasons why this shift has been recommended, two of them were the superior scoring method and the accurate sampling method [23–25]. For instance, the PDCAAS score of Whey Protein Isolate (WPI) and Soy Protein Isolate (SPI) is 1 and 0.98 (no significant difference). But the DIAAS score of WPI's is 1.09 and for SPI it reduces to 0.90. This gives a clear distinction of protein quality and in turn helps to make informed decisions. Knowledge of the IAA (Indispensable amino acid) content from protein sources, is not sufficient to accurately determine the requirement of the type of amino acid, because it varies with respect to physiological conditions, age etc. Therefore, FAO concludes that the current data of digestibility is insufficient and suggests that additional data is required, on ileal digestibility of human foods, determined in animal as well as human models [25].

Other alternate ways to determine protein digestibility, such as *in vitro* digestion methods that are less time consuming, controllable and easy to perform are INFOGEST, and *in vitro* PDCAAS [26, 27]. In a recent study, INFOGEST was used to study the digestion of pea proteins using enzymes under simulated gastrointestinal conditions [16].

4. Factors affecting protein digestibility (extrinsic and intrinsic factors)

The full benefits of legumes depend on how easily the proteins are digested. Proteins are polymers of amino acids. Amino acids are linked together by a peptide bond formed between the amino group of one amino acid and the carboxyl group of the adjacent amino acid. The sequence of amino acids defines its primary structure. The organization of amino acids into secondary and tertiary structures is what defines the ultimate protein structure, an attribute that is unique and dependent on the primary structure. The polypeptide chain is not linear, but adopts a three-dimensional structure and can be interlinked via disulphide bonds, making for a stable structure. Breakdown of this structure is required before peptides or amino acids can be released, either by internal digestion or by processing methods.

Different legumes contain different types of proteins. Hence, the increase in digestibility of legume proteins varies, depending on the type of protein they contain. When compared to animal proteins, the digestibility of legume protein is low. Among legumes, there are variances in the digestibility of proteins, with ease of digestibility increasing in the following order: soyabean, lentil, chickpea and common bean [7, 8]. Protein structure and functionality, compartmentalization, the permeability of cell walls, the protective seed coat, and enzyme accessibility are all important aspects of this trait.

The digestibility of proteins, can be influenced by several factors that can be classified as extrinsic factors or intrinsic factors. Extrinsic factors include pH, temperature, ionic strength conditions, and the food matrix, as well as the presence of secondary molecules present in the environment of the protein. Intrinsic factors are those factors that contribute to the inherent property of the protein, and impart its characteristics. These include protein amino acid sequence and protein structural characteristics. Furthermore, growth conditions (e.g., drought and heat stress) can influence both internal and exterior elements throughout plant development [28, 29]. The pre-harvest characteristics influencing plant protein digestibility, on the other hand, are beyond the scope of this chapter.

4.1 Extrinsic factors

Extrinsic factors can affect the digestibility of legume proteins: these include interaction with other compounds such as carbohydrates, lipids, and antinutritional factors like tannins, phytates, trypsin inhibitors and lectins. These are described in detail, in another section in this chapter. In the seed matrix, proteins are complexed with other compounds like phenolic compounds and carbohydrates, causing a physical entrapment of cellular structures that shield the proteins from the action of proteases. Drulyte et al. suggested that cell wall rigidity and fiber content may influence protein digestibility. Particle size reduction disrupts the cell wall integrity; thus, the reported improvement of digestibility attributed to milling could also be due to the alteration of the cell wall, which enhances legume seed protein digestibility [30]. In a study, by Melito et al., physical or enzymatic removal of the cell walls enhanced legume digestion by up to 50%. This shows that physiological barriers such as the cell wall have an impact on protein digestion [31].

4.2 Intrinsic factors

The low digestibility of legume proteins is attributed to their amino acid composition and protein quaternary structure. Proline-rich regions often diminish protein chain flexibility and are renowned for their high resistance to peptidase hydrolysis. Legume seed storage proteins are classified into globulins, albumins, glutelins, and prolamins according to their solubility properties in water, salted water, or ethanol/water solutions. Among these, globulins and albumins are the most abundant proteins found in legumes. Albumins are soluble in water. Examples of albumin proteins are Kunitz trypsin inhibitor and Bowman-Birk trypsin/chymotrypsin inhibitors [8].

Globulins are extracted in salt solutions, and represent approximately 70% of legume seed proteins. They consist mainly of the 7S proteins called vicilins, and 11S proteins called legumins, [32]. Soyabean protein contains three major fractions such as 2S, 7S, and 11S. In soyabean, 11S and 7S fractions represent approximately 70% of total protein. 11S fraction consists only of glycinin, which typically exists as a hexamer and 7S fraction majorly consists of β-conglycinin. The molecular weight of seed proteins ranges from 8 to 600 kDa [33]. Albumins have a molecular weight ranging from 50 to 80 kDa. These proteins generally exist in oligomeric form. The 7S globulins are typically trimers of molecular weight about 150 kDa, while the 11S proteins form hexamers of molecular weight about 350–400 kDa, or higher association of subunits, such as the 15–18S globulins found in soyabean globulins [34].

One of the factors influencing the stability of proteins, is their secondary structure. In legumes proteins, the predominant secondary structure is the β-sheet conformation, as compared to the α-helix structure [35]. This β-sheet conformation contributes to its resistance to proteolysis in the gastrointestinal tract. The β-sheet structure of legume proteins is a contributing factor to aggregation which occurs during the processing of legume proteins. Protein aggregation affects the biological value and technological usefulness of the raw materials when used in food production. Another contributing factor to increased stability is the presence of disulphide bonds, formed between the polypeptide chains. Globulins showed better *in vitro* digestibility than albumins due to the presence of lower cysteine content and hence less number of disulphide bond as compared to albumins [7, 36].

The amino acid sequence of a protein determines the type of peptides formed on digestion. Peptidases have a high specificity for hydrolysing peptide bonds that are next to a specific type of amino acid. In processing, the sequence of peptides formed, depends on the legume protein used, and the specificity of the enzyme used. This determines the antioxidant activity of the resultant peptide. **Figure 4** shows an outline for the production of peptides, produced by enzymatic methods.

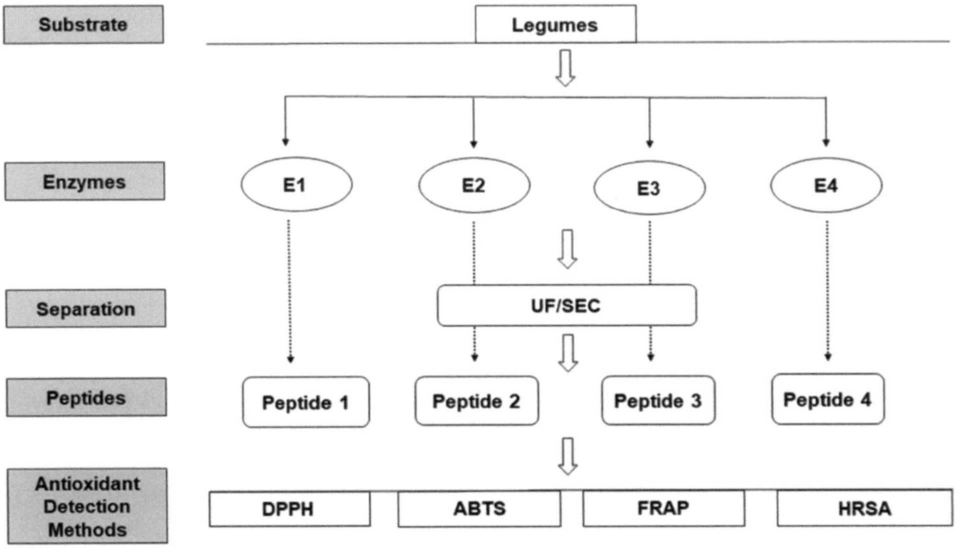

Figure 4.
Digestion of proteins into peptides by specific enzymes and selection for antioxidant property. Abbreviations: *E (different enzymes), UF (ultrafiltration), SEC (size-exclusion chromatography), DPPH (2,2-diphenyl-1-picrylhydrazyl), ABTS (2,2′-azino-bis,3-ethyl benzoline-6-sulfonic acid), HRSA (hydroxyl radical scavenging activity).*

5. Enhancement of protein digestibility using enzymatic treatment

Protein hydrolysis includes the breakage of peptide bonds, resulting in smaller peptides and free amino acids, which improves digestibility and functional characteristics [37]. Chemical hydrolysis (by acids or alkalis) has significant drawbacks since it can produce harmful amino acid residues (e.g., lysinoalanine) and produce goods with lower nutritional quality [38, 39]. Protein enzymatic hydrolysis by enzymes was previously used in the food industry to enhance the biological value and functional qualities of these molecules [40]. Protein hydrolysates produced by enzymatic treatment (e.g., cellulases, hemicellulases, proteases) may improve protein availability and digestibility by reducing undesired compounds found in legumes [38, 40, 41]. Proteases (or peptidases) have been used to improve product nutritional value by modifying protein structures [39, 42]. Protein hydrolysis has been shown to lower protein antigenicity, increase tolerance, and create peptides that do not stimulate *in vitro* IgE antibody binding activity, therefore decreasing allergenicity.

Protein enzymatic hydrolysis was found to be effective in enhancing protein solubility, foaming capacity and stability, and gelation capability [38, 39]. However, there are some challenges with the application of protein hydrolysates, because protein hydrolysis can result in the formation of hydrophobic peptides, which causes the development of bitterness and off-flavors, negatively impacting taste and limiting the use of protein hydrolysates in food products [37].

To improve the availability of protein in fava beans, enzymatic treatments were performed in four cultivars (ON, OPNS, TAL and VC3). The greatest change was observed in the OPNS cultivar treated with protease, which increased its digestibility from 54.4% (control treatment) to 81.6% [40]. Legume preparations when treated with pepsin/pancreatin in an *in vitro* digestion simulation, have resulted in 20–46% increase in the degree of hydrolysis [43].

6. Problems encountered in the digestion of legumes

6.1 Insufficient digestive enzymes

Digestive enzymes are synthesized by the stomach, small intestine, and pancreas. The pancreas have an essential role in the digestion, absorption, and metabolism of carbohydrates, fats, and proteins hence is the enzyme "powerhouse" of digestion. Insufficient secretion of digestive enzymes by the pancreas is called exocrine pancreatic insufficiency. Some enzyme insufficiencies are genetic, hereditary and congenital or develop over time, and with age. Any impairment of digestive enzymes over a prolonged period results in deficiencies of vitamins and minerals, gastrointestinal irritation, malnutrition, and complications, leading to poor quality of life.

Impaired enzyme-related digestion can be alleviated by prescription digestive enzymes. These over-the-counter digestive enzyme supplements are used to treat health issues such as acid reflux, gas, bloating and diarrhea. Enzyme supplements, like VegPeptase™ can be used to improve the digestibility of legumes. These supplements aid in better digestion of "hard-to-digest" proteins in food and absorption of nutrients. Pancreatic enzyme replacement therapy is the most popular and the only FDA-approved enzyme replacement therapy (PERT). PERT is the use of medications that contain enzymes to replace what the pancreas is deficient in producing. These medications contain proteases, amylases and lipases. Microbial sources of enzymes viz. cellulase, protease, and lipase can be used to improve digestion and access the required nutrients, when shifting to a plant-based diet. Similarly, plant-sourced enzymes like bromelain (from pineapple) and papain (from papaya) are proteolytic enzymes, which are included in many digestive formulas. They have an additional use as systemic enzymes and against inflammation. This helps people follow a less restricted diet on a long term basis.

6.2 Antinutritional factors (ANFs)

One of the main factors affecting the protein digestibility of legumes is the presence of antinutritional factors. Antinutritional factors are compounds that are known to affect the digestibility and thus impair the nutritional quality of various foods, including legume food proteins [44]. These antinutritional factors are present in unprocessed food or foods, as a result of processing (e.g., Maillard reaction products in soyabean-based products) [45]. Major antinutritional factors, which are found in legumes include saponins, tannins, phytic acid, gossypol, lectins, protease inhibitors, amylase inhibitors, and goitrogens [46]. These antinutritional factors cause unfavorable effects when consumed in large quantities. They are also known to cause allergic responses in some individuals, which is a cause for concern [47]. Thus, the exclusion or deactivation of these antinutritional factors and allergenic compounds can promote protein digestibility.

Among the ANFs found in legumes, the following are known to interfere with protein digestion in humans and animals: protease inhibitors (trypsin inhibitors), tannins, lectins, and phytic acid (**Figure 5**).

6.2.1 Protease inhibitors (trypsin inhibitors)

One of the main ANFs found in legumes are protease inhibitors. They are small proteins, which have evolved as defense strategies in plants [48]. As the name

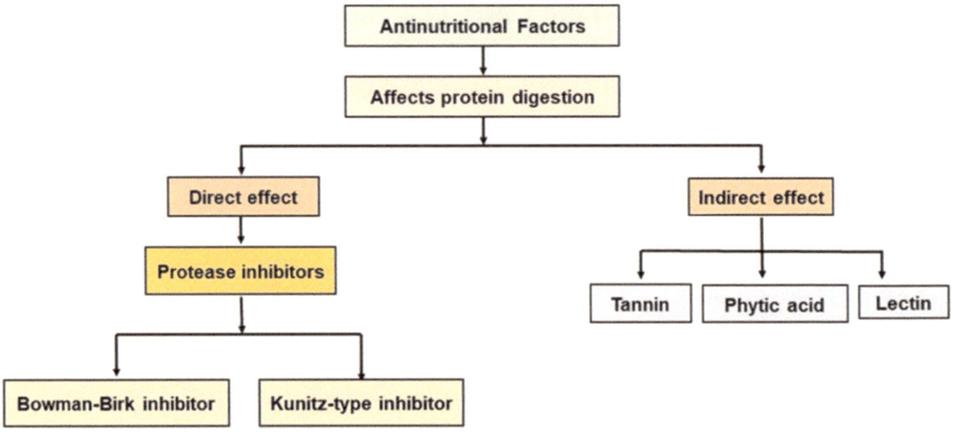

Figure 5.
Antinutritional factors that interfere in protein digestion.

suggests, these inhibitors inhibit the action of proteases in mammals, thus impairing protein digestion [49] and affecting the nutritional value of foods [50].

Trypsin and chymotrypsin are the main proteases, in the lumen of the upper gastrointestinal tract, where they exercise their digestive functions [51]. The presence of trypsin inhibitors in the diet leads to the formation of irreversible enzyme-trypsin inhibitor complexes. These complexes are indigestible, even in the presence of high amounts of digestive enzymes [52]. Trypsin inhibitors block the active site of trypsin/ chymotrypsin, through the N- or C-terminus and exposed loop [51], effectively preventing these enzymes from acting on the protein substrate (**Figure 6**). Therefore, when legumes are eaten raw or without being cooked properly, they upset digestive functions and cause diarrhea or excessive gas [52]. In such cases, even

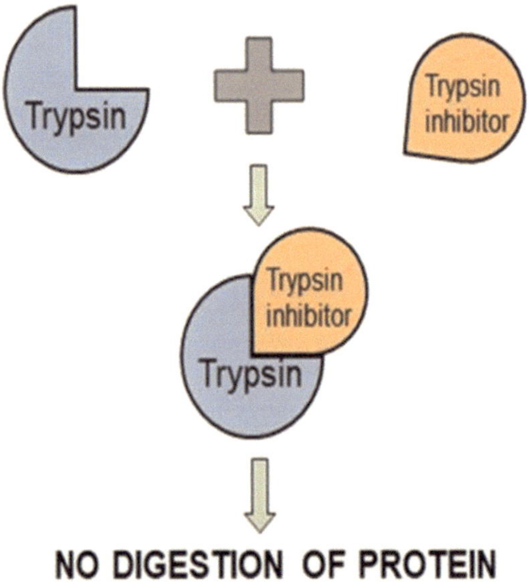

Figure 6.
Trypsin inhibitor competitively binds with trypsin, and prevents it from digesting the protein.

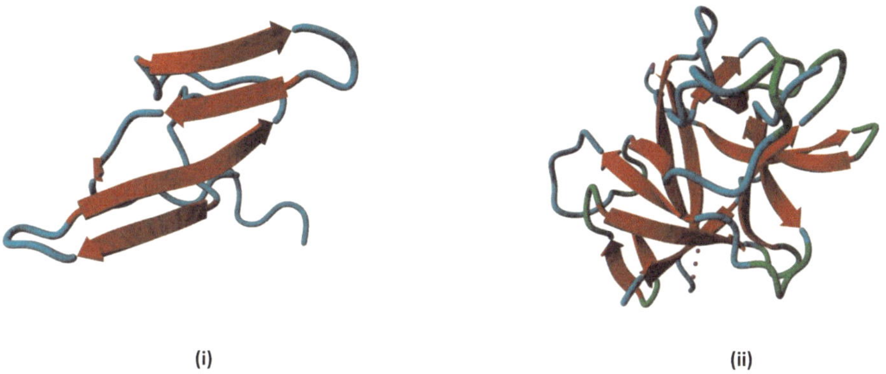

Figure 7.
Protein structure of trypsin inhibitors, (i) Bowman-Birk inhibitor (BBI), and (ii) Kunitz-type inhibitor, from soyabean. Images are prepared using PDB ids, 1BBI and 6NTT, using YASARA, version 22.9.24. The beta sheets are depicted in red.

Antinutritional factors	Concentration in raw soyabean seeds
Protease inhibitors	25–50 mg/g
Glycinin	150–200 mg/g
β-conglycinin	50–100 mg/g
Lectins	2100–3500 ppm
Phytic acid	6 mg/g

Table 2.
Antinutritional factors in raw soyabean seeds [58].

though the intake of protein is high, the complete mobilization of amino acids is prevented.

In legumes, the trypsin inhibitor content ranges from 3 to 84 U/mg, while the chymotrypsin inhibitor content varies from 0 to 17 U/mg [53, 54]. The prominent trypsin inhibitors in legumes are the Bowman-Birk inhibitor and Kunitz-type inhibitor (**Figure 7**) [55–57]. Kunitz-type inhibitor (molecular weight 18–24 kDa) and Bowman-Birk inhibitors (molecular weight 7–9 kDa) are both capable of inhibiting trypsin and chymotrypsin enzymes. In soyabeans, glycinin and β-conglycinin constitute 65–80% of the protein fraction or 25–35% of the soya seed weight (**Table 2**) [59]. Because of their predominant beta-barrel structure, they are very stable.

6.2.2 Lectins

Lectins are proteins that have specificity for carbohydrates. When combined with the glycoprotein components of red blood cells, they cause agglutination of the cells. Lectins bind to epithelial membrane of glycoproteins, such as brush-border membrane enzymes, gangliosides, glycolipids, receptors, secreted mucins, and transport proteins [60]. They disturb intestinal permeability and interfere with the absorption of digestive end products in the small intestine [61]. Protein digestion is affected, leading to nitrogen loss; the undigested and unabsorbed proteins in the small intestines reach the colon where they are fermented to short chain fatty acids and release gases leading to gastrointestinal disorders. The affected intestinal permeability allows the entrance of the bacteria and their endotoxins into the bloodstream, causing a toxic response. Moreover, lectins may also be internalized directly and cause systemic effects. They can disrupt protein, carbohydrate, and lipid metabolism [62]. Lectins are also resistant to heat and digestive processes, during their intestinal passage their activity is retained [63].

6.2.3 Phytic acid

Phytic acid (myo-inositol-1,2,3,4,5,6-hexakis dihydrogen phosphate) (**Figure 8a**), is a secondary compound found in plant seeds of legumes [64]. Generally, phytates contain about 50–80% of the total phosphorus present in the seeds [65]. Due to its chelating property, phytic acid complexes with metal ions, like iron, magnesium and calcium, reducing their bioavailability, and resulting in mineral ion deficiencies in human nutrition [66, 67]. In addition, phytic acid interferes with the digestion of proteins. In both acidic and basic pH, phytic acid forms a complex with proteins and alters the protein conformation. It also binds trypsin and thus affects the action of trypsin on proteins [68–70].

6.2.4 Tannins

Tannins are located in the layer between the external tegument and the aleuronic layer inside the seeds, protecting the plant embryo from mechanical and oxidative damage and maintaining its dormancy [71]. They are also present in plant leaves, fruits, and bark [72].

The consumption of tannins can cause hardening of the gastrointestinal mucosa, resulting in reduced nutrient absorption. Tannins affect protein digestibility, by forming reversible and irreversible complexes between the hydroxyl group of tannins (**Figure 8b**) and the carbonyl group of proteins, leading to a decrease in essential amino acid availability [28, 73, 74]. These complexes are relatively large and hydrophobic in nature [75]. The breakdown products constitute a large number of compounds, which can be toxic. In the oral cavity, tannins bind to proline-rich proteins in saliva, and this helps to protect dietary and endogenous protein. However, in the

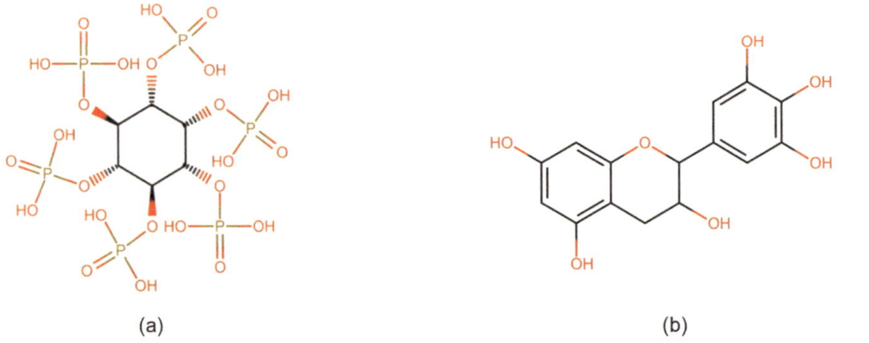

Figure 8.
(a) Chemical structure of phytic acid (b) Chemical structure (basic unit) of tannin. (chemical structures are prepared using Marvin JS).

absence of sufficient salivary secretion, tannins are then free to interact with digestive enzymes [76, 77]. Tannins are known to inhibit the digestion of proteins by 28% [46].

6.3 Methods to eliminate antinutritional factors

Some of the common methods employed to diminish or eliminate antinutritional factors include soaking, heating, cooking, germination, fermentation, extraction, irradiation, and enzymatic treatment [78]. The application of a single technique is frequently insufficient for effective treatment and so combinations of methods are usually employed. These treatments can be classified based on the processing techniques—physical, chemical, biological and enzymatic.

6.3.1 Physical treatment

Soaking overnight is the most common method used to reduce the antinutritional content in legumes and improve their nutritional value. Most of the antinutrients in these foods are found in the upper layer. Since many are water-soluble, they can be eliminated by prolonged soaking. In legumes, soaking has been found to decrease phytate, protease inhibitors, lectins, and tannins. Soaking is typically used in combination with other methods, like thermal treatment, germination, and fermentation.

Thermal treatments, like cooking, boiling, autoclaving and microwave cooking are the most popular methods for processing legumes, because it improves protein digestibility. Processing by heat is an effective technique to limit ANFs and improve nutrient digestibility in legumes [79]. Heating results in denaturation of the protein, an increase in surface area and exposure of cleavage sites that are otherwise inaccessible to protease enzymes [80]. Thus, a reduction in the concentration of ANFs, due to heat treatment is responsible for improved protein digestibility [81].

However, not all heat treatment is advantageous. Excessive or intensive heating may result in the degradation of heat sensitive amino acids and micronutrients and limit their bioavailability [30]. It may also lead to the formation of new products called neoantigens, which can elicit an allergic response. These neoantigens result from the Maillard reaction, by interaction of proteins with sugar residues upon heating [33]. Allergenic legume proteins elicit an allergenic response by surviving the acidic gastric conditions and action of digestive proteases. However, many are resistant to heat. Allergenic proteins in peanut are heat-resistant, while those in soya are partially heat-stable.

6.3.2 Biological treatment

During the germination of legume seeds, enzymes like amylase, protease, and lipase are activated to degrade starch, storage-protein and proteinaceous antinutritional factors. Germination is reported to suppress the amount of phytate, tannins, and trypsin inhibitors in different legume seeds [82], thus improving protein digestibility.

Fermentation is a traditional technique, where microorganisms facilitate enzymatic reactions that reduce the antinutrient content and thus increase the digestibility of plant proteins [83–85]. During this process, hard-to-digest proteins, like glycinin and β-conglycinin, of soyabean, are hydrolyzed to bioactive peptides. This results in improved solubility and hence higher protein digestibility of complex storage proteins [86]. This reduces the levels of undigested proteins that can cause food allergies [87]. Unfortunately, the microorganisms involved in the fermentation process can also utilize amino acids and proteins, resulting in the loss of amino acids and proteins [85]. Therefore, due to lack of specificity and optimum conditions, which could lead to maximum protein digestibility with minimal loss of protein, the use of this technique remains unpredictable. Future food processing methods may need to incorporate techniques that reduce these antinutritional factors, and are economically feasible, for both the environment and customers.

6.3.3 Enzymatic treatment

The universal use of enzymes in food and feed processing is due to their unmatched specificity, operating under mild conditions of pH, temperature and pressure while displaying high activity, high turnover numbers and high biodegradability [88]. Thus, the application of enzymes is considered as a promising approach for plant protein modifications. Major groups of enzymes used in food applications are proteases, amylases, and lipases for the manipulation of proteins, starch, and lipids, respectively. Proteases can enhance protein digestibility by reducing the amount of trypsin inhibitors [38, 40, 41] and lectins. Phytase may also be applied in the industrial processing of soyabean to prepare certain foods for human consumption. Phytases have gained attention in human nutrition, especially to counteract zinc and iron deficiencies [89], by improving their bioavailabilities [90]. Saito et al. have developed a novel process for removal of the major soyabean storage proteins β-conglycinin and glycinin, using phytase added to defatted soy milk at pH 6 with incubation at 40°C [91]. Phytic acid reduction by bioprocessing as a tool for improving the *in vitro* digestibility of fava bean flour has been demonstrated by Rosa-Sibakov et al. The improvement in protein digestibility was dose dependent and correlated to phytic acid content reduction, which explains the influence of enzymatic phytase treatment and LAB (lactic acid bacteria) fermentation on food digestibility, protein quality and protein solubility [92].

Food security is a global issue; hence increasing the nutritional value of food that is underutilized, will be an important part of the solution. Therefore, it will be interesting to explore the potential of enzymes in legume processing for human and animal health.

6.4 Legumes in animal nutrition

Legumes are used as a protein source in animal nutrition. Soyabean is the most important protein source in poultry and swine diets. Legumes are increasingly being used as a sustainable replacement for fish meals in aquafeed and pet diets. Globally, approximately 98 percent of soyabean meal is used as animal feed. Among the most significant ANFs in animal nutrition, are the trypsin inhibitors, found in raw soyabeans. By interfering with trypsin and chymotrypsin activity, they impair digestion in monogastric animals and some young ruminant animals [93]. Other young monogastric, such as swine, have also responded to soyabean meal, with reduced growth performance [94, 95]. Trypsin inhibitors have deleterious effects on animals. They result in stunted growth, reduced feed efficiency and pancreatic hypertrophy [93]. Lectins attach to mucosa cells damaging the intestinal wall and reducing the absorption of nutrients [63]. Glycinin and β-conglycinin are two allergenic soyabean proteins that are not digested easily. Glycinin damages intestinal morphology, causing intestinal atrophy and necrosis [94, 96, 97]. β-conglycinin causes a hypersensitive immune response and negatively affects the growth performance of animals [98, 99]. Other antinutritional factors like tannins cause decreased feed consumption in animals, as they bind dietary protein and digestive enzymes to form complexes that are not readily digestible [100], reducing palatability and growth rate [101]. Higher concentrations of undigested protein, result in fermentation in the distal intestinal tract of poultry, and are attributed to the proliferation of pathogenic bacteria such as *Clostridium perfringens* [102–105], leading to diseases like coccidiosis and necrotic enteritis. Coccidiosis is the most frequently reported and economically important poultry-related disease worldwide [106].

6.4.1 Use of enzymes in animal feed

Monogastrics lack endogenous enzymes to break down soyabean anti-nutrients [107, 108]. Animal feed is not processed and hence ANFs that would normally be reduced in human nutrition by pre-processing, are not eliminated before they are consumed. Moreover heat treatment greatly reduces the nutritional value of the feed. Hence, an effective treatment to counteract these ill effects of ANFs, is the use of exogenous enzymes, added as feed additives to soyabean meal (SBM). Since trypsin inhibitors are proteins, they can be broken down and eliminated by the action of proteases. In an interesting study, protease inclusion in broiler diets, led to improved nutrient digestibility and upregulation of growth-related genes [109]. Enzyme supplementation of proteases (e.g., DigeGrain Pro 6), thus improves growth performance, by increasing protein digestibility. This results in better utilization of the protein content in the feed, leading to minimum wastage.

6.4.2 Use of legumes as an alternative to fish meal

Fish meal, due to its high protein content and palatability is the primary choice of feed in aquaculture [110, 111]. Small fishes like sardines and anchovies are extensively used for fishmeal, leading to overfishing and depletion of fish stocks in the oceans. In addition to not being a sustainable source of feed ingredient, fishmeal is associated with high cost, and hence alternative sources of protein and energy need to be investigated. Hence, recent research has focussed on the evaluation of plant proteins like soyabean meal, lupin meal, and various legumes (cowpea, green mung bean, rice bran) [112–115] as ingredients in feeds for aquatic animals. In diets where fishmeal was replaced by SBM (30%) in the feed of European seabass, optimum growth and feed utilization was maintained. No case of enteritis was observed in histological analysis, and nutritional status was similar as with fish meal [116]. Soy white flakes, a product obtained during soybean processing, was used to prepare aquafeed with suitable properties (lower water absorption and higher solubility indices, high durability, lower bulk density) [117]. Fermentation of SBM by a bacterial strain *Shewanella sp. MR-7*, prior to feeding, led to improved performance and alleviation of soy-related inflammation, caused due to ANFs [118]. In another study, the use of protease allowed slightly lower protein content to be used in the feed of Nile tilapia. Growth parameters, feed intake and feed conversion efficiency was unaffected. As an added benefit, water quality was improved due to lower ammonia and nitrite content [119].

Thus the replacement of fish meal with SBM, when coupled with protease treatment can avoid problems associated with trypsin inhibitors, use proteins efficiently and prevent excretion of undigested products that lead to contamination of water.

7. Conclusion

In 2022, the world population touched 8 billion and is estimated to reach 9.7 billion by 2050 [120]. An increase in legume production by ~25% is needed to fulfill the protein demand of the world's population. Legumes have the additional advantage of having a low GHG footprint. However, efficient processes, both *in vitro* and *in vivo* must be employed in order to unlock the potential of legumes in nutrition. The use of enzymatic treatment, not only offers a greener alternative but also added health benefits. In spite of several health benefits, a considerable number of people are reluctant to include legumes in their daily diet. To increase the popularity of legumes in the diet, future research must focus on processes that improve the taste and texture of legume preparations, without stripping them of vital nutrition. The problem of low content of essential amino acids like methionine, can be circumvented by genetic engineering of legumes to increase the synthesis of amino acids like methionine, through metabolic engineering or through the engineering of legume proteins so that they contain higher concentrations of methionine.

The use of legumes coupled with enzymatic treatment in animal feed, will prevent unnecessary use of antibiotics and culling of animals due to disease, while improving their overall health, and result in economic benefits. Recently, the food systems have been threatened by the three C's, i.e., climate change, conflict, and Covid-19 pandemic [121]. The solution then lies, in maximizing the use of resources. Rather than following the mantra "more is better", optimum use of resources, is the need of the hour. Large production volatility and lesser profitability, relative to other crops are barriers to expanded legume use. A future transition to using legumes as a primary source of dietary protein may be made possible by increased consumer knowledge and investment in growing new varieties of legumes. Moreover, breeding of drought resistant varieties will enable legumes to be grown locally, and avoid dependence on supply chains. Overall, improving the protein digestibility of legumes will allow complete utilization of its nutritional components, prevent the wastage of food, and contribute to sustainability.

Acknowledgements

We thank Anil R. Narooka for his assistance in preparation of figures.

Conflict of interest

The authors declare no conflict of interest.

Abbreviations

ANFs	antinutritional factors
ABTS	2,2′-azino-bis (3-ethylbenzothiazoline-6-sulfonic acid)
BBI	Bowman-Birk inhibitor
DIAAS	Digestible indispensable amino acid score
DPPH	2,2-diphenyl-1-picrylhydrazyl

EAA	essential amino acid
FAO	Food and Agricultural Organization
FAOSTAT	Food and Agriculture Organization Corporate Statistical Database
FDA	food and drug administration
FRAP	ferric reducing antioxidant power
GHG	greenhouse gases
HRSA	hydroxyl radical scavenging activity
INFOGEST	an international network of excellence on the fate of food in the gastrointestinal tract
IgE	immunoglobulin type E
IAA	indispensable amino acid
LAB	lactic acid bacteria
ON	Ouro Negro
OPA	o-phthalaldehyde
OPNS	OP-NS-331
PDCAAS	protein digestibility corrected amino acid score
PERT	pancreatic enzyme replacement therapy
Ppm	parts per million
mg/g	milligram per gram
SBM	soyabean meal
SPI	soy protein isolate
SEC	size exclusion chromatography
TAL	Talisma
TCA	trichloroacetic acid
TD	true digestibility
UF	ultrafiltration
UN	United Nations
U/mg	Unit per milligram
VC3	VC-3
WHO	World Health Organization
WPI	Whey Protein Isolate

Author details

Stephanie A. Misquitta*, Deepika N. Kshirsagar, Pooja R. Dange,
Vikram G. Choudhari and Mukund M. Kabra
Advanced Enzymes Technologies Ltd., Thane, Maharashtra, India

*Address all correspondence to: stephanie@advancedenzymes.com

References

[1] FAOSTAT. Available from: https://www.fao.org/faostat/en/#home [Accessed: December 15, 2022]

[2] Klupšaitė D, Juodeikienė G. Legume: Composition, protein extraction and functional properties. A review. ChemTech. 2015;**66**(1):5-12. DOI: 10.5755/j01.ct.66.1.12355

[3] Maphosa Y, Jideani VA. The role of legumes in human nutrition. In: Functional Food-Improve Health Through Adequate Food. Vol. 1. Rijeka: IntechOpen; 2017. p. 13. DOI: 10.5772/intechopen.69127

[4] Messina MJ. Legumes and soybeans: Overview of their nutritional profiles and health effects. The American Journal of Clinical Nutrition. 1999;**70**(3):439s-450s. DOI: 10.1093/ajcn/70.3.439s

[5] Bessada SMF, Barreira JCM, Oliveira MBPP. Pulses and food security: Dietary protein, digestibility, bioactive and functional properties. Trends in Food Science and Technology. 2019;**93**: 53-68

[6] Gondwe TM, Alamu EO, Mdziniso P, Maziya-Dixon B. Cowpea (*Vigna unguiculata* (L.) Walp) for food security: An evaluation of end-user traits of improved varieties in Swaziland. Scientific Reports. 2019;**9**:15991. DOI: 10.1038/s41598-019-52360-w

[7] Carbonaro M, Maselli P, Nucara A. Structural aspects of legume proteins and nutraceutical properties. Foodservice Research International. 2015;**76**:19-30. DOI: 10.1016/j.foodres.2014.11.007

[8] Carbonaro M, Nucara A. Legume proteins and peptides as compounds in nutraceuticals: A structural basis for dietary health effects. Nutrients. 2022;**14**(6):1188. DOI: 10.3390/nu14061188

[9] Akbarian M, Khani A, Eghbalpour S, Uversky VN. Bioactive peptides: Synthesis, sources, applications, and proposed mechanisms of action. International Journal of Molecular Sciences. 2022;**23**(3): 1445. DOI: 10.3390/ijms23031445

[10] Kitts DD, Weiler K. Bioactive proteins and peptides from food sources. Applications of bioprocesses used in isolation and recovery. Current Pharmaceutical Design. 2003;**9**(16): 1309-1323. DOI: 10.2174/1381612033454883

[11] Li Y, Jiang B, Zhang T, Mu W, Liu J. Antioxidant and free radical-scavenging activities of chickpea protein hydrolysate (CPH). Food Chemistry. 2008;**106**(2): 444-450. DOI: 10.1016/j.foodchem.2007.04.067

[12] Fan H, Liu H, Zhang Y, Zhang S, Liu T, Wang D. Review on plant-derived bioactive peptides: Biological activities, mechanism of action and utilizations in food development. Journal of Future Foods. 2022;**2**(2):143-159. DOI: 10.1016/j.jfutfo.2022.03.003

[13] Ashaolu TJ. Applications of soy protein hydrolysates in the emerging functional foods: A review. International Journal of Food Science and Technology. 2020;**55**(2):421-428. DOI: 10.1111/ijfs.14380

[14] Gao MT, Hirata M, Toorisaka E, Hano T. Acid-hydrolysis of fish wastes for lactic acid fermentation. Bioresource Technology. 2006;**97**(18): 2414-2420. DOI: 10.1016/j.biortech.2005.10.002

[15] Liu TX, Zhao M. Physical and chemical modification of SPI as a potential means to enhance small peptide contents and antioxidant activity found in hydrolysates. Innovative Food Science and Emerging Technologies. 2010;**11**(4):677-683. DOI: 10.1016/j.ifset.2010.08.004

[16] Jadhav SB, Gaonkar T, Rathi A. In vitro gastrointestinal digestion of proteins in the presence of enzyme supplements: Details of antioxidant and antidiabetic properties. LWT. 2021;**147**: 111650. DOI: 10.1016/j.lwt.2021.111650

[17] Orgeron ML, Stone KP, Wanders D, Cortez CC, Van NT, Gettys TW. The impact of dietary methionine restriction on biomarkers of metabolic health. Progress in Molecular Biology and Translational Science. 2014;**121**:351-376. DOI: 10.1016/B978-0-12-800101-1.00011-9

[18] Kudełka W, Kowalska M, Popis M. Quality of soybean products in terms of essential amino acids composition. Molecules. 2021;**26**(16):5071. DOI: 10.3390/molecules26165071

[19] Gharibzahedi SMT, Smith B. The functional modification of legume proteins by ultrasonication: A review. Trends in Food Science and Technology. 2020;**98**:107-116. DOI: 10.1016/j.tifs.2020.02.002

[20] Joint FAO/WHO/UNU Expert Consultation on Protein and Amino Acid Requirements in Human Nutrition (2002: Geneva S, Nations F and AO of the U, Organization WH, University UN. Protein and Amino Acid Requirements in Human Nutrition: Report of a Joint FAO/WHO/UNU Expert Consultation. Geneva: World Health Organization; 2007. Available from: https://apps.who.int/iris/handle/10665/43411

[21] Katz DL, Doughty KN, Geagan K, Jenkins DA, Gardner CD. Perspective: The public health case for modernizing the definition of protein quality. Advances in Nutrition. 2019;**10**(5): 755-764. DOI: 10.1093/advances/nmz023

[22] Gomes SD, Fuess LT, Mañunga T, Feitosa de Lima Gomes PC, Zaiat M. Bacteriocins of lactic acid bacteria as a hindering factor for biohydrogen production from cassava flour wastewater in a continuous multiple tube reactor. International Journal of Hydrogen Energy. 2016;**41**(19): 8120-8131. DOI: 10.1016/j.ijhydene.2015.11.186

[23] Hertzler SR, Lieblein-Boff JC, Weiler M, Allgeier C. Plant proteins: Assessing their nutritional quality and effects on health and physical function. Nutrients. 2020;**12**(12):3704. DOI: 10.3390/nu12123704

[24] Shivakumar N, Jackson AA, Courtney-Martin G, Elango R, Ghosh S, Hodgkinson S, et al. Protein quality assessment of follow-up formula for young children and ready-to-use therapeutic foods: Recommendations by the FAO Expert Working Group in 2017. The Journal of Nutrition. 2020;**150**(2): 195-201. DOI: 10.1093/jn/nxz250

[25] Dietary Protein Quality Evaluation in Human Nutrition: Report of an FAO Expert Consultation [on Protein Quality Evaluation in Human Nutrition]; 31 March–2 April, 2011; Auckland, New Zealand. Rome, Food and Agriculture Organization of the United Nations; 2013. 64 p. (FAO Food and Nutrition Paper)

[26] Minekus M, Alminger M, Alvito P, Ballance S, Bohn T, Bourlieu C, et al. A standardised static in vitro digestion method suitable for food—An international consensus. Food &

Function. 2014;**5**(6):1113-1124. DOI: 10.1039/c3fo60702j

[27] Tavano OL, Neves VA, da Silva Júnior SI. In vitro versus in vivo protein digestibility techniques for calculating PDCAAS (protein digestibility-corrected amino acid score) applied to chickpea fractions. Food Research International. 2016;**89**(Pt 1):756-763. DOI: 10.1016/j.foodres.2016.10.005

[28] Joye I. Protein digestibility of cereal products. Foods. 2019;**8**(6):199. DOI: 10.3390/foods8060199

[29] Impa SM, Perumal R, Bean SR, Sunoj VSJ, Jagadish SVK. Water deficit and heat stress induced alterations in grain physico-chemical characteristics and micronutrient composition in field grown grain sorghum. Journal of Cereal Science. 2019;**86**:124-131. DOI: 10.1016/j.jcs.2019.01.013

[30] Drulyte D, Orlien V. The effect of processing on digestion of legume proteins. Food. 2019;**8**(6):224. DOI: 10.3390/foods8060224

[31] Melito C, Tovar J. Cell walls limit in vitro protein digestibility in processed legume seeds. Food Chemistry. 1995; **53**(3):305-307. DOI: 10.1016/0308-8146(95)93937-M

[32] Nath A, Ahmad AS, Amankwaa A, Csehi B, Mednyánszky Z, Szerdahelyi E, et al. Hydrolysis of soybean milk protein by papain: Antioxidant, anti-angiotensin, antigenic and digestibility perspectives. Bioengineering. 2022;**9**(9): 418. DOI: 10.3390/bioengineering9090418

[33] Bennetau-Pelissero C. Plant proteins from legumes. In: Mérillon JM, Ramawat KG, editors. Bioactive Molecules in Food. Cham: Springer International Publishing; 2019. pp. 223-265. (Reference Series in Phytochemistry). Available from: http://link.springer.com/10.1007/978-3-319-78030-6_3

[34] Yang J, Zamani S, Liang L, Chen L. Extraction methods significantly impact pea protein composition, structure and gelling properties. Food Hydrocolloids. 2021;**117**:106678. DOI: 10.1016/j.foodhyd.2021.106678

[35] Shevkani K, Singh N, Chen Y, Kaur A, Yu L. Pulse proteins: Secondary structure, functionality and applications. Journal of Food Science and Technology. 2019;**56**(6):2787-2798. DOI: 10.1007/s13197-019-03723-8

[36] Ohanenye IC, Ekezie FGC, Sarteshnizi RA, Boachie RT, Emenike CU, Sun X, et al. Legume seed protein digestibility as influenced by traditional and emerging physical processing technologies. Food. 2022; **11**(15):2299. DOI: 10.1016/j.tifs.2020.05.003

[37] Liceaga AM, Hall F. Nutritional, functional and bioactive protein hydrolysates2019. DOI: 10.1016/B978-0-08-100596-5.21776-9

[38] Potier M, Tomé D. Comparison of digestibility and quality of intact proteins with their respective hydrolysates. Journal of AOAC International. 2008;**91**(4):1002-1005. DOI: 10.1093/jaoac/91.4.1002

[39] Vaz Patto MC, Amarowicz R, Aryee ANA, Boye JI, Chung HJ, Martín-Cabrejas MA, et al. Achievements and challenges in improving the nutritional quality of food legumes. Critical Reviews in Plant Sciences. 2015;**34**(1–3):105-143. DOI: 10.1080/07352689.2014.897907

[40] Dias DR, de Abreu CMP, Silvestre MPC, Schwan RF. In vitro

protein digestibility of enzymatically pre-treated bean (*Phaseolus vulgaris* L.) flour using commercial protease and Bacillus sp. protease. Food Science and Technology. 2010;**30**(1):94-99. DOI: 10.1590/S0101-20612010005000010

[41] Fawale OS, Gbadamosi SO, Ige MM, Kadiri O. Effects of cooking and fermentation on the chemical composition, functional, and antinutritional properties of kariya (*Hildergardia barteri*) seeds. Food Science & Nutrition. 2017;**5**(6):1106-1115. DOI: 10.1002/fsn3.501

[42] Kapravelou G, Martínez R, Andrade AM, Sánchez C, Chaves CL, López-Jurado M, et al. Health promoting effects of Lupin (*Lupinus albus* var. *multolupa*) protein hydrolyzate and insoluble fiber in a diet-induced animal experimental model of hypercholesterolemia. Foodservice Research International. 2013;**54**(2):1471-1481. DOI: 10.1016/j.foodres.2013.10.019

[43] Torres J, Rutherfurd SM, Muñoz LS, Peters M, Montoya CA. The impact of heating and soaking on the in vitro enzymatic hydrolysis of protein varies in different species of tropical legumes. Food Chemistry. 2016;**194**:377-382. DOI: 10.1016/j.foodchem.2015.08.022

[44] Sarwar Gilani G, Wu Xiao C, Cockell KA. Impact of antinutritional factors in food proteins on the digestibility of protein and the bioavailability of amino acids and on protein quality. The British Journal of Nutrition. 2012;**108**(Suppl 2):S315-S332. DOI: 10.1017/S0007114512002371

[45] Samtiya M, Aluko RE, Dhewa T. Plant food anti-nutritional factors and their reduction strategies: An overview. Food Production, Processing and Nutrition. 2020;**2**(1):6. DOI: 10.1186/s43014-020-0020-5

[46] Ohanenye IC, Tsopmo A, Ejike CECC, Udenigwe CC. Germination as a bioprocess for enhancing the quality and nutritional prospects of legume proteins. Trends in Food Science and Technology. 2020;**101**:213-222. DOI: 10.1016/j.tifs.2020.05.003

[47] Mookerjee A, Tanaka T. Influence of enzymatic treatments on legume proteins for improved functional and nutritional properties: Expansion of legume protein utilization as food ingredients. Current Opinion in Food Science. 2023;**49**:100974. DOI: 10.1016/j.cofs.2022.100974

[48] Adeleye OO, Awodiran ST, Ajayi AO, Ogunmoyela TF. Effect of high-temperature, short-time cooking conditions on in vitro protein digestibility, enzyme inhibitor activity and amino acid profile of selected legume grains. Heliyon. 2020;**6**(11):e05419. DOI: 10.1016/j.heliyon.2020.e05419

[49] Hill GD. Plant antinutritional factors: characteristics. In: Encyclopedia of Food Science and Nutrition. Amsterdam: Elsevier; 2003. pp. 4578-4587. DOI: 10.1016/B0-12-227055-X/01318-3

[50] Muzquiz M, Varela A, Burbano C, Cuadrado C, Guillamón E, Pedrosa MM. Bioactive compounds in legumes: Pronutritive and antinutritive actions. Implications for nutrition and health. Phytochemistry Reviews. 2012;**11**(2/3):227-244. DOI: 10.1007/s11101-012-9233-9

[51] Vergnolle N. Protease inhibition as new therapeutic strategy for GI diseases. Gut. 2016;**65**(7):1215-1224. DOI: 10.1136/gutjnl-2015-309147

[52] Thakur A, Sharma V, Thakur A. An overview of anti-nutritional factors in food. International Journal of Chemical Studies. 2019;7(1):2472-2479

[53] Pasqualone A, Costantini M, Coldea TE, Summo C. Use of legumes in extrusion cooking: A review. Food. 2020; **9**(7):958. DOI: 10.3390/foods9070958

[54] Pedrosa MM, Guillamón E, Arribas C. Autoclaved and extruded legumes as a source of bioactive phytochemicals: A review. Food. 2021; **10**(2):379. DOI: 10.3390/foods10020379

[55] Kårlund A, Paukkonen I, Gómez-Gallego C, Kolehmainen M. Intestinal exposure to food-derived protease inhibitors: Digestion physiology- and gut health-related effects. Healthcare (Basel). 2021;**9**(8):1002. DOI: 10.3390/healthcare9081002

[56] Werner MH, Wemmer DE. Three-dimensional structure of soybean trypsin/chymotrypsin Bowman-Birk inhibitor in solution. Biochemistry. 1992; **31**(4):999-1010. DOI: 10.1021/bi00119a008

[57] McPherson A, Day J, Larson SB. Lattice interactions in crystals of soybean trypsin inhibitor (Kunitz) produced by inclusion of 1,5-disulfonylnaphthalene. Crystal Growth and Design. 2019;**19**(5):2963-2969. DOI: 10.1021/acs.cgd.9b00164

[58] U.S. Soybean Export Council, Author at U.S. Soy. U.S. Soy. Available from: https://ussoy.org/author/ussoy/

[59] Hammond EG, Murphy PA, Johnson LA. Soy (soya) beans | properties and analysis. In: Encyclopedia of Food Sciences and Nutrition. Amsterdam: Elsevier; 2003. pp. 5389-5392. Available from: https://linkinghub.elsevier.com/retrieve/pii/B012227055X011111

[60] Pusztai L, Lewis CE, Lorenzen J, McGee JO. Growth factors: Regulation of normal and neoplastic growth. The Journal of Pathology. 1993;**169**(2):191-201

[61] Banwell JG, Howard R, Kabir I, Costerton JW. Bacterial overgrowth by indigenous microflora in the phytohemagglutinin-fed rat. Canadian Journal of Microbiology. 1988;**34**(8):1009-1013. DOI: 10.1139/m88-177

[62] Fereidoon S. Beneficial health effects and drawbacks of antinutrients and phytochemicals in foods. Applied Microbiology and Biotechnology. 2014;**97**:45-55. DOI: 10.1021/bk-1997-0662.ch001

[63] Pusztai A, Ewen SWB, Grant G, Peumans W, Damme E, Bardocz S. Relationship between survival and binding of plant lectins during small intestinal passage and their effectiveness as growth factors. Digestion. Digestion. 1990;**46**(Suppl 2):308-316. DOI: 10.1002/path.1711690204

[64] García-Estepa RM, Guerra-Hernández E, García-Villanova B. Phytic acid content in milled cereal products and breads. Foodservice Research International. 1999;**32**(3):217-221. DOI: 10.1016/S0963-9969(99)00092-7

[65] JNA L, Ockenden I, Raboy V, Batten GD. Phytic acid and phosphorus in crop seeds and fruits: A global estimate. Seed Science Research. 2000; **10**(1):11-33. DOI: 10.1017/S096025 8500000039

[66] Grases F, Simonet BM, Prieto RM, March JG. Dietary phytate and mineral bioavailability. Journal of Trace Elements in Medicine and Biology. 2001; **15**(4):221-228. DOI: 10.1016/S0946-672X (01)80037-7

[67] Bora P. Anti-nutritional factors in foods and their effects. Journal of Academia and Industrial Research. 2014; **3**(6):285-290

[68] Nissar J, Ahad T, Hussain S, Naik HR. A Review Phytic Acid: As Antinutrient or Nutraceutical. Journal of Pharmacognosy and Phytochemistry.2017;**6**(6):1554-1560

[69] Kies AK, De Jonge LH, Kemme PA, Jongbloed AW. Interaction between protein, phytate, and microbial phytase. In vitro studies. Journal of Agricultural and Food Chemistry. 2006;**54**(5): 1753-1758. DOI: 10.1021/jf0518554

[70] Lathia D, Hoch G, Kievernagel Y. Influence of phytate on in vitro digestibility of casein under physiological conditions. Plant Food for Human Nutrition. 1987;**37**(3):229-235. DOI: 10.1007/BF01091787

[71] Demonsais L, Utz-Pugin A, Loubéry S, Lopez-Molina L. Identification of tannic cell walls at the outer surface of the endosperm upon Arabidopsis seed coat rupture. The Plant Journal. 2020;**104**(3):567-580. DOI: 10.1111/tpj.14994

[72] Timotheo CA, Lauer CM. Toxicity of vegetable tannin extract from *Acacia mearnsii* in *Saccharomyces cerevisiae*. International Journal of Environmental Science and Technology. 2018;**15**(3):659-664. DOI: 10.1007/s13762-017-1430-z

[73] Lampart-Szczapa E, Siger A, Trojanowska K, Nogala-Kalucka M, Malecka M, Pacholek B. Chemical composition and antibacterial activities of lupin seeds extracts. Die Nahrung. 2003;**47**(5):286-290. DOI: 10.1002/food.200390068

[74] Raes K, Knockaert D, Struijs K, van Camp J. Role of processing on bioaccessibility of minerals: Influence of localization of minerals and anti-nutritional factors in the plant. Trends in Food Science and Technology. 2014; **37**(1):32-41. DOI: 10.1016/j.tifs.2014.02.002

[75] Frutos P, Hervás G, Giráldez FJ, Mantecón AR. Review. Tannins and ruminant nutrition. Spanish Journal of Agricultural Research. 2004;**2**(2): 191-202. DOI: 10.5424/sjar/2004022-73

[76] Jansman AJ, Frohlich AA, Marquardt RR. Production of proline-rich proteins by the parotid glands of rats is enhanced by feeding diets containing tannins from faba beans (*Vicia faba* L.). The Journal of Nutrition. 1994;**124**(2):249-258. DOI: 10.1093/jn/124.2.249

[77] Haile M, Asquith TN, Butler LG, Rogler JC, Carlson DM. Tannin-mediated induction of proline-rich protein synthesis. Journal of Agricultural and Food Chemistry. 1992;**40**(1):93-97. DOI: 10.1021/jf00013a018

[78] Khokhar S, Apenten RK. Anti-nutritional factors in Food Legumes and effects of processing. In: Squires VR, editor. The Role of Food, Agriculture, Forestry and Fisheries in Human Nutrition. Oxford, UK: Encyclopedia of Life Support Systems; 2003. pp. 82-116

[79] Alonso R, Aguirre A. Effect of extrusion and traditional processing methods on antinutrients and in vitro digestibility of protein and starch in faba and kidney bean. Food Chemistry. 2000; **68**:159-165. DOI: 10.1016/S0308-8146(99)00169-7

[80] Day L. Proteins from land plants—Potential resources for human nutrition and food security. Trends in Food

Science and Technology. 2013;**32**(1): 25-42. DOI: 10.1016/j.tifs.2013.05.005

[81] van der Poel A, Thomas FB, Stolp W, Van Zuilichem DJ. Twin-screw extrusion of two pea varieties: Effects of temperature and moisture level on antinutritional factors and protein dispersibility. Journal of Science and Food Agriculture. 1992;**58**(1):83-87. DOI: 10.1002/jsfa.2740580114

[82] Sangronis E, Machado CJ. Influence of germination on the nutritional quality of *Phaseolus vulgaris* and *Cajanus cajan*. LWT–Food Science and Technology. 2007;**40**(1):116-120. DOI: 10.1016/j.lwt.2005.08.003

[83] Ali MAM, El Tinay AH, Abdalla AH. Effect of fermentation on the in vitro protein digestibility of pearl mille. Food Chemistry. 2003;**80**(1):51-54. DOI: 10.1016/s0308-8146(02)00234-0

[84] El Hag ME, El Tinay AH, Yousif NE. Effect of fermentation and dehulling on starch, total polyphenols, phytic acid content and in vitro protein digestibility of pearl millet. Food chemistry. 2002;**77**: 193-196. DOI: 10.1016/S0308-8146(01)00336-3

[85] Pranoto Y, Anggrahini S, Efendi Z. Effect of natural and *Lactobacillus plantarum* fermentation on in-vitro protein and starch digestibilities of sorghum flour. Food Bioscience. 2013;**2**:46-52. DOI: 10.1016/j.fbio.2013.04.001

[86] Babar VS, Chavan JK, Kadam SS. Effects of heat treatments and germination on trypsin inhibitor activity and polyphenols in jack bean (*Canavalia ensiformis* L. DC). Plant Foods for Human Nutrition. 1988;**38**(4):319-324. DOI: 10.1007/BF01091729

[87] Untersmayr E, Jensen-Jarolim E. The role of protein digestibility and antacids on food allergy outcomes. The Journal of Allergy and Clinical Immunology. 2008; **121**(6):1301-1308; quiz 1309–10. DOI: 10.1016/j.jaci.2008.04.025

[88] Fernandes P. Enzymes in food processing: A condensed overview on strategies for better biocatalysts. Enzyme Research. 2010;**2010**:862537. DOI: 10.4061/2010/862537

[89] Kaur P, Kunze G, Satyanarayana T. Yeast phytases: Present scenario and future perspectives. Critical Reviews in Biotechnology. 2007;**27**(2):93-109. DOI: 10.1080/07388550701334519

[90] Zimmermann MB, Hurrell RF. Improving iron, zinc and vitamin A nutrition through plant biotechnology. Current Opinion in Biotechnology. 2002; **13**(2):142-145. DOI: 10.1016/s0958-1669(02)00304-x

[91] Saito T, Kohno M, Tsumura K, Kugimiya W, Kito M. Novel method using phytase for separating soybean beta-conglycinin and glycinin. Bioscience, Biotechnology, and Biochemistry. 2001;**65**(4):884-887. DOI: 10.1271/bbb.65.884

[92] Rosa-Sibakov N, Re M, Karsma A, Laitila A, Nordlund E. Phytic acid reduction by bioprocessing as a tool to improve the in vitro digestibility of faba bean protein. Journal of Agricultural and Food Chemistry. 2018;**66**(40): 10394-10399. DOI: 10.1021/acs.jafc.8b02948

[93] Liener IE. Implications of antinutritional components in soybean foods. Critical Reviews in Food Science and Nutrition. 1994;**34**(1):31-67. DOI: 10.1080/10408399409527649

[94] Li DF, Nelssen JL, Reddy PG, Blecha F, Klemm R, Goodband RD.

Interrelationship between hypersensitivity to soybean proteins and growth performance in early-weaned pigs. Journal of Animal Science. 1991; **69**(10):4062-4069. DOI: 10.2527/1991.69104062x

[95] Friesen KG, Goodband RD, Nelssen JL, Blecha F, Reddy DN, Reddy PG, et al. The effect of pre- and postweaning exposure to soybean meal on growth performance and on the immune response in the early-weaned pig. Journal of Animal Science. 1993; **71**(8):2089-2098. DOI: 10.2527/1993.7182089x

[96] Zhao Y, Qin GX, Sun ZW, Zhang B, Wang T. Effects of glycinin and β-conglycinin on enterocyte apoptosis, proliferation and migration of piglets. Food and Agricultural Immunology. 2010;**21**(3):209-218

[97] Zhao Y, Qin G, Sun Z, Zhang X, Bao N, Wang T, et al. Disappearance of immunoreactive glycinin and beta-conglycinin in the digestive tract of piglets. Archives of Animal Nutrition. 2008;**62**(4):322-330. DOI: 10.1080/17450390802190318

[98] Chen L, Gao LX, Huang QH, Lu QP, Sa RN, Zhang HF. Prediction of digestible energy of feed ingredients for growing pigs using a computer-controlled simulated digestion system. Journal of Animal Science. 2014;**92**(9):3887-3894. DOI: 10.2527/jas.2013-7092

[99] Zhu J, Gao M, Zhang R, Sun Z, Wang C, Yang F, et al. Effects of soybean meal fermented by *L. plantarum*, *B. subtilis* and *S. cerevisieae* on growth, immune function and intestinal morphology in weaned piglets. Microbial Cell Factories. 2017;**16**(1):191. DOI: 10.1186/s12934-017-0809-3

[100] Aletor VA. Allelochemicals in plant foods and feedingstuffs: 1. Nutritional, biochemical and physiopathological aspects in animal production. Veterinary and Human Toxicology. 1993;**35**(1):57-67

[101] Roeder E. Medicinal plants in Europe containing pyrrolizidine alkaloids. Die Pharmazie. 1995;**50**(2): 83-98

[102] Bryan DDLS, Abbott DA, Classen HL. The influence of indigestible protein on the performance and meat quality of broilers vaccinated for coccidiosis. Poultry Science. 2019; **98**(10):4815-4828. DOI: 10.3382/ps/pez216

[103] Kocher A, Choct M, Ross G, Broz J, Chung TK. Effects of enzyme combinations on apparent metabolizable energy of corn-soybean meal-based diets in broilers. Journal of Applied Poultry Research. 2003;**12**(3):275-283. DOI: 10.1093/japr/12.3.275

[104] Irish GG, Balnave D. Non-starch polysaccharides and broiler performance on diets containing soyabean meal as the sole protein concentrate [chickens]. Australian Journal of Agricultural Research (Australia). 1993;**44**:1483-1499. DOI: 10.1071/AR9931483

[105] Marsman GJ, Gruppen H, van der Poel AF, Kwakkel RP, Verstegen MW, Voragen AG. The effect of thermal processing and enzyme treatments of soybean meal on growth performance, ileal nutrient digestibilities, and chyme characteristics in broiler chicks. Poultry Science. 1997;**76**(6):864-872. DOI: 10.1093/ps/76.6.864

[106] Dalloul RA, Lillehoj HS. Poultry coccidiosis: Recent advancements in control measures and vaccine development. Expert Review of

Vaccines. 2006;**5**(1):143-163. DOI: 10.1586/14760584.5.1.143

[107] M H. Quality of soybean meals (SBM) and effect of microbial enzymes in degrading soya antinutritional compounds (ANC). 2nd International Soybean Processing and Utilization Conference; 1996; Bangkok, Thailand. 1996; Available from: https://cir.nii.ac.jp/crid/1573105975187739008

[108] Jørgensen H, Zhao XQ, Eggum BO. The influence of dietary fibre and environmental temperature on the development of the gastrointestinal tract, digestibility, degree of fermentation in the hind-gut and energy metabolism in pigs. The British Journal of Nutrition. 1996;**75**(3):365-378. DOI: 10.1079/bjn19960140

[109] Park JH, Lee SI, Kim IH. The effect of protease on growth performance, nutrient digestibility, and expression of growth-related genes and amino acid transporters in broilers. Journal of Animal Science and Technology. 2020; **62**(5):614-627. DOI: 10.5187/jast.2020.62.5.614

[110] Henry M, Gasco L, Piccolo G, Fountoulaki E. Review on the use of insects in the diet of farmed fish: Past and future. Animal Feed Science and Technology. 2015;**203**:1-22. DOI: 10.1016/j.anifeedsci.2015.03.001

[111] Chakrabarti S, Guha S, Majumder K. Food-derived bioactive peptides in human health: Challenges and opportunities. Nutrients. 2018; **10**(11):1738. DOI: 10.3390/nu10111738

[112] Ramachandran S, Ray AK. Nutritional evaluation of fermented black gram (*Phaseolus mungo*) seed meal in compound diets for rohu, Labeo rohita (Hamilton), fingerlings. Journal of Applied Ichthyology. 2007;**23**(1):74-79. DOI: 10.1111/j.1439-0426.2006.00772.x

[113] Latif KA, Alam MT, Sayeed MA, Hussain MA, Sultana S, Hossain MA. Comparative study on the effects of low cost oil seed cakes and fish meal as dietary protein sources for *Labeo rohita* (Hamilton) fingerling. University Journal of Zoology, Rajshahi University. 2008;**27**:25-30. DOI: 10.3329/ujzru.v27i0.1949

[114] Lim SJ, Lee KJ. Supplemental iron and phosphorus increase dietary inclusion of cottonseed and soybean meal in olive flounder (*Paralichthys olivaceus*). Aquaculture Nutrition. 2008; **14**(5):423-430. DOI: 10.1111/j.1365-2095.2007.00546.x

[115] Tahir MZI, Ahmed I, Mateen A, Ashraf M, Hussain Z, Ali H. Studies on partial replacement of fish meal with oilseeds meal in the diet of major carps. International Journal of Agriculture & Biology. 2008;**10**(4):455-458

[116] Bonvini E, Bonaldo A, Mandrioli L, Sirri R, Dondi F, Bianco C, et al. Effects of feeding low fishmeal diets with increasing soybean meal levels on growth, gut histology and plasma biochemistry of sea bass. Animal. 2018; **12**(5):923-930. DOI: 10.1017/S1751731117002683

[117] Singh SK, Muthukumarappan K. Effect of feed moisture, extrusion temperature and screw speed on properties of soy white flakes based aquafeed: A response surface analysis. Journal of the Science of Food and Agriculture. 2016;**96**(6):2220-2229. DOI: 10.1002/jsfa.7339

[118] Li C, Zhang B, Wang X, Pi X, Wang X, Zhou H, et al. Improved

utilization of soybean meal through fermentation with commensal Shewanella sp. MR-7 in turbot (*Scophthalmus maximus* L.). Microbial Cell Factories. 2019;**18**(1):214. DOI: 10.1186/s12934-019-1265-z

[119] Saleh ESE, Tawfeek SS, Abdel-Fadeel AAA, Abdel-Daim ASA, Abdel-Razik ARH, Youssef IMI. Effect of dietary protease supplementation on growth performance, water quality, blood parameters and intestinal morphology of Nile tilapia (*Oreochromis niloticus*). Journal of Animal Physiology and Animal Nutrition. 2022; **106**(2):419-428. DOI: 10.1111/jpn.13591

[120] Nations U. World population to reach 8 billion on 15 November 2022. United Nations. United Nations. Available from: https://www.un.org/en/desa/world-population-reach-8-billion-15-november-2022

[121] Devos Y, Arena M, Ashe S, Blanck M, Bray E, Broglia A, et al. Addressing the need for safe, nutritious and sustainable food: Outcomes of the "ONE – Health, Environment & Society—Conference 2022". Trends in Food Science and Technology. 2022;**129**: 164-178. DOI: 10.1016/j.tifs.2022.09.014

Chapter 8

Weed Management in Pulses: Overview and Prospects

Rajan Sagar Chaudhary and Suman Dhakal

Abstract

Pulses, the world's second-most consumed food, are an important source of food. They face several major challenges, including weed infestations, as a wide variety of weeds compete with them. Because of their competition with weeds, pulses can suffer a significant yield reduction. So as to alleviate such a menace, growers rely on different management tools, such as tillage, intercropping systems, and herbicides. Each method has been effective, albeit to varying degrees, in resolving the issue. Chemical herbicides, however, have served as double-edged swords over the past few decades due to their indiscriminate use. The repetitive use of the same herbicide or herbicides with the same mode of action confers resistance, thereby, leading to a serious impact on only nontargets. Therefore, it requires well-thought-out planning for a weed management strategy to maximize yields without creating environmental issues concomitantly. At the present, the integrated weed management approach has been accepted as the most reasonable tool for many farmers, which includes using preventive strategies, mechanical tools, crop rotation, intercropping, and herbicides with different modes of action, but cautiously. Modeling and robotics are the cutting-edge technologies that growers will be using for weed management in the coming days, thanks to the advent of such new innovation.

Keywords: weed flora, herbicides, weed resistance, Site-Specific Weed Management (SSWM), AI-driven machines

1. Introduction

The Fabaceae or Leguminosae family, also referred to as the legume, pea, or bean family, is the third-largest group of flowering plants, with more than 20,000 species [1]. The term "pulse" is limited to the annual legume crops that are specifically grown for dried and edible seeds. Chickpea, cowpea, pigeon pea, faba beans, lentils, and dry beans are some of the types of pulses [2]. Pulses are the second-most consumed food crop in the world, right behind cereal grains. They are a crucial source of food for the poor, particularly in developing and underdeveloped countries. Moreover, pulse-based products are in high demand among consumers around the world due to the significant nutritional value for the human diet they offer in terms of protein and mineral quality and bioavailability [3]. Incorporated into cropping systems, pulses increase the efficiency of both water and nutrient use, as they can fix atmospheric nitrogen into soils and allow companion crops to use stratified soil water, thereby contributing to sustainability in crop production [4].

A total of 89.8 million metric tons of pulses were produced worldwide in 2020, with India being the largest pulse producer [5]. A wide range of pulse crops are cultivated around the world, including chickpea (Cicer arietinum), pigeonpea (Cajanus cajan), mungbean (Vigna radiata), urdbean (Vigna mungo), cowpea (*Vigna unguiculata*), lentil (Lens culinaris *Medikus ssp. culinaris*), horse gram (Macrotyloma uniflorum), French bean (Phaseolus vulgaris), and lathyrus (Lathyrus sativus). There have been major challenges in increasing total pulse production to meet its global demand due to both biotic and abiotic stresses. Since pulses take so long to reach maturity, weeds often get a head start on the crops and end up smothering them. Furthermore, most pulses are grown in conjunction with nonlegume crops, and 84% of that area is grown under rain-fed conditions. For this reason, pulses are vulnerable to a wide range of biotic and abiotic stresses [6]. Weed infestation in crops accounts for the highest yield loss, i.e., 34%, compared to the losses associated with any pests, such as insects and pathogens, depending upon crops and weed's emergence time, density and nature [7, 8]. Weeds not only reduce crop yields but also impede other agricultural operations and serve as an alternative host for a wide variety of pests and diseases. It is vital to bring the weed density below the threshold level and maximize the crop yield and quality. In this review article, a specific focus is given on pulse's weed control choices for growers at the present and in the days to come.

1.1 Major weed flora

Various types of weeds have been reported to be associated with pulse crops, varying with the agro-ecological conditions and practices of crop management. However, the most abundant ones are presented in **Table 1**. The type of weed flora and the level of infestation in the field determine the extent to which crop growth and yield are affected. Reference [9] reported that non-grass types and sedges had a greater impact on the case of pigeonpea and sorghum intercropping than grass types. *Cyperus rotundus* L., more commonly known as nut grass, is a rhizospheric competitor with its network of underground tubers and is most prevalent during the summer and wetter months. Lambs quarter (*Chenopodium album*) is the most common and destructive weed in pulse crops. It thrives quickly and easily disseminates through seeds carried by the breeze. It not only competes with them for moisture but also spreads viral diseases [10]. Furthermore, WSSA [11] is in agreement with the fact that the aforementioned weed is the most prevalent weed in gardens.

A better understanding of environmental practices is by either increasing germination to kill seedlings or suppressing germination [12]. As a strategy for depleting weed seed banks, Gallandt [13] suggests influencing seed germination. In a similar way, understanding weed phenology could lead to more specific control methods by accurately estimating when and how weed competition affects crop yield [14]. It is important to note that most studies on the biology and ecology of weeds are based on a small number of populations. One region's population, however, may differ from another due to differences in management practices, rainfall, climate, soil type, etc. Consequently, it is necessary to include multiple populations in future studies.

1.2 Crop loss

The reduction in yield due to weeds can be up to 97% (**Table 2**); however, it varies with crops, weed intensity, crop management practices, and agro-climatic conditions.

DOI: http://dx.doi.org/10.5772/intechopen.110208

Weeds	Family	Types	Seasons		
			Kharif	Winter	Spring/ Summer
Ageratum conyzoides	Asteraceae	Broad-leaf weed		*	
Amaranthus viridis	Amaranthaceae	Broad-leaf weed			*
Anagallis arvensis	Myrsinaceae	Broad-leaf weed		*	
Argemone maxicana	Papaveraceae	Broad-leaf weed		*	
Asphodelus tenuifolius	Asphodelaceae	Broad-leaf weed		*	
Avena ludoviciana	Poaceae	Narrow-leaf weed		*	
Carthamus oxycantha	Asteraceae	Broad-leaf weed		*	
Celosia argentea	Amaranthaceae	Broad-leaf weed	*		
Chenopodium album	Chemopodiaceae	Broad-leaf weed		*	*
Cleome viscose	Capparaceae	Broad-leaf weed	*		
Commelina benghalensis	Commelinaceae	Broad-leaf weed	*		
Convolvulus arvensis	Convovulaceae	Broad-leaf weed		*	
Coronopus didymus	Brassicaceae	Broad-leaf weed		*	
Cucumis trigonus	Cucurbitaceae	Broad-leaf weed	*		*
Cynodon dactylon	Poaceae	Narrow-leaf weed	*		*
Cyperus difformis	Cyperaceae	Sedge	*		
Cyperus iria	Cyperaceae	Sedge	*		
Cyperus rotundus	Cyperaceae	Sedge	*	*	*
Dactyloctenium aegyptium	Poaceae	Narrow-leaf weed			*
Digera arvensis	Poaceae	Narrow-leaf weed	*		
Digitaria sanguinalis	Poaceae	Narrow-leaf weed			*
Echinochloa colona	Poaceae	Narrow-leaf weed	*		
Echinochloa crus-gall	Poaceae	Narrow-leaf weed	*		
Eclipta alba	Asteraceae	Broad-leaf weed			*
Eleusine indica	Poaceae	Narrow-leaf weed			*
Eragrostis tenella	Poaceae	Narrow-leaf weed	*		
Euphorbia hirta	Euphorbiaceae	Broad-leaf weed	*		
Fimbristylis spp.	Cyperaceae	Narrow-leaf weed	*		
Fumaria parviflora	Papaveraceae	Broad-leaf weed		*	
Gnaphalium indicum	Asteraceae	Broad-leaf weed		*	
Lathyrus aphaca	Fabaceae	Broad-leaf weed		*	
Launaea nudicaulis	Asteraceae	Broad-leaf weed		*	
Lolium temulentum	Poaceae	Narrow-leaf weed		*	
Medicago denticulate	Fabaceae	Broad-leaf weed		*	
Melilotus alba	Fabaceae	Broad-leaf weed		*	

Weeds	Family	Types	Seasons		
			Kharif	Winter	Spring/ Summer
Panicum maximum	Poaceae	Narrow-leaf weed			*
Phalaris minor	Poaceae	Narrow-leaf weed		*	
Phyllanthus niruri	Phyllanthaceae	Broad-leaf weed	*		
Physalis minima	Solanaceae	Broad-leaf weed			*
Poa annua	Poaceae	Narrow-leaf weed		*	
Polygonum plebejum	Polygonaceae	Broad-leaf weed			*
Polypogon monspeliensis	Poaceae	Narrow-leaf weed		*	
Portulaca quadrifida	Portulacaceae	Broad-leaf weed			*
Rumex dentatus	Polygonaceae	Broad-leaf weed		*	
Saccharum spontaneum	Poaceae	Narrow-leaf weed	*		
Setaria glauca	Poaceae	Narrow-leaf weed	*		*
Solanum nigrum	Solanaceae	Broad-leaf weed		*	*
Sorghum halepense	Fabaceae	Narrow-leaf weed	*		
Spergula arvensis	Caryophllaceae	Broad-leaf weed		*	
Trianthema monogyna	Aizoaceae	Broad-leaf weed	*		*
Vicia hirsute	Fabaceae	Broad-leaf weed		*	
Vicia sativa	Fabaceae	Broad-leaf weed		*	

**Indicates the active season for the corresponding weeds. Source: [9].*

Table 1.
Significant weeds and their growing seasons associated with pulses.

Pulses	Critical period [15]	Yield loss (%)	
		Ali M. et al. [8]	Other references
Pigeon pea	15-60 DAS	21-97	31.0-52.8 [16]
Green Gram	15-30 DAS	40-50	38.6 [17]
Black gram	15-30 DAS	44-83	43.3 [18]
Chickpea	30-60 DAS	29-70	77.8 [19]
Lentil	30-60 DAS	70-87	37.7 [20]
Pea	30-45 DAS	25-35	50 [21]

Table 2.
Critical period and yield loss associated to major pulses.

2. Weed Management practices

Understanding weed biology and ecology is essential for developing a sustainable weed management program. We still lack fundamental information on many important species, necessitating additional research. Nevertheless, there are many approaches that have been put into practice in farmers' fields with the intention of limiting the effects of weeds in effective and economically sound ways.

2.1 Tillage

It is one of the oldest preventive measures to avoid weed infestation. It uproots and leaves weeds exposed, taking control of weeds by burying their seeds deep enough to impede their germination and altering the soil-based growing environment. Taking an effective approach to controlling perennial weeds requires covering them deeply in the soil or drying them out by starving tactics [22]. There are several methods of tillage that are applicable to pulses. However, the efficacy of tillage varies with its methods, as we can observe in **Table 3**.

The use of moldboard plows prior to sowing had no discernible impact on chickpea yield, as demonstrated by Barzegar et al. [24]. Their findings state that, compared to moldboard, disk harrows were more effective against yield loss. Nighttime (photocontrol) tillage has been proven to be advantageous over weed management; nonetheless, due to its inconsistent results, questions have arisen about its effectiveness [25].

2.2 Intercropping system

Intercropping has been identified to be an effective approach in establishing agricultural systems and enabling sustainable agriculture goals. Hiltbrunner et al. [26] concluded that one of the greatest benefits of intercropping systems is weed control. Intercropping increases soil surface cover and plant diversity, two principles that control weeds better than monocropping. It has been shown in several studies that intercropping improves yields and eliminates weeds. Banik et al. [27] found that planting wheat and chickpeas together increases total yield productivity, makes better use of the land, and keeps weeds from growing. **Table 4** shows the efficiency of different inter-cropping systems in managing weeds in pulses [28].

Furthermore, according to Rai et al. [29], in pigeonpea + blackgram, and pigeonpea + greengram intercropping systems, weed suppression efficiency was found to be 69.6% and 69.4%, respectively, which were significantly higher than that of pigeonpea monocropping. This finding also concurs with the conclusion that intercropping is superior to monoculture for reducing weed damage to crops.

Treatments	Weed density(No./0.25m^2)			Weed control efficiency (%)	
	Broad- leaf weeds	Grasses	Sedges		
Zero tillage	6.52	6.58	1.31	6.6	49.6
Conventional Tillage	12.13	9.4	1.73	10.28	40.8

Source: [23].

Table 3.
Effect of different tillage practices for weed management in mung bean.

Intercropping systems	WSE (%)
Pigeon pea + Black gram	32.8
Pigeon pea + Green gram	31
Pigeon pea + Cowpea	39.1
Pigeon pea + Sesame	36.6
Pigeon pea + Pearlmillet	50.8
Black gram + Maize	17.3
Pigeon pea + Maize	16.4

Source: [28].

Table 4.
Weed-Smothering Efficiency (WSP) of different pulse-based intercropping systems.

2.3 Herbicides

Herbicides are a significant piece of agricultural technology that has contributed, at least in part, to the agricultural revolution that has occurred in recent decades and to the accompanying rise in the amount of food that has been produced. Herbicides, a major component of pesticides, are one of the external factors and a group of synthetic chemical and biochemicals used to suppress or kill unwanted vegetation [30]. Increasing labor shortages in agriculture, coupled with the need to maximize crop productivity to meet the needs of a growing global population, have led to the widespread use of herbicides for weed control, leading to their adoption as one of agriculture's most popular weed control strategies [31]. An author [32] added that reducing soil erosion resulting from tilling is another advantage of the approach. Nevertheless, maintaining the efficiency of existing weed control options necessitates that herbicide use practices and recommendations be regularly updated and revised to keep up with the ever-changing weed ecology (**Table 5**).

It is imperative that herbicides be applied only at the time specified on the label and in accordance with the recommended intervals between the time of treatment and the time of planting or harvesting the crops. Whenever there is a possibility of rain within 2–4 hours of application, it is best to avoid herbicide applications. The use of herbicides requires a great deal of caution from us [34]. Several countries have restricted the use of some herbicides because of the health risks they pose. Paraquat, for example, is restricted in some countries due to its acute toxicity and association with Parkinson's disease. That means, the aforementioned chemical can only be applied by certified applicators for the purposes of scientific research and observation.

2.4 Integrated Weed management

Herbicidal technology has faced significant shifts in its effectiveness in agricultural systems, which can, in some instances, result in the failure of weed control applications. This is primarily attributable to the perpetuating development of weed tolerance and resistance, as well as the development of the herbicide industry and its associated limitations. We have some data on cases of herbicide-associated resistance as expressed in **Figures 1** and **2** [35].

Herbicides	Trade names	Active ingredients (lb a.i)	Site of action	Application Time	Targets
Pendimethalin	Acumen	0.95-1.43	3	PPI	Annual grasses, small-seeded annual broadleaf weeds
Trifluralin	Treflan	0.5-1	3	PPI	Grasses and some small-seeded broadleaf weeds
Ethalfluralin	Sonalan	0.55-0.75	3	PPI	Certain grasses and broadleaf weeds
S-metolachor	StreliuS II	0.95-1.9	15	PPI or PRE	Annual grasses and some broadleaf weeds
Saflufenacil	Sharpen	0.02-0.04	14	EPP or PRE	Broadleaf weeds
Imazethapyr	Praxis	0.03-0.047	2	PRE, EPOST	Several annual broadleaf weeds and some foxtail
Dimethenamid-p	Slider	0.56-1	15	PPI & PRE	Annual grasses
Carfentrazone	Aim	0.008-0.031	14	EPP	Small weeds
Flumioxazin	Flumi	0.095	14	POST	Various grasses and boardleaf weeds
Quizalofop	Targa	0.035-0.08	1	POST	Annual grasses and quack grass
Glyphosate	Roundup PowerMAX	5.5	9	POST	Wide range
Triallate	Avadex MinTill	1.5	8	PPI	Wild oat
Sethoxydim	Poast	0.1-0.5	1	POST	Actively growing grasses
Clethodim	Tapout	0.07-0.25	1	POST	Annual grasses
Imazamox	Beyond	0.031-0.047	2	EPOST	Actively growing small broadleaf and grasses
Sulfentrazone	Sulfin	0.07-0.25	14	EPP or PRE, PPI	Annual broadleaf weeds including pigweed
S-metolachor + Glyphosate	Sequence	0.75-1.5 + 0.56-1.13	15+9	EPP or PRE	Grasses and some broadleaf weeds
Paraquat*	Paraquat	0.3-0.5	22	POST	For harvest aid and desiccation of green weed foliage

lb a.i. = *Pounds active ingredient,* **EPP** = *Early Preplant,* **PPI** = *Preplant Incorporated,* **PRE** = *Preemergence,* **EPOST** = *Early Postemergence,* **POST** = *Postemergence*
Sites of action (groups): **1** = *ACCase Inhibitor,* **2** = *ALS Inhibitor,* **3** = *Microtuble Inhibitor,* **8** = *Lipid Synthesis Inhibitor,* **9** = *EPSP Inhibitor,* **14** = *Cell Membrane Disruptor (PPO Inhibitor),* **15** = *Seedling Shoot Inhibitor,* **22** = *Cell Membrane Disruptor (PSI Inhibitor)*indicates Restricted Use Herbicide.*

Table 5.
Environmental Protection Agency (EPA)-approved herbicides recommended for pulse crops by Johnson et al. [33] based on research conducted at the South Dakota Agricultural Experiment Station and other studies.

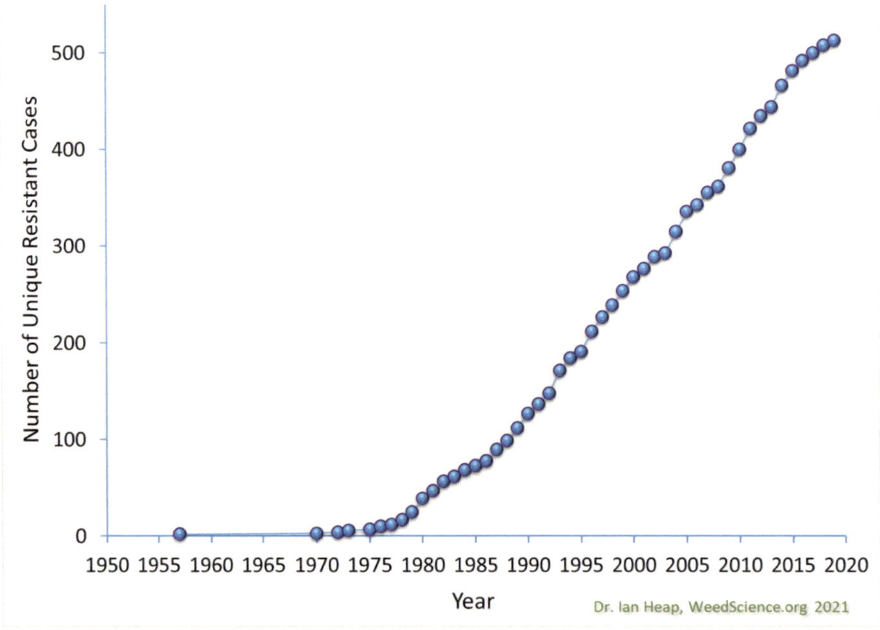

Figure 1.
A global increase in unique resistant cases at different years.

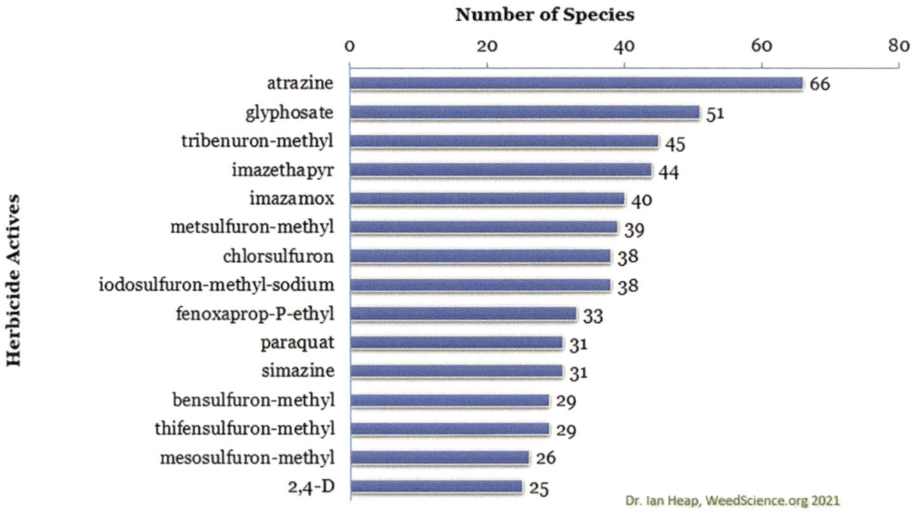

Figure 2.
The top 10 herbicides, along with the number of associated resistant species. Source: [35].

The widespread use of herbicides that primarily have the same or a similar mode of action is hamstrung by the emerging risks of environmental hazards, the introduction of herbicide resistance in various biotypes of weeds, and the nonselectivity and narrow spectrum of herbicides, all of which contribute to limiting the scope of herbicide use. To develop an effective and sustainable weed

DOI: http://dx.doi.org/10.5772/intechopen.110208

management strategy, it is essential to first comprehend the selection pressure of an organism. Selection pressure is an outcome of virtually anything as long as the survival and reproductive pattern of a species are influenced, provided that it acts in a relatively consistent manner over and over again [36]. It is worth pointing out that this is the case with herbicide resistance. The repeated use of the same active ingredient or of the same mode of action eliminates susceptible weeds from a population, leaving only the resistant ones, which become dominant species over time; the development of herbicide resistance can be considered an evolutionary process [37].

The development of herbicide-resistant weeds is associated with several factors, including selection pressure, the weed's genetic variability, inheritance patterns, gene flow, herbicides' nature, agro-ecosystem factors, and others [38]. In light of this, it is not always possible to come up with a single management strategy for controlling and preventing the spread of herbicide-resistant weeds; instead, an integrated weed management (IWM) approach is required.

Integrated weed management (IWM) strategies for managing resistant weeds:

1. Regularly scout fields and identify weeds, as well as respond swiftly to changes in weed populations, to prevent the spread of weeds.

2. Choose herbicides based on the types of the target weeds present and use it prudently.

3. Crop rotation is an effective method for interrupting the life cycles of weeds, and certain weed problems are more easily managed in certain crops than in others.

4. Refrain from using the same herbicide or another herbicide with the same mode of action for 2 years or more in a row in the same field.

5. Consider using a tank mixture or sequential applications of herbicides with varying modes of action.

6. Keep tillage and harvesting equipment clean to avoid spreading weeds from field to field.

2.5 Modeling and robotics for SSWM

Site-specific weed management (SSWM) is a state-of-the-art weed management approach that allows optimization of weed treatment for each unique agronomical site, with precise and continuous monitoring and mapping of weed infestations, which has been proven highly efficient and environmentally safe for control of weed populations [39, 40].

This system relies on multidisciplinary technologies such as image sensing techniques (multiple-dimensional cameras and multispectral imaging), GPS, remote sensors, artificial intelligence (AI), and machine learning algorithms for discerning a specific weed and its population, thereby allowing unmanned vehicles for weed management via targeted spraying, automated hoeing, or other techniques. In conjunction with the new sensor technologies, decision support systems (DSS) can help farmers apply weed control treatments at the right time, with the right intensity, and in the right places [41].

2.5.1 Drones

Precision agriculture has adopted unmanned aerial vehicles (UAVs), primarily drones, as a common tool [42, 43]. Due to their affordability, user-friendliness, and adaptability, UAVs are frequently the preferred option for rapid and accurate in situ remote sensing or survey operations. Despite their adaptability, these systems can serve a variety of purposes depending on the sensors they carry. UAVs, as one of the most effective tools for weed mapping, are critical for SSWM. The workflow consists of three significant phases: 1) collection of field images, via sensor cameras, 2) image processing, which recognizes weeds and pinpoints their whereabouts and patches via deep neural networks or other AI techniques, 3) training-specific algorithms to eliminate the targeted weeds with herbicide spraying by drones or mechanically with unmanned terrestrial vehicles (UTVs). There are three types of sensors attached to UAVs, depending on the payload and weed/crop recognition system and other purposes: 1) RGB (Red, Green, and Blue) or VIS (visible) sensors, 2) multispectral sensors, and 3) hyperspectral sensors. With up to 80% precision, hyperspectral sensors can differentiate between glyphosate-resistant and glyphosate-susceptible Kochia biotypes [44]. And the accuracy rate is 96% for *Amaranthus palmeri* in real field bases [45]. A novel alternative to UAVs could be laser-equipped robots.

2.5.2 Autonomous laser weeding

Andreasen et al. [46] highlighted that Autonomous Laser Weeding is a cutting-edge technique for weed management that is a prototype, not yet widely used or sold commercially. Artificial intelligence and deep learning are being deployed to precisely locate and distinguish weeds [47, 48] and burn the meristems of the targets with laser beams released by robotic actuators for real-time weed control. Beam quality is a crucial parameter for laser applications, particularly weeding, as it determines the maximum power density that can be achieved. At least 54 joules of laser energy per plant were required to cause lethal damage to each treated plant with a 95% probability. Lethal damages are contingent upon weed species, growth stage, laser spot position and area, and laser energy (J) applied [49–51]. Papadopoulos [52] reported that LaserWeeder, a product of Carbon Robotics, is an autonomous laser robot that has the capacity of eliminating 200,000 weeds per hour by incinerating active ones, with a performance increase of 100 percent over the system's first version.

Need-based spatial spraying minimizes selection pressure on herbicide-resistant weeds and herbicide diffusion with only minimal interference with nontargeted plants. Importantly, laser robots offer substantially less interference with biodiversity and the environment, achieving the goal. Due to their lighter weight, UTVs perform site-specific weeding with acceptable soil impacts, creating a more favorable environment for crop growth. There have been positive impacts on ecological and agro-economic aspects, as depicted in **Figure 3**. It is possible for these robotic devices to replace organic growers' manual weeding practices. However, it can be challenging or may take some time, particularly for developing countries, to introduce and adopt such a novel approach.

3. Conclusion

To overcome the weed infestation, farmers have been using different tools and methods, and among them, the herbicide-use approach is widely adopted due to

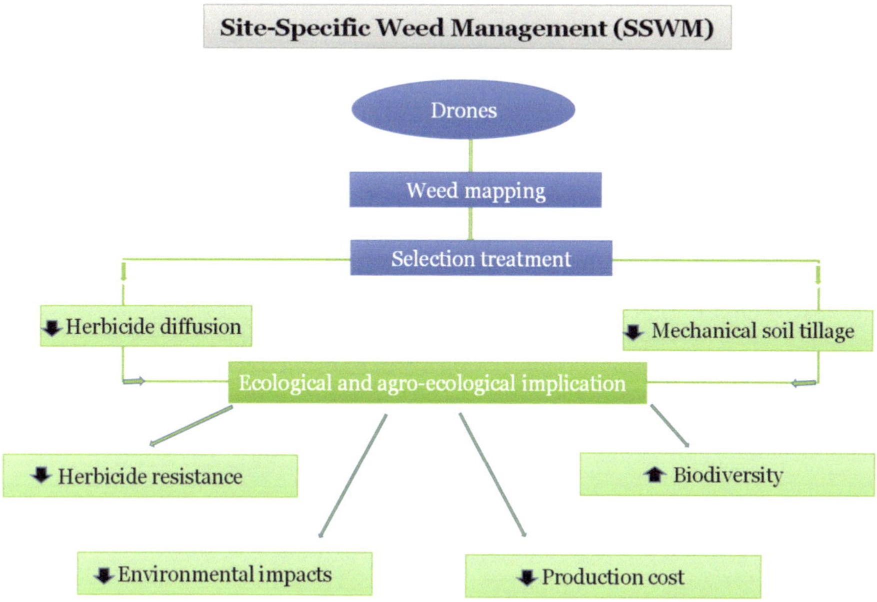

Figure 3.
Drone-based site-specific weed management (SSWM) and its impact on the Agri-economy and ecology. Source: [53].

its ease of use and labor shortage. Long-term weed management is unlikely to be achieved through the use of a single method of weed control, since this approach often leads to the development of weed resistance. This is not only the case with herbicides; even repetitive hand hoeing over and over may force weeds to adapt to such a stressed environment and build resistance/tolerance. Over the past few years, herbicide resistance and resistance management have been of great interest to weed scientists. Site-specific weed management (SSWM) is likely to improve the sustainability of weed management by treating only the weed species community, using image analysis and machine learning techniques. Further studies are crucial and in high demand to make this novel approach applicable in real agricultural situations.

Author details

Rajan Sagar Chaudhary[1*] and Suman Dhakal[2]

1 Agroforestry Polytechnic Institute, Lumbini Province, Nepal

2 Agriculture and Forestry University (AFU), Rampur, Chitwan, Nepal

*Address all correspondence to: rajandang031@gmail.com

References

[1] Christenhusz MJM, Byng JW. The number of known plants species in the world and its annual increase. Phytotaxa. 2016;**261**(3):201. DOI: 10.11646/phytotaxa.261.3.1

[2] Balasubramanian P. Pulse crops [Internet]. The Canadian Encyclopedia. 2015. [cited 2022 Dec 14]. Available from: https://www.thecanadianencyclopedia.ca/en/article/pulse-crops

[3] Singh N. Pulses: An overview. Journal of Food Science and Technology. 2017;**54**(4):853-857

[4] Mashungwa GN. Grain legume production and their potential for sustainable agriculture in Botswana between 2008 and 2015: A review. Botswana Journal of Agriculture and Applied Sciences. 2019;**13**(1):80-90

[5] Shahbandeh M. Pulses: Production Volume Worldwide 2020 [Internet]. New York: Statista; 2022 [cited 2022Dec7]. Available from: https://www.statista.com/statistics/721945/pulses-production-volume-worldwide/

[6] Sinchana JK, Raj SK. Weed management in pulses: A review. Legume Research-An International Journal. 2020;**1**:8. DOI: 10.18805/lr-4375

[7] Gharde Y, Singh PK, Dubey RP, Gupta PK. Assessment of yield and economic losses in agriculture due to weeds in India. Crop Protection. 1 May 2018;**107**:12-18

[8] Oerke EC. Crop losses to pests. The Journal of Agricultural Science. Feb 2006;**144**(1):31-43

[9] Ali M, Kumar S, Singh M. 25 Years of Pulses Research at IIPR 1984-2009. Lucknow: Army Printing Press; 2009. Available from: https://iipr.icar.gov.in/pdf/pulses_research_atiipr.pdf

[10] Gervase. The 10 types of weeds that are most dangerous for your crops [internet]. GVC Farm Supply. 2018 [cited 2022Dec7]. Available from: https://www.gvcfarmsupply.com/the-10-types-of-weeds-that-are-most-dangerous-for-your-crops#:~:text=Lambsquarter%20(Chenopodium%20Album)&text=Vegetable%20and%20pulse%20crops%20such,easily%20blown%20by%20the%20wind

[11] WSSA. WSSA Survey Ranks most Common and most Troublesome Weeds in Broadleaf Crops, Fruits and Vegetables [Internet]. Weed Science Society of America; 2017 [cited 2022Dec7]. Available from: https://wssa.net/2017/05/wssa-survey-ranks-most-common-and-most-troublesome-weeds-in-broadleaf-crops-fruits-and-vegetables/

[12] Chauhan BS, Johnson DE. The role of seed ecology in improving weed management strategies in the tropics. Advances in Agronomy. 2010;**105**:221-262

[13] Gallandt ER. How can we target the weed seedbank? Weed Science. 2006;**54**(3):588-596

[14] Ghersa CM, Holt JS. Using phenology prediction in weed management: A review. Weed research. 1995;**35**(6):461-470

[15] Reddy TY, Reddy GHS. In Weed Management. In: Principles of agronomy. 5th ed. Ludhiana: Kalyani Publishers; 2016

[16] Singh G, Sekhon HS. Integrated weed management in pigeonpea [Cajanus cajan (L.) Millsp.]. World Journal of Agricultural Sciences. 2013;**9**(1):86-91

[17] Kumar N, Hazra KK, Nadarajan N. Efficacy of post-emergence application of Imazethapyr in summer mungbean (*Vigna radiata* L.). Legume Research. 2016;**39**(1):96-100

[18] Choudhary VK, Kumar PS, Bhagawati R. Integrated weed management in blackgram (Vigna mungo) under mid hills of Arunachal Pradesh. Indian Journal of Agronomy. 2012;**57**(4):382-385

[19] Patel BD, Patel VJ, Patel JB, Patel RB. Effect of fertilizers and weed management practices on weed control in chickpea (Cicer arietinum L.) under middle Gujarat conditions. Indian. Journal of Crop Science. 2006;**1**(1and2):180-183

[20] Yadav RB, Singh RV, Yadav KG. Weed management in lentil. Indian Journal of Weed Science. 2013;**45**(2):113-115

[21] Singh M, Kumar R, Kumar S, Kumar V. Critical period for weed control in field pea. Legume Research-An International Journal. 2016;**39**(1):86-90

[22] Jorgensen MH. The effect of tillage on the weed control: An adaptive approach. In: Radhakrisnan R, editor. Biological Approaches for Controlling Weeds. London, UK: InTech; 2018. pp. 17-25. DOI: 10.5772/intechopen.76704

[23] Singh PK, Singh SK, Shukla MK, Singh C, Kumari M, Singh R, et al. Effect of different tillage practice, herbicide and rhizobium on weed, yield and economics of mung bean (Vigna radiata L.). Internationl Journal of Multidisciplinary Research and Development. 2016;**3**(7):257-259

[24] Barzegar AR, Asoodar MA, Khadish A, Hashemi AM, Herbert SJ. Soil physical characteristics and chickpea yield responses to tillage treatments. Soil and Tillage Research. 2003;**71**(1):49-57

[25] Photocontrol – Tilling in the Dark? [Internet]. Dalhousie University. [cited 2022Dec7]. Available from: https://www.dal.ca/faculty/agriculture/oacc/en-home/resources/pest-management/weed-management/organic-weed-mgmt-resources/weeds-photocontrol.html

[26] Hiltbrunner J, Liedgens M, Bloch L, Stamp P, Streit B. Legume cover crops as living mulches for winter wheat: Components of biomass and the control of weeds: Semantic scholar [internet]. European Journal of Agronomy. 1970 [cited 2023Jan7]. Available from: https://www.semanticscholar.org/paper/Legume-cover-crops-as-living-mulches-for-winter-of-Hiltbrunner-Liedgens/60988b6ccdf0ed4db95c05b69ae906fb35955b4b

[27] Banik P, Midya A, Sarkar BK, Ghose SS. Wheat and chickpea intercropping systems in an additive series experiment: Advantages and weed smothering. European Journal of agronomy. 2006;**24**(4):325-332

[28] Ali M. Weed suppressing ability and productivity of short duration legumes intercroppped with pigeonpea under rainfed conditions. International Journal of Pest Management. 1 Jan 1988;**34**(4):384-387

[29] Rai CL, Tiwari RK, Sirothia P, Pandey S. Intercropping and weed management effects on weed dynamics, productivity and economics of pigeonpea. Weed Science. 2016;**48**(1):44-47. DOI: 10.5958/0974-8164.2016.00010.1

[30] Qasem JR. Herbicide Resistant Weeds: The Technology and Weed Management. In: Price AJ, Kelton JA, editors. Herbicides–Current Research and Case Studies in Use [Internet]. London: IntechOpen; 2013 [cited 2023 Jan 14]. Available from: https://www.intechopen.com/chapters/44981 DOI: 10.5772/56036

[31] Gianessi LP. The increasing importance of herbicides in worldwide crop production. Pest Management Science. 2013;**69**(10):1099-1105

[32] Pacanoski Z. Herbicide use: Benefits for society as a vvhole-A review. Pakistan Journal of Weed Science and Research. 2007;**13**(1-2):135-147

[33] Johnson PO, Vos A. Weed control: Pulse crops [internet]. SDSU Extension. 2021 [cited 2023Jan7]. Available from: https://extension.sdstate.edu/weed-control-pulse-crops

[34] Dhaker DL, Maurya S, Singh K. Chemical Weed Management increasing herbicide efficiency. Agriculture and Environment. 2021;**2**(10):31-32. Available from: https://www.researchgate.net/publication/357327269_Chemical_Weed_Management_Increasing_Herbicide_Efficiency

[35] Heap I. International Herbicide-Resistant Weed Database [Internet]. Weedscience.org. 2021 [cited 2022Dec17]. Available from: http://www.weedscience.org/Pages/Graphs.aspx

[36] Anissimov M. What Is Selection Pressure? [Internet]. San Francisco: All the Science; 2022 [cited 2023Jan7]. Available from: https://www.allthescience.org/what-is-selection-pressure.htm

[37] Sosnoskie C. Selective forces that act on weeds [Internet]. Progressive Crop Consultant. 2019 [cited 2023Jan7]. Available from: https://progressivecrop.com/2019/09/selective-forces-that-act-on-weeds/

[38] Powles SB, Yu Q. Evolution in action: plants resistant to herbicides. Annual review of plant biology. 2 Jun 2010;**61**:317-347

[39] Hunter JE III, Gannon TW, Richardson RJ, Yelverton FH, Leon RG. Integration of remote-weed mapping and an autonomous spraying unmanned aerial vehicle for site-specific weed management. Pest Management Science. 2020;**76**(4):1386-1392

[40] John KN, Valentin V, Abdullah B, Bayat M, Kargar MH, Zargar M. Weed mapping technologies in discerning and managing weed infestation levels of farming systems. Research on Crops. 2020;**21**(1):93-98

[41] Christensen S, Heisel T, Walter AM, Graglia E. A decision algorithm for patch spraying. Weed Research. 2003;**43**(4):276-284

[42] Radoglou-Grammatikis P, Sarigiannidis P, Lagkas T, Moscholios I. A compilation of UAV applications for precision agriculture. Computer Networks. 2020;**172**:107148

[43] Daponte P, De Vito L, Glielmo L, Iannelli L, Liuzza D, Picariello F, et al. A review on the use of drones for precision agriculture. In: IOP Conference Series: Earth and Environmental Science. Vol. 275, No. 1. Bristol, UK: IOP Publishing; 2019. p. 012022

[44] Scherrer B, Sheppard J, Jha P, Shaw JA. Hyperspectral imaging and neural networks to classify herbicide-resistant weeds. Journal of Applied Remote Sensing. 2019;**13**(4):044516

[45] Reddy KN, Huang Y, Lee MA, Nandula VK, Fletcher RS, Thomson SJ, et al. Glyphosate-resistant and glyphosate-susceptible palmer amaranth (Amaranthus palmeri S. wats.): Hyperspectral reflectance properties of plants and potential for classification. Pest Management Science. 2014;**70**(12):1910-1917

[46] Andreasen C, Scholle K, Saberi M. Laser weeding with small autonomous vehicles: Friends or foes? [Internet]. Frontiers. 2022 [cited 2023Jan7].

Available from: https://www.frontiersin.org/articles/10.3389/fagro.2022.841086/full

[47] Gikunda PK, Jouandeau N. Modern CNNs for IoT based farms. In: International Conference on Information and Communication Technology for Development for Africa. Cham: Springer; 2019. pp. 68-79

[48] Rakhmatulin I, Kamilaris A, Andreasen C. Deep neural networks to detect weeds from crops in agricultural environments in real-time: A review. Remote Sensing. 2021;**13**(21):4486

[49] Mathiassen SK, Bak T, Christensen S, Kudsk P. The effect of laser treatment as a weed control method. Biosystems Engineering. 2006;**95**(4):497-505

[50] Marx C, Barcikowski S, Hustedt M, Haferkamp H, Rath T. Design and application of a weed damage model for laser-based weed control. Biosystems Engineering. 2012;**113**(2):148-157

[51] Rakhmatulin I, Andreasen C. A concept of a compact and inexpensive device for controlling weeds with laser beams. Agronomy. 2020;**10**(10):1616

[52] Papadopoulos L. This new farming robot uses lasers to kill 200,000 weeds per hour [Internet]. Interesting Engineering. Interesting Engineering; 2022 [cited 2023Jan7]. Available from: https://interestingengineering.com/innovation/farming-robot-lasers-200000-weeds-per-hour

[53] Esposito M, Crimaldi M, Cirillo V, Sarghini F, Maggio A. Drone and sensor technology for sustainable weed management: A review. Chemical and Biological Technologies in Agriculture. Dec 2021;**8**(1):1-1

Chapter 9

Future Use Prospects of Legumes through Improvement and the Challenges Faced

Briggx Xavier

Abstract

Legumes are important crops, being one of the most protein containing species of grain plants from their seeds which are used as food among other uses of the crop such as Nitrogen fixation (in most), which helps maintain soil nutrition at bay. The uses extend to key ingredients in livestock feeds manufacture even for marine life diets. Their roots go deep into the soil to find water and in the process hold soil particles together aiding in soil erosion control. However, low performance and production levels have been recorded over the years with Africa, for example, contributing only 10% of the entire world legume production per year. This is attributed to little breeding programs being conducted on the legume plants among less improvements aiding in the plants' performance and production for sustainability. This book chapter therefore seeks to outline in depth some of the future prospects of legume plants species in relation to improvements that should be done on the crop such as breeding programs to sustain diverse functions, among which, increasing food security. The improvements not only aim at helping humanity, but rather the environment in general including marine life.

Keywords: nitrogen fixation, soil erosion, marine life, sustainability, food security

1. Introduction

The leguminous family of plants is the largest pods-producing flowering plants family with over 18,000 different species classified into 650 generic classes [1], under the 1/1/12th of all known flowering plants on the planet earth. Not all legumes fix atmospheric nitrogen. Among the *Leguminosae* subfamily, the *Fabaceae* species are recognized as those with the primary agricultural role in the group. Herbaceous and woody legume plant types from the *Fabaceae* species have been used for pastures, animal feeds, erosion control, agro-forestry purposes and as sources of green manure traditionally. Above the uses, they also yield important industrial substances such as tannin, resin for making gums and glues, synthetic dyes, perfumes, insecticides and bio-fuels. Some of these leguminous family valuable food crops include, peas, common beans, peanuts and soybean, which produce high protein grains for human consumption, making an important constituent in their diet. Of all the plants that man used as food, only the grasses are more stable as compared to the legumes [2]. Despite

IntechOpen

considerable resources being directed towards the development of grasses such as rice, maize and wheat, only peanuts and soybeans within the leguminous family have been thoroughly given priority on the same. The world's increasing population needs adequate food to feed its citizens so as to prevent common malnutrition problems, which is prospected to be greatly contributed by dietary legumes in order to achieve food security in our nations.

Through improvements that aim in increasing the performance and yields of legumes, these plants are super contributors to the economy to ensure food security among nations in the word. Breeding programs such as gene mapping to identify and isolate traits aid in the selection and isolation of genes of interest from plants which are improved and modified then used in legumes to boost the performance [3]. Other technologies include breeding to suit performance roles such as adaptability to environments, for example deep roots in search for water. Legume produces can be improved for uses in the food industry for humanity, in feed industries such as in ruminants dies replacements and in industries and in the pharmaceutical industries in the manufacture of drugs.

Besides the improvements, there are many breeding technologies which are aimed at improving performance and yield currently. An example is the breeding for lodging resistance which reduces yield losses especially during heavy rainfall seasons by avoiding plant bends which promote rotting once the pods come into contact with moisture. Breeding is also done to increase the general yields of the plant by increasing the number of produces per plant in many agricultural crops. Breeding is done to reduce grain shattering in legumes especially during harvesting stage. This is by preventing the chances of the pods to open which leads to losses through spillage [4, 5]. All these are some of the many examples which are believed to form the basis for this chapter. This is because in order for improvements to occur, much grains must be produced, and of high quality as the grains are the requirements in implementation of most of the improvement prospects.

As agronomists, scientists and researchers, our main perspective is to think of legumes in the primary role of aiding in nitrogen fixation to otherwise deficient soils. Despite, other scientists outside the "agriculture" field view the crop for diverse benefits and uses, such as use as a vital source of food and forage, use in rotation with other crops to improve yields and also as a forest commodity essential for providing firewood traditionally or shelter. However, some scientists from the medical field now view the crops as a source of pharmaceutical ingredient in the manufacture of major drugs for hospital use in a range of maladies. This role should not be under looked when we display that legumes have been a major component of traditional medicine among communities for centuries. Despite the purpose you intend to grow the crop for, its symbiotic role, that is, the association between the nitrogen fixing bacteria in the root nodules (rhizobia) and the plants, play a significant role in agriculture production sector by reducing ca. 100 million metric tons of atmospheric nitrogen into ammonia [6], thus saving the world about US$30 billion on Nitrogen fertilizer every year. Following photosynthesis process in plants, we might consider viewing Biological Nitrogen Fixation (BNF) by legumes as the next most important essential natural occurring biological process in plants. There is still a challenge on the realization of this process as many developing and developed countries all over the world have not fully embraced Biological Nitrogen Fixation but instead rely upon nitrogen fertilizer to drive agricultural productivity. This lack of adoption of the process is majorly attributed to many factors ranging from little knowledge and expertise in both the manufacture of inoculants and in the growing of inoculated legumes with rhizobia. Some governments in many countries across the world with advanced economies also are viewed to participate in this by providing subsidies which mitigate against the use of Biological Nitrogen Fixation (BNF). Unfortunately, with the fossil fuel prices hiking, small economies will most likely be faced with either food shortages, high food costs or inflated fertilizer nitrogen prizes. Many developing countries such as those in South Eastern parts of Asian continent rely upon buying of urea (a nitrogenous fertilizer) for rice production [7]. This is a problem that needs to be addressed as soon as possible due to the current forecast that food production will have to double by the next 10 years so as to feed and sustain the expanding population. This can only be avoided with employment of Biological Nitrogen Fixation (BNF) inputs.

Apart from direct benefits of artificial nitrogen fixation from legumes, they also provide additional importance in aiding in weeds, pests and pathogens control, improving soil fertility when the plants die and form organic manure and ensuring stability from rotation in different and diverse cropping systems with different species of crops. Taking a look at a country like the United States of America (USA) alone for example, alfalfa, *Medicage sativa,* is currently estimated to be the third most valuable crop worth up to $7 billion annually [8]. However, intense pressure from biological, environmental, human health as well as economic sectors dictate that the legumes suite and their use in the modern civilization to be dynamic rather than fixed. This chapter outlines how legumes can be developed, more so rhizobia, for future diverse uses not only in agriculture but outside fields as well.

2. Legumes future breeding improvement prospects

2.1 Legumes use in pharmaceutical industry to solve health problems

The strong consumer-driven trend for natural products in the world has pushed for shift to natural active ingredients in medicines manufacture. Of the active ingredients prescribed in pharmaceuticals, 25% are flowering plants-derived, expected to increase to about 30% in the next 10 years to come. On this, of the antineoplastic drugs that are prescribed in the Western countries and in Japan, 54% are natural occurring products or their analogs [9]. Many consumers in the world aim at natural drugs, believing that they are safer that synthetics. This has also pushed many, more so in African countries, to go the herbal medicine direction rather than buying drugs from chemists and pharmacies. The current global market for natural pharmaceutical products is estimated at US$30 billion growing at an increasing rate of 6% per annum [10]. Herbs (which also includes many legumes), possessing anti-cancer or penile potency properties are the main focus of smuggling into the European, Japan and the USA markets. Advances in analytical chemical techniques in plants, such as High-Performance Liquid Chromatography (HPLC), Mass Spectroscopy (MS) and Nuclear Magnetic Resonance (NMR) have allowed the rapid identification of proteins in plant cells that are responsible for increasing the legumes value, particularly in regards to the pharmaceutical industry. References proposed that legume plants species combine essential genomic materials with biochemistry thus forming a compound which is of acute relevance to human health.

Non-traditional benefits of legumes in human diets have been emphasized also in the recent years commonly. These benefits include, alfalfa sprouts and soybeans use as a source of phytoestrogens which aims at reducing menopause symptoms majorly in women and also aiding in maintaining bones health. In the Chinese medicine for example, one of the old-dating known useful plants is the licorice, (*Glycyrrhiza glabra,* a popular legume herb known for its anti-ulcer and anti-inflammatory properties. Legumes also contain useful chemical compounds in their protein-DNA that are essential for their ant-diabetic, anti-allergenic as well as anti-inflammatory properties [11]. Plant Genetic Resource Conservation unit (PGRC) within the United States Department of Agriculture (USAID) is currently conserving 17 different legumes species containing essential phytochemical properties with positive human health impact. Some of these plant legume species include the butterfly pea, *Clitoria ternatea l.,* known for its anti-fungal properties, hyacinth bean, *Lablab purpureus.,* known for its anti-hypertensive properties and kudzu, *Pueraria montana* var. *Lobata willd,* known to containing isoflavone daidzein properties essential as an anti-inflammatory, anti-microbial and cancer preventive treatments. The five pyran isoflavones isolated from a *Fabaceae* family species rootstock, *Eriosema kraussianum,* contains 75% properties of Viagra which increases blood flow in rats' penile tissue as the active ingredient. *Trigonella foenum-graecum l.* plant popularly known in the Indian medicine for increasing lactation in women [12], also contains numerous chemical properties of interest in the modern pharmaceutical sector, for example, diosgenin and coumarin.

Legumes also contain phytoestrogens with great biological activities currently being applied to humans for menopause and osteoporosis treatments. These phytoestrogens are plant-derives chemicals, so named due to their possession of both estrogenic and anti-estrogenic traits, although much less effective than the genetically human produced estrogens. Isoflavonoids are one major phytoestrogen class that includes genistein, daidzein and equol compounds. They are also among the most extensively classes of phytoestrogens to be researched. Isoflavonoids are the most particular prevalent classes in the *Fabaceae* sub-family of leguminous plants the most studied being the ones from soybeans and red clover, *Trifolium pratense l.,* species. The isoflavonoids extracted from red clover and soybeans are now being used as alternative compounds in the Hormonal Replacement Therapies (HRT) for the treatment of the menopause-related disorders [13].

Soybeans are the main dietary source of food of the two isoflavonoids, genistein and daidzein, in humans, present in their glycoside forms. A huge consumption of foods containing high soy-based products may result in high plasms levels, high urine and prostate phytoestrogen fluid concentrates. Epidemiological studies on the other hand suggests that women in Asian countries with a high phytoestrogens dietary intakes have a decreased breast cancer risk rates and also a lower menopause-incidence symptoms. As well, the study still suggests that men consuming high-soy product traditional foods have a lower prostate cancer incidences especially Asian men as compared to European and American men. Although these claims may not provide sufficient evidence and still awaits further study, numerous in vitro studies support a role of genistein in inhibition of the growth of a number of cancers [14].

Laboratories in vitro studies have produces alcohol extracts from a wide range of legume leaves and stem tissues that aid in in inhibiting the growth of MCF7 breast and LNCaP prostate cancer cells [15]. Soybean isoflavonoids is also suspected to have a role in the maintaining of healthy brain tissues and also in the treatment of age-associated cognitive declines such as Alzheimer's disease, loss of memory episodes, and improving the general cognitive functions in the brain.

Many of these mentioned secondary plant compounds are mostly found in small quantities and tend to be synthesized in specialized cells in the plants or at specific growth stages. This makes their identification, extraction, separation and purification processes more challenging. Nevertheless, equipment has been invented and now currently available, which are aided to speed up the extraction of the useful legume compounds for use in human medicine improvements in the pharmaceutical industry.

2.2 Legumes use in food industry

Due to most of the underutilized legume plants' high nutritional properties, some essential proteins can be extracted from the plants and used in the food industries in the manufacture of various products. For example, edible products such as cooking oil can be extracted from soybean and the African yam bean. This is due to their high lipid contents [4]. These lipids used in the manufacture of the cooking oils is obtained from the seed grains, which are processed to produce the final product "oil".

Underutilized legumes can also be processed into flour. This will not only extend the shelf life, but also diversify food by increasing the options for the legume produce use. The process is done after the grains have recorded a reduced moisture content of 4% or less [5]. After that, the grains are taken to the grinding machine after which processed into flour. This flour can now be stored for up to six months depending on the storage conditions. On another option, the flour can be used in preparation of foods such as the famous "ugali" in many African countries. The flour can also be used in a combination with other grain flours such as maize flour, millet flour and sorghum flour in making of porridge which is a good example of breakfast foods for use with either bread or other breakfast food choices.

The processed flour can be used in the baking industries [16]. Here, the flour is processed into legume breads. Some of these breads can be made from undermined legume crops such as soybean. This will very much aid in diversifying food uses too not only consuming the grains directly for lunch dishes, but through processing, legume-bread can also be made which is a good breakfast choice and even for export to other countries.

2.3 Legumes use for ruminants benefits

When it comes to the emergence of herbicides resistance in weed control, development and implementation of chemical control method for gastrointestinal parasites in grazing animals is an equilibrium between seeking of efficiency and avoiding the resistance development. Nematodes in sheep such as *Osterstagia circumcincta, Haemonchus contortus and Trichostrongylus spp.* are a major cause of livestock mortalities and reduced production, and further widespread resistance to anti-helminthics treatment effective control. However, there is sufficient evidence that plant natural occurring tannins in majority of forage legumes can reduce worm infestation issues in grazing animals, hence reducing the requirement for deworming. This in turn provides a new weapon in the management of anti helminthic parasites resistance. The potential anti-helminthic tannin or CTs containing properties are described as proanthrocyanidins, phenolic compounds present in varying concentrates in wide range of leguminous forage plants. CTs form an important part of the plants defense against bacterial and insect predation and also against invasion into grazing vegetation for herbivores. The CTs may also have a positive impact on ruminant nutrition by increasing the efficiency of utilization of proteins. Through the reversible of binding to plant proteins, CTs are postulated to interfere with the protease activities produced by the rumen micro-organisms thus reducing the protein degradation process in the rumen and in return allowing a larger portion of protein to reach the ileum [17].

However, despite the discussed benefits of leguminous CT plants in increasing the wool growth more so in sheep, milk production in mostly dairy livestock, increasing reproductive rates and aiding in bloat control, high tannin concentrations can also reduce the voluntary feed intake rates in ruminants resulting to reduced animal performance. All these effects of CTs towards ruminants vary evidently according to the nature, concentration and the structure of different compounds and potential anti-helminthic properties.

Positive benefits of various leguminous CT forage plants in reducing worm infestation challenges in sheep have been identified in numerous studies. For example, in feed experiment trials, significant reduction in worm infestation levels have occurred in sheep grazing in tannin containing forage plants such as sulla, *Hedysarum coronarium,* lotus, *Lotus pedunculatus,* birdsfoot, trefoil, *L. corniculatus* and chicory, *Cichorium intybus.* pen studies conducted with tannin extracts also indicate that there is a large decrease in sheep-worm egg count and also a lowered worm infestation rate. In goats, pen studies as well also indicate a decreased *Haemonchus contortus* and their significant anti-parasitic effects with *Sericia lespedeza* forages in all pens in the trials. in a general view, the worms egg counts are lowered within a week post the introduction to CT-containing pasture legumes or rotations [18], with much decreases in total worm numbers up to 30–35% in relation to introduction to non-CT legume groups.

2.4 Legumes use in aquaculture and marine feeds

Aquiculture sector over the years has expanded very quickly that it currently provides over 30% of the world`s global fishery products to industrial ones. Although marine-based ingredients such as fishmeal and fish oil are manufactured in industries and remain many people's preferrable protein and oil sources from aquaculture products, it is projected that by the next 10 years or so, 50% of the world's fish catch will most likely be directed towards legume feeds [19]. The current and modern intensive aquaculture practices is therefore viewed as a net fish user rather than producer which is very much undesirable and should not be the trend. Almost much of the soybean meal extracts have already been approved and verified for use as alternative protein and energy source by the aquaculture industry sector. On top of that, sweet lupin, *L. angustifolius,* and other legume grain extracts are currently underway in evaluation appearing to be current substitutes of fish manufactured feed products. Can other legumes specifically those that can be produced intensively satisfy the increasing protein and energy demand in the aquaculture industry at large?

Fish do not require carbohydrates in their diets and their presence in grain legumes can reduce fishmeal digestibility produced from the grain legumes and cause huge decrease in protein retention in fish yet they require S-rich amino acid proteins and fatty acid or lipid oils in their diets. Even though these compounds are provided by legumes in different ratios, anti-nutritional factors similar to the ones previously discussed for humans and other monogastric animals also affect fish [20]. Most notably are the saponins, protein inhibitors, oligosaccharides and high cellular or fiber content. All these and other potential tainting molecules, for example, coumarins cannot be assumed in the formulation of fish diets, however, extracting them from legume grains requires expensive procedures or an extensive breeding program approaches to achieve.

One of the important roles of fish in human health is related to the long chain omega-3 to omega-6 oil ratios with more than 18-carbon atoms on a straight chain in marine products. Two issues of importance arise from here in relation to oil from legume plants. First, legumes produce predominantly C18 oils rather than C20 and C22 oils from fish proven to have beneficial importance to human health. Fish from fresh waters can synthesize C22 fats from C18 precursors as compared to marine fish, mainly cold-water ones, which are much less able to do so. Secondly, the omega-3-omega-6 ratio considerably between leguminous plants and fishmeal, with a much difference of up to more than 100 folds [21]. For more improved human health, a high omega-3-omega-6 ratio is essential, and if lower oil levels are ultimately reflected in fatty acid content of aquaculture end products, the legume-fed fish value in human diets needs to be supplemented.

Nevertheless, dietary substitution of fishmeal in aquaculture fish feed diets containing high protein grains is attractive, particularly those containing omega-3 and omega-6 oil fats rates.

2.5 Perennial legume improvement for increase water access from deeper roots

Another prospect for the future use of legumes is in the provision of a hydrological stable to low input agriculture ecosystems which are pocket friendly. When left undisturbed, grass fields and ecosystem ranges often contain different several annual and perennial plants species mix including herbs, shrubs, trees, grass and also legume family species as well. This unique mix of natural biological plants in the temperate climates contributes to the hydrological stability in the ground and underground water systems of the most part of the world's land mass, with the species with deeper rooting systems translocating water from deeper depths during the drier periods of summer and autumns. In South Australia for example, the natural perennial mixes of shrubs, trees, annual grasses and herbs was violently disturbed and destroyed with the people's ruthless clearing of 25 million hectares for agriculture in the nineteenth and twentieth centuries. In return, larger areas in the region have since been seriously affected by a combination of high salinity levels and waterlogging as a result of the rising water tables due to decrease in water utilization as a result of deforestation and vegetation clearing practices. Currently, in South Australia where the example was picked, the total affected unit land area is estimated to exceed 5 million hectares [22]. On this, the largest scale land use is observed to be under pasture for livestock use which is then the greatest potential for the disaster cause. Farming systems therefore, not only in Southern Australia but all the regions faced with the same challenge across the globe needs to be resolved by employing redesigning strategies in the current Century so as to restore the water use pattern of native flora with the main aim being the discovery of plants and improvements for both economical and hydrological benefits, including legumes.

Perennial legumes are speculated to play a significant role in the redesignation agriculture. Many studies estimate *M. sativa* to being adopted to 96% of most soil types in the entire world even where the soils are fertile or alkaline making the suitable for adaptability. Much of the perennial legume species that are found in the rangelands of the Mediterranean basin surroundings can be elevated to welcome *M. sativa* in the setting more so where improvements are required. This will not only help in water utilization but the diverse benefits which come with legumes as well as discussed previously. However, when it comes to the acidic and more coarse-textured soils, which represents approximately 30% of most agricultural lands in many regions, a different suite of perennial legumes and rhizobia to those exploited in agriculture will need to be developed as a result of breeding programs for adaptability and suitability [23]. This is because none of the current commercial legume species all over the world is adapted to the combination of edaphic aridity stresses, infertility nor acidity stresses in any region. By the development and improvement breeding programs as well, this will provide a major opportunity for the development of legumes by many upcoming scientists and breeders in the near future to serve for purposes.

3. Challenges faced in breeding improvement prospects for legumes

3.1 Health concerns

On the breeding of new legumes with high nutritional quality for monogastric or human consumption, many anti-nutritional and health factors have to be considered, more so ethical issues and points of concerns from the wild legume types and varieties. These concerns include non-protein amino acids, alkaloids, glycosides, tannins, saponins and protease inhibitors from wild legumes, which require further testing as they are ethically not yet viewed as safe healthwise. Even though some societies have found a way to deal with these anti-nutritional factors through processing techniques such as high heat boiling for long duration, soaking, leaching, fermentation and dehulling, this is often not a common practice in today's large economies in both developing and developed worlds. Even though some of the anti-nutritional properties are driven by single genes, it will not be an easy task to isolate and combine all the necessary genes required for the domestication traits among species into a single new superior species that will in return displace the contemporary grain legumes suite in farming systems and markets across the world. The most recent example of the domestication was seen in *L. angustifolius* in the 1970s, following its adoption on acid sandy infertile soils in Western Australia [24]. This advancement in the crop was faced with several highlighted difficulties into the legume market by the novel legumes due to the health concern suspicion among the people thus making its utilization difficult. Despite *L. angustifolius* acquiring an important ground from its rotation with many cereal crops on more than 750,000 hectares of land annually, the price paid by its seeds constrained include;

i. Breeding acceptance for its quality traits in the legume industry for human consumption,

ii. Placing of legumes into farming systems which is a difficult idea especially for forages in the warmer climates,

iii. Selection of legumes and rhizobia well suited and adapted to both harsh soils and severe climates, adoption and

iv. Discovery and acquisition of germplasms across the continent [25].

Lupin is considered primarily as an animal feed in many marketplaces whereas traditional other common grain legumes are cultivated for human consumption and fetch higher market prices, for example Cicer, Vicia and Lens legumes. However, despite this negative faced by the crops, lupins remain popular across many farming systems due to their ability to fix over 100 units of nitrogen per hectare, while still providing many additional rotational benefits associated with legumes in coexistence with other crop species in the field [26].

3.2 Social and technical adoption challenges

There exists other many social and technical barriers to the legume adoption as well in the current world. For example, farming systems are distorted by high price subsidization more often, ignoring the direct and associated benefits of legumes-cultivation especially in the rural regions. Also, much direct financial support to farmers is needed to ensure arable lands remain occupied and busy but eliminating the incentive to develop efficient farming systems which are based upon Biologically-fixed nitrogen. The recognition of the environmental pollution in manufacturing and utilization of nitrogen fertilizers should be considered as it slowly increases embracing of Biological Nitrogen Fixation (BNF) in many regions across the world. In other circumstances as a result, investment in legumes is not much often realized for long recurrent growing seasons and thus, the legumes growing of the crop that generates higher quicker instant cash flow is significantly instead lost. When it comes to communally owned lands, it often even makes it more difficult to manage the long-term practice of improved forages to incur return benefits to the investor as well which may bring disputes in the future resulting to implementation challenges [27].

3.3 Growth environment challenges

Complex hurdles are also encountered in legume adoption. These include the unfavorable soil types or climates that affect the components of legumes symbiosis benefits with other crops mainly on rotation and the presence of competition from rhizobia that compromises the process of nitrogen fixation, although yet ineffective. Legumes are also more difficult to grow many times than many cereals in an agronomic perspective. The other consideration is the introduction of the legumes to new environments which requires thorough selection of appropriate rhizobia-containing inoculants followed by their industrial manufacture which is a difficult process. Also, expertise required in the process to nature high-quality inoculant in manufacturing industries should be well trained in handling process and should not be underestimated [28].

Some of the factors limiting legume exploitation remains to be acknowledged from the key role of woody and herbaceous annual and perennial legumes in communal rangelands the drier and forest regions across the world. Where vegetation has not been disturbed or cleared for human benefits, majority of legumes and rhizobia are found in situ in these precious non-arable grounds. These repositories are now currently recognized for their extremely high conservation values particularly in ex situ germplasm centers which are becoming expensive to retain [29]. It is from there in situ natural repositories where many plant legumes and their root nodule bacteria (rhizobia) with unique prospect future roles in the field of agriculture, horticulture products and pharmaceutical medicine will be drawn.

3.4 Difficulties in understanding and studying of the CT plants

Despite this, the role of CT legume forage plants as an alternative to chemical anti-helminthic drugs is far from clear due to the results and conclusions from various research studies which vary greatly. This is for example in a study where little or no effect was noted in grazing experiments with neither sulla nor *L. pedunculatus*, where also variations in the effect on different worm-species were also observed. Several authors have reported reduction in *Teladorsagia circumcincta* infestation burdens but not on *Trichostrongylus spp,* where effects were found on the intestines but not in the abomasum [30]. It is therefore not clear whether these disparities vary in CTs concentrations or the presence of different CT compounds in the feed diets.

3.5 Uncertainties

There are uncertainties regarding the CTs mode of action on worm population in the ruminants' stomachs. This is particularly driven in a case where there is unclarity whether the effects are due to direct anti-helminthic actions of CTs on various nematode stages in their life cycles to be specific. The effects of high protein diet intakes on the immunological competence of livestock have been well-established, although it does not necessarily explain all the anti-parasitic effects observed in pasture-grazing sheep which are high in meat protein as a result. Direct effects of worms have been also numerously reported in in-vitro studies, including worm-eggs inhibition and hatching and larvae migration of *H. contortus, T. circumcincta* and *Tr. colubriformis* with sulla extracts and its similar effects, birdsfoot trefoil, lotus, sainfoin, *Onobrychus viciifolia* and *Dorycnium spp.* on *Tr. colubriformis* on sheep and nematodes of deer. Similarly, there was decreased larval development in faecal droppings from sheep that were fed on chicory, *Dorycnium spp.* and *L. pedunculatus.* However, the significance of these study effects for the ideal natural situations is unclear as in vitro egg-hatching results have not been in accordance with the results from field experimental trials [31].

Therefore, further studies, both in vitro and in the fields, need to be conducted to indicate whether CT legumes containing forages will likely be a reliable effective addition to the non-chemical worm control strategies in livestock. The studies should as well report the CT concentration levels and proportions of the different worm species involved, as well as noting any production effects in relation to the animal in question. These mechanisms as well require much elucidation to explain any form of variable results that might be obtained in the proposed grazing trials. The identification of specific compounds linked with dose-administered dependent inhibitory effects against nematode developmental stages will aid in provision of an objective basis for the laboratory assay results in relation to those occurring in the field trials [32].

3.6 Cost

Authors of experimental sites have also reported that CT-containing legume forages are relatively more difficult and expensive to develop, establish and maintain than the traditional pastures [33]. Unless new legumes' economic importance is clear, both in terms of anti-helminthic effects and pasture-management cost and the sociological effects are considered, their general adoption may be compromised.

3.7 Lack of knowledge and familiarity of many legumes

Before we embark on a mass legume breeding program specifically for fish feeds, we should ask ourselves whether any natural occurring plant legume seeds contains the essential nutritional range considerations essential for aquaculture feeds. On research conducted by Assefam (2021), among the legume species adapted to different alkaline soils, *Trigonella balansa* was found to contain a relatively high significant omega-3 and omega-6 fats levels but a lower omega-3-omega-6 ratio that *T. glanduriferum.* A future broader legume family search may very clearly outline other agronomically adapted plant legume species nutritionally-richer for aquaculture diets. Also, little is known regarding the essential reproductive, agronomic, rhizo-biological and physiological perennial legume forage trends in relation to other species such as *M. sativa, T. repens, T. pratense* and *Lotus corniculatus* which are much used commercially in many parts of the world [34]. This lack of knowledge is a serious constraint and challenge to the developing of other perennial legumes for future agricultural purposes.

4. Conclusion

Despite legumes widespread diverse benefits, most have neither been observed for their potential contribution to the primary production systems nor indeed their biologically active grain produce constituents. This book chapter has attempted to bring out some of the future use prospects to which legumes may be improved or manufactured for and the pathway to achieving these advancements. The genetic biodiversity of legume crops is currently constantly under much threat through the loss of natural habitats by humans for various benefits such as livestock rearing as discussed, overgrazing challenges or even illegal trading of medicinal plants across the globe. Of the 6000 known species of legumes, many are considered to be at a higher risk rate of extinction in the coming years. Currently, 10 *Trifolium* species native to the United States of America (USA) have been red flagged to be at a higher threat risk and their 16-world known common taxonomic classes are said to be endangered and vulnerable [35]. Medicinal plants for many centuries have also been used by farmers and pastoralists as a primary source of prevention and in the control of various diseases affecting livestock. With the rapid fading of ethnic traditional customs and cultures, some of the legume plants used in the making of organized traditional medicine will also, with no doubt, fade away too. It should become like a normal cultural practice now than ever more before that we should explore and try to put measures to preserve and conserve these plant species before they fade away and get lost from science completely. Just as most of the research in the field of Agriculture, and agronomy to be specific, on legumes is focused on yield increase in food and fiber crops, equally more emphasis should be put on research to identify the legume plants with potential to supplying of essential products in the pharmaceutical and nutrition industries in the current modern evolving society. This book chapter as well has put much attempt on the way forward prospections and anticipation on some of the roles that might be applicable and useful to the legume plants and their rhizomes. To quote, "We need to nodulate prokaryote plants". Researches focused on continued exploitation of the enormous natural genetic variations available in both legume forage plants and their constituent micro-symbionts will contribute greatly in the application of Biological Nitrogen Fixation (BNF), which is unarguably one of the key essential biological processes on the entire planet.

This chapter closes by concluding with a very important quote for Agriculturalists in whatever diverse fields, in general, and the entire people on planet earth always to remember to save essential plants with positive benefits to the ecosystem including man, therefore, "Save Plants that Save Lives".

Thanks

I would like to send my sincere gratitude and thanks to Blanka Gugic, who has been the personal Author Service Manager, IntechOpen, in the pioneering of the writing of this chapter by extending the offer to contribute a chapter to this book entitled, "Production and Utilization of Legumes - Progress and Prospects", for all the support, encouragement and the advice as well as communication progress she has been offering all along. I am really glad and honored for her and much importantly I could not have done it without her, and thus, it would be a huge misfortune failing to honor her.

Thank you once again Blanka Gugic.

Author details

Briggx Xavier
Kenya Methodist University, Meru, Kenya

*Address all correspondence to: xavierbriggx@gmail.com

References

[1] Food and Agriculture Organization of the United Nations Definition and Classification of Commodities: Pulses and Derived Products. Available from: http://www.fao.org/es/faodef/fdef04e.htm. [Accessed: January 6, 2021]

[2] Chen Y, McGee R, Vandemark G, Brick M, Thompson HJ. Dietary fiber analysis of four pulses using AOAC 2011.25: Implications for human health. Nutrients. 2016;**8**:829

[3] Wu TD, Watanabe C. GMAP: A genomic mapping and alignment program for mRNA and EST sequences. Bioinformatics. 2015;**21**:1859-1875. DOI: 10.1093/bioinformatics/bti310

[4] Tako E, Glahn RP, Laparra JM, et al. Iron and zinc bio availabilities to pigs from red and white beans (*Phaseolus vulgaris* L.) are similar. Journal of Agricultural Food Chemistry. 2019;**57**(8):3134-3140

[5] Shitta NS, Edemodu AC, Abtew WG, Tesfaye AA. A Review on the Cooking Attributes of African Yam Bean (*Sphenostylis stenocarpa*). London, UK: IntechOpen; 2021

[6] Rütting T, Aronsson H, Delin S. Efficient use of nitrogen in agriculture. Nutrient Cycling in Agroecosystems. 2018;**110**:1-5. DOI: 10.1007/s10705-017-9900-8

[7] Niles M, Ahuja R, Barker T, Esquivel J, Gutterman S, Heller M, et al. Climate change mitigation beyond agriculture: A review of food system opportunities and implications. Renewable Agriculture and Food Systems. 2018;**33**:297-308. DOI: 10.1017/S1742170518000029

[8] Berg WK, Cunningham SM, Brouder SM, Joern BC, Johnson KD, Santini J, et al. Influence of phosphorus and potassium on alfalfa yield and yield components. Crop Science. 2015;**45**:297-304

[9] Morris JB. Bio-functional legumes with nutraceutical, pharmaceutical, and industrial uses. Economics Botany. 2013;**57**:254-261

[10] Marimuthu M, Gurumoorthi P. Phytochemical screening and ft-ir studies on wild and common South Indian legumes. Asian Journal of Pharmaceutical and Clinical Research. 2013;**6**(2):141-144

[11] Geil PB, Anderson JW. Nutrition and health implications of dry beans: A review. Journal of American College Nutrition. 2014;**13**(6):549-558

[12] Caprioli G, Giusti F, Ballini R, et al. Lipid nutritional value of legumes: Evaluation of different extraction methods and Determination of fatty acid composition. Food Chemistry. 2016;**192**:965-971

[13] Mawani M, Ali SA, Bano G. Iron deficiency anemia among women of reproductive age, an important public health problem: Situation analysis. Reproductive System Sex Disorders. 2016;**5**(3):1-6

[14] Fung T et al. Major dietary patterns and the risk of colorectal cancer in women. Archives of Internal Medicine. 2013;**163**:309-314

[15] Velie EM, Schairer C, Flood A, et al. Empirically derived dietary patterns and risk of postmenopausal breast cancer in a large prospective cohort study. American Journal of Clinical Nutrition. 2015;**82**(6):1308-1319

[16] Soetan K. Antinutritional factors of five selected underutilized legumes. Food Science Quality Management. 2018;**76**:92-100

[17] Das G, Sharma A, Sarkar PK. Conventional and emerging processing techniques for the post-harvest reduction of antinutrients in edible legumes. Applied Food Research. 2022;**2**:100112

[18] Caprioli G, Cristalli G, Ragazzi E, et al. A preliminary matrix-assisted laser desorption/ionization time-of-flight approach for the characterization of Italian lentil varieties. Rapid Communications in Mass Spectrometry. 2010;**24**:2843-2848

[19] Tacon AG, Hasan MR, Metian M. Demand and supply of feed ingredients for farmed fish and crustaceans: Trends and prospects. FAO Fisheries and Aquaculture technical paper. 2011;**564**:I

[20] Henry M, Gasco L, Piccolo G, Fountoulaki E. Review on the use of insects in the diet of farmed fish: Past and future. Animal Feed Science and Technology. 2015;**203**:1-22. DOI: 10.1016/j.anifeedsci.2015.03.001

[21] Tacon AG, Metian M. Feed matters: Satisfying the feed demand of aquaculture. Reviews in Fisheries Science & Aquaculture. 2015;**23**:1-10

[22] Brockwell J, Bottomley PJ, Thies JE. Manipulation of rhizobia microflora for improving legume productivity and soil fertility: A critical assessment. Plant and Soil. 2015;**174**:143-180

[23] Rao IM, Beebe SE, Polania J, Grajales M, Cajiao C, Ricaurte J, et al. Evidence for genotypic differences among elite lines of common bean in the ability to remobilize photosynthate to increase yield under drought. Journal of Agricultural Science. 2017;**155**:857-875

[24] Neill S, Lee DR. Explaining the adoption and disadoption of sustainable agriculture: The case of cover crops in Northern Honduras. Economic Development and Cultural Change. 2011;**49**:793-820

[25] Feder G, Umali DL. The adoption of agricultural innovations: A review. Technological Forecasting and Social Change. 2013;**43**:215-239

[26] Adesina AA, Baidu-Forson J. Farmers' perceptions and adoption of new agricultural technology: Evidence from analysis in Burkina Faso and Guinea, West Africa. Agricultural Economics. 2015;**13**:1-9

[27] Yigezu YA, Bishaw Z, Niane AA, Alwang J, El-Shater T, Boughlala M, et al. Institutional and farm-level challenges limiting the diffusion of new varieties from public and CGIAR centers: The case of wheat in Moroccan. Food Security. 2021;**13**:1359-1377

[28] Bailey-Serres J, Parker JE, Ainsworth EA, Oldroyd GED, Schroeder J. Genetic strategies for improving crop yields. Nature. 2019;**575**:109-118

[29] Wendimu GY, Moral TM. The challenges and prospects of Ethiopian agriculture. Cogent in Food Agriculture. 2021;**7**:1923619

[30] Stagnari F, Maggio A, Gailien A, Pisante M. Multiple benefits of legumes for agricultural sustainability: An overview. Chemical, Biological Technological Agriculture. 2017;**4**:2

[31] Mamuye W. Determinants of smallholder farmers participation in formal credit and challenges faced by institutions: The case of Mojana Wodera District, Amhara Region, Ethiopia. International Journal of Finance Bank Research. 2021;**7**:9-20

[32] Geda SA, Kuhl R. Exploring smallholder farmers' preferences for climate-smart seed innovations: Empirical evidence from Southern Ethiopia. Sustainability. 2021;**13**:2786

[33] Yigezu YA, El-Shater T, Boughlala M, Bishaw Z, Niane AA, Maalouf F, et al. Legume-based rotations have clear economic advantages over cereal monocropping in dry areas. Agronomy for Sustainable Development. 2019;**39**:58

[34] Assefam BT, Reidsma P, Chamberlin J. Farm- and community-level factors underlying the profitability of fertilizer usage for Ethiopian smallholder farmers. Agrekon. 2021;**60**:460-479

[35] Baskin JM, Snyder KM, Walck JL, Baskin CC. The comparative autecology of endemic, globally-rare, and geographically widespread, common plant species: Three case studies. Southwestern Naturalist. 2017;**42**:384-399